A SHEARWATER BOOK

# Beyond the Last Village

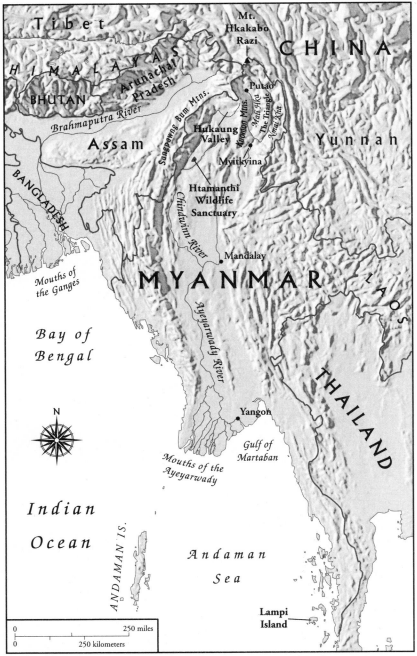

Myanmar. The author's explorations have occurred in four main parts
of the country: Lampi Island, Htamanthi Wildlife Sanctuary, Hukaung Valley,
and the mountainous region surrounding Mount Hkakabo Razi.

# Beyond the Last Village

## A JOURNEY OF DISCOVERY IN ASIA'S FORBIDDEN WILDERNESS

ALAN RABINOWITZ

AURUM PRESS

The journey is difficult, immense, at times impossible, yet that will not deter some of us from attempting it. We cannot know all that has happened in the past, or the reason for all of the events, any more than we can with surety discern what lies ahead. We have joined the caravan, you might say, at a certain point; we will travel as far as we can, but we cannot in one lifetime see all that we would like to see or learn all that we hunger to know. . . .

—Loren Eiseley

Major topographic features of the greater Myanmar region. Note that far northern Myanmar is at the intersection of the rugged north–south mountain chains of southern China and the eastern edge of the Himalayas.

# Contents

# *Author's Note*

The historic and better-known name of the Union of Myanmar, where most of this story takes place, is Burma (or the Union of Burma). Some writers still prefer to use the more familiar term, but the government's name change has been in effect since 1989 and is now recognized by other nations. The government changed many city and river names throughout the country as well—the capital city of Rangoon is now Yangon, for example, the historic city of Pagan is now Bagan, the Chindwin River became the Chindwinn River, and the spelling of the country's best-known river went from Irrawaddy to Ayeyarwady. Although some are hesitant to use these revised names because they were mandated by the present military government, a case can be made that they are in greater accord with original Myanmar pronunciation or with the actual place names before they were pidginized by the British in the 1800s. The revised names are used in this book, except where other authors are quoted or reference is made to a site in the period when the former names were used.

The official language of Myanmar is described in this book as Burmese because it is derived from the internationally accepted Tibeto-Burman family of languages. A distinction, however, should be noted between the Bamar (formerly called Burman) people, who comprise the country's major ethnic group that speaks the Burmese language, and the people of Myanmar in general, who are referred to in this book as the Myanmar people.

To transliterate the names in the remote northern regions into English, our expedition teams did their best to piece together phonetic spellings that, if not completely correct linguistically, could at least be understood and used by others who came after us. Finally, when the names of Myanmar people are written, *U* (pronounced "oo") is placed before the given name of an adult male, a sign of respectful address with the literal translation of "uncle." Similarly, *Daw* means "aunt," and by convention it is placed before the name of an adult woman of any age, married or single.

# Prologue

We live in a time when we are reminded almost daily of the numbers of species sliding toward extinction and the acreage of rain forest being lost to a rapidly expanding human population. We are confronted by a growing list of personal ailments that are blamed, in one form or another, on the desecration of the earth's natural environment. Little wonder that, as we enter the second millennium of the modern era, cynicism abounds over the future of what is perceived as a self-destructive global community, hell bent on a winner-take-all attitude, plummeting toward oblivion.

In such a climate, the excitement and wonders of the world are not oft discussed. The idea of exploring uncharted terrain, discovering new species, and probing perceptions of little-known cultures has been all but relegated to the history books. The world's newest wonders are now defined instead by the latest advances in computer technologies as we invent the species of our choice or bring back the dinosaurs in virtual reality.

"The time for great discoveries is past," pronounced Louis Agassiz in 1867 on an expedition to explore Brazil. "No student of nature should go out now expecting to find a new world."

Many people still share these sentiments, convinced that our knowledge of the world's large creatures and cultures is all but complete. They are wrong. And so was Agassiz. Within the first ten years of his pronouncement, Nikolay Prezhevalsky explored the Gobi

Desert from end to end, the one-armed John Wesley Powell traveled 1,000 miles down the Colorado River and through the Grand Canyon by boat, Luigi D'Albertis penetrated the interior of New Guinea, and Henry Morton Stanley traced the length of the Congo River. During the first half of the twentieth century, Roald Amundsen reached the South Pole, Candido Rondon surveyed the Mato Grosso of Brazil, Roy Chapman Andrews discovered dinosaur fossils in the Gobi, and William Beebe dove in a bathysphere to more than 3,000 feet. And in just the last decade of the twentieth century, scientists uncovered a biological "lost world" in the Annamite Mountains between Laos and Vietnam, complete with evidence of at least five mammal species new to science, as well as the rediscovery of living members of two large mammal species thought long extinct.

Our world remains a wondrous place. You can still find your way to the end of the last dirt roads, where maps show nothing but river blue and forest green. You can still go where no television antennas are perched upon the thatched roofing of village huts, and where the animals and plants have not all found their way into museum collections. There are still worlds to be explored where few have come before you and where mystery is waiting to be turned into knowledge.

This is a book about a journey to such a place, about exploration and scientific discovery in a remote corner of wilderness wedged between the eastern edge of the Himalayas and the ancient mountains of western China. It is also a story of physical hardship and emotional turmoil, about a person who once found comfort only with animals because he couldn't speak the way others did. Now he enters a world where the greatest necessity is salt, where people plow the earth using themselves as the beasts of burden, and where the main source of meat is a group of primitive species that are little known outside the region. But when the last village is left behind for the final time, an angry, stuttering boy gives way to a man ready to stop running and come home to embrace the world anew.

## CHAPTER 1

# Yangon, 1993

I will care not to go towards the dark. I will go towards
the sky.
—Igulik Eskimo words spoken before a long journey.

THIS TIME WOULD BE DIFFERENT. Different from
all the other times in the previous ten years that had been different.
I sensed that when the plane broke through the clouds and my first
sight was of a pagoda-studded landscape amid an expanse of forest
greenery. We landed hard, bumping several times on the runway
before taxiing to a stop near a small crowd that had gathered by the
arrival gates. Men in their skirtlike *longyis* were in animated conversation with one another, puffing away on Myanmar cheroots.
Women with plaited waist-length hair, yellow-chalked faces, and
colorful sarongs stood to the side, smiling demurely. Everything
about the scene evoked images of George Orwell's *Burmese Days,*
with his vivid descriptions of life here during the waning days of
British rule. A maintenance crew moved tentatively below the
underbelly of the plane, as if they had only recently become familiar with these giant machines of the sky.

I was surprised by the intense feeling of "rightness" that crept up from deep inside my gut. I had forgotten what it felt like. Nearly a decade had passed since I had studied leopards and tigers in the forests of Thailand, searched for the last Sumatran rhinos in the interior of Borneo, trained wildlife staff in China and Malaysia, and carried out the first biological surveys of the Annamite Mountains between Laos and Vietnam. What was there to show for it? Proof that extinction is inevitable for species containing body parts valued by a superstitious, sometimes desperate segment of human society? Or perhaps simply the realization that government bureaucracy can be just as self-serving in the so-called democracies as in the struggling socialist and communist regimes of the region?

I had grown tired of grappling with issues that never got resolved, despite my best efforts. And just when I thought my cynicism about the future of wildlife conservation in the region couldn't get any deeper, I learned of the suicide of Seub Nakasathien, a Thai wildlife officer and good friend, who lived by the conviction that other animals had as much right to life as human beings. In the end, he succumbed to despair over the corruption and politics of a system that neither appreciated him nor let him do his job.

Now here I was, 40 years old and the director of Asia programs for the Wildlife Conservation Society (WCS), based halfway around the world at the Bronx Zoo, with the task of trying to save wildlife in some of the most populated countries on earth with some of the world's most arbitrary and corrupt governments. Despite my excitement at the moment, a part of me wanted to turn around and take the next flight back out. I wasn't sure I still had it in me to deal with a military government that went by the acronym of SLORC (State Law and Order Restoration Council) and was on trial in the world press as one of the world's greatest current abusers of human rights.

Yet it wasn't politics or human rights or even my own despair that was on my mind as I stepped out of the airplane and into the steamy heat of a country that had been closed to the Western world for more than three decades. Somewhere within this little pocket of humanity, known to most of the world as Burma but renamed Myanmar in 1989 by the current military regime, lurked some of the world's remaining strongholds of tigers, Asian elephants, and Sumatran rhinos. That was where I hungered to go: into the hinterland of a country that contained the world's last great stands of teak trees, rugged, unexplored mountain ranges, and a diversity of wildlife almost unparalleled in the Asia-Pacific region.

I had worked for four years to make this trip happen, time and again seeking an invitation to speak with government officials about initiating a wildlife research and conservation program here. Almost nothing was known about the state of Myanmar's wildlife, and the government showed no inclination toward allowing Western scientists to wander the country's forests. Back in New York, some of my peers had told me to stop wasting my time, to instead wait until the country was safer and the politics improved. I was warned that raising funds for such a program, if I did get one started, would be difficult at best. But none of that concerned me at the moment. Given the state of wildlife elsewhere in the region, I knew that this was no time to wait.

While doing research in Thailand, I had spent countless hours talking with Myanmar Embassy officials and had sent dozens of letters and faxes to government offices in Yangon requesting an audience. Most inquiries had gone unanswered. The responses I did receive were typically noncommittal. Finally, someone in the Forest Department read my letters and inquired after William Beebe, the former director of tropical research for the New York Zoological Society, now the Wildlife Conservation Society, who had traveled in Myanmar in the early 1900s and written about pheasants. I wrote back, breaking the news gently that Beebe had died in 1962, but implying that I had replaced him (a minor exaggeration of the facts) and declaring that I wanted to follow up on his excellent work in Myanmar.

The reply to my letter was swift, informing me that I had been granted a one-week official visa, with an invitation to visit the Forest Department "to discuss wildlife." I was ecstatic; it was the Forest Department that dealt with all wildlife and conservation issues in the country.

On the drive into downtown Yangon, officials of the Forest Department went over my schedule of meetings, asked me what sights I wanted to see around town, and bombarded me with questions about the United States. I answered politely as we bumped along the potholed streets and I stared outside, past crumbling, weather-beaten buildings of colonial British architecture showing decades of neglect. It seemed a strangely charming city, with trishaws hugging the curbs, passed by rickety local buses built in the 1950s—all moving at their own slow pace along broad, tree-lined streets laid out in a British grid system.

My eyes were drawn to the throngs of longyi-clad traders plying their wares, and to the groups of men sitting around dollhouse-sized tables in coffee shops. When I rolled down my window, I was physically jolted by the blast of damp, hot air that struck my face. But now I could almost taste the pungent aromas emanating from the countless street-side food stalls, and hear amid the other noises of the street the laughter of the children bathing at public wells. This was a comparatively young city, having become the country's capital only in 1885 when the British completed their conquest of upper Myanmar. Now it seemed a city in transition, trying to put a modern facade on a culture that was still firmly entrenched in past values and superstitions.

I thought again about what I would have done to get here. For the truth was that this trip for me was not just about saving wildlife. It was a last-ditch effort to convince myself that I still cared enough to try to make a difference in the world. That I still gave a damn. And that the passion which had always burned so strongly inside had not died completely that night when my friend Seub sat alone in the forest and put a bullet cleanly through his brain.

# CHAPTER 2

# Tarnished Golden Land

In Rangoon the imagination strains forward into years
that are yet to come, for some hint of the great Destiny
that awaits it.

—V. C. Scott O'Connor

THE 1,200-MILE LENGTH OF MYANMAR forms
a land bridge between the main Asian continent and the Malay
Peninsula, with India and Bangladesh to the west and China to the
north. As the largest country in mainland southeast Asia, with a
landscape stretching from the rain forests of the south to the icy
Himalayan Mountains in the north, Myanmar was known for its
biological wealth. It was said to be home to at least 7,000 different
species of plants, 300 species of mammals, 360 species of reptiles,
and 1,000 species of birds. But with an ethnic population as diverse
as its landscape, Myanmar had also been plagued by continual civil
strife since the country gained independence from the British in
1948.

What was once called "The Golden Land" had gone from having one of the richest economies in Asia during the first half of the

5

twentieth century to becoming one of the ten poorest countries in the world. Although Burma was touted as a major destination for the sport hunting of large mammals during the early 1900s, subsequent political instability and insurgency had kept people from traveling safely throughout the countryside for decades. When I arrived in the capital city for the first time in 1993, most of Myanmar's forests were still off-limits to foreigners for "national security" reasons, and the true status of the country's once spectacular wildlife populations was anyone's guess.

After driving through much of Yangon, my Forest Department hosts and I arrived at a large, gated compound housing their offices. Following my companions into the nearest building, I listened to our footsteps echo through the halls as we walked by mostly empty offices and silent typewriters. Everywhere I looked were signs of decay, inactivity, and neglect, a replication in miniature of what I had seen on the drive through the city.

Not sure exactly with whom I'd be speaking, I had played out various dialogues in my head the night before, making a case to let the Wildlife Conservation Society set up a conservation program in this country. But in the ensuing hours, as I was shuttled from meeting to meeting, served countless cups of heavily sweetened coffee, and smothered in Myanmar politeness, I was given little chance to talk about what was on my mind. Instead, despite the niceties, which are a genuine part of Myanmar upbringing, my motives were constantly questioned. "Why are you coming to this country now when it is so hard to accomplish anything?" "Why are you interested in only the most remote and dangerous areas?" "Why don't you look more like a scientist?" Some questions were easier to field than others. But I soon realized that the questions were only a prelude to heartfelt discussions about the country and its wildlife. It was my first glimpse of the passion that lay beneath the seemingly austere exteriors of these Forest Department officials, who were to play a pivotal role in my work in the years to come.

Though outwardly now only a shadow of its former self, the Burmese Forest Department, established after the British annexed lower Burma as part of their Indian Empire in 1856, had a venerable past. Under the direction of Dr. Detrick Brandis, the new department began by designing a system for sustainable, long-term commercial teak production. As a result of these efforts, forest revenues in Burma had climbed to all-time highs by the end of World War I.

Though the Burmese Forest Department became the envy of Asia, that status was not to last, as its fate became increasingly tied to the country's shifting political fortunes. In 1937, the British split Burma away from India as a separate colony, but a growing underground nationalist movement, led primarily by University of Yangon student U Aung San, continued to push for full self-rule. During the early years of World War II, U Aung San formed the Burma National Army, siding first with the Japanese and then with the Allies. Forest management was severely disrupted by the fighting that took place in these first war years and later by the timber requisitions of the Japanese during their occupation of the country.

In the early postwar period leading up to independence, U Aung San and six of his ministers were assassinated, ethnic strife erupted anew, and the system of sustainable use introduced by the British and managed by the Burmese Forest Department completely disintegrated. After independence in 1948, the new government took over the timber industry and created the State Timber Board to oversee all timber extraction, leaving the Forest Department with only the role of implementing forest conservation activities. As opposition to the new government began to turn violent in the countryside, even this role was diminished; the Forest Department's authority often extended little beyond Yangon.

A military coup in 1962 led by General Ne Win, one of the original members of U Aung San's Burma National Army, intensified the civil wars, and commercially important forests in the country became not only the sites of conflict but the subject of conflict as well. These protracted conflicts, fueled by General Ne Win's attempt to impose a centrally planned economy, led to continued economic stagnation, massive external debt, and further deterioration of the country's natural resources.

The people in power when I arrived in 1993 had emerged only a few contentious years earlier. In 1988, large popular demonstrations had forced General Ne Win's "retirement," while subsequent confrontations between pro-democracy demonstrators and the military led to an estimated 3,000 deaths over a six-week period—Burma's Tiananmen Square. What arose from the flames was a collective ruling body of several dozen ministers calling itself SLORC, which established martial law and promised to hold democratic elections in 1989. The elections were held, but the results, which would have placed the leader of the opposition (Aung San Suu Kyi, the daughter of U Aung San) as head of a new government, were never implemented. Instead, Aung San Suu Kyi was placed under house arrest.

Under SLORC, all Forest Department activities were now closely controlled by the military. What had been the State Timber Board became the Myanmar Timber Enterprise, and it played an important part in the nation's economy. During 1989, timber exports, mostly teak, brought in approximately U.S.$136 million, accounting for nearly half of that year's export earnings, and in subsequent years the value of timber exports rose even higher. As the country's forests increasingly came to be seen as the government's most dependable "cash cow," the military leaders began to recognize the need for more positive long-term environmental management.

There was pressure from outside the country as well. In an attempt to integrate Myanmar into the global economy, the government reacted to international criticism of widespread deforestation by beginning to give greater weight to forest conservation and wildlife issues. In 1990, SLORC created a commission to develop an integrated national environmental policy. In 1992, in the wake of the Earth Summit held in Rio de Janeiro, a new Forest Law was enacted that for the first time linked forest exploitation to such environmental considerations as biodiversity conservation, watershed protection, and private-sector participation.

The policies looked good on paper, but there was a complicating factor. Ostracized by much of the international community because of its human rights record, and needing funds for continued military expansion to keep control of the country, SLORC had pushed for greater, and increasingly unsustainable, exploitation of the country's forests and other natural resources.

In this context, despite their extremely low salaries (the director-general of the Forest Department was making less than U.S.$25/month when I arrived) and severe morale problems, senior Forest Department officials had become deeply concerned about the accelerated loss and exploitation of their forests and wildlife. While the statistics the government released looked good, these officials suspected that the reality behind the numbers was grim, particularly for wildlife. Without realizing it, I had picked an opportune moment to offer my services on behalf of WCS to the Forest Department.

The Myanmar government claimed that 43 percent of the country's land area at the time was still covered in healthy forest and was appropriately managed by the Forest Department's estimated 14,000 technical and clerical staff. But the country's protected areas, in the form of national parks and wildlife sanctuaries, made up only about 1 percent of the total land area, one of the lowest proportions in the world. The protected areas that did exist were "protected" mostly in name only, with no on-site staff or management. Worst of all, with continued exploitation of the country's natural resources by both the government and ethnic insurgents, the survival of even high-profile species such as tigers, rhinos, and elephants had become questionable in most regions.

Surprisingly, it was not until I actually met the minister of forestry that I felt a glimmer of hope regarding what might be done in this country. Yet I had dreaded that first meeting from the moment I was summoned. General Chit Swe, a senior military officer in the regime and a powerful member of the SLORC cabinet, did not reach his position without breaking eggs. And now that he had become minister of perhaps the most lucrative sector of the government, there was no shortage of rumors regarding timber deals he had brokered and personal wealth he'd acquired while in office. Yet his cooperation was the key to any exploration I wanted to do and to my hopes of accomplishing anything for conservation in this country.

General Chit Swe entered the room, a short, stocky man with the body of a wrestler and what seemed like a permanent scowl etched on his face. We shook hands and he motioned for me to sit beside him. He said nothing at first, just stared at me. When he began to speak, I had to bend forward to catch the words; his soft, gentle voice seemed completely out of character with his demeanor. He was uncomfortable speaking English, and his words were halting. He asked after the health of my family and then questioned the origin of my surname. I was careful with my answers, trying to figure out as I went along what lay beneath each query. When I mentioned I was Jewish, he seemed intrigued.

"You have suffered much," he said quietly.

"Not me, but others." I answered. "My own suffering has nothing to do with being a Jew."

I was uneasy with the direction of the conversation, so I changed the subject. Why was he interested in animals, I asked, and did he believe that the conservation of forests and wildlife was really possible in this country? One of his assistants stiffened. General Chit Swe smiled.

"You people are straight," he said. I wondered if he meant conservationists or Jews.

"Yes, there is a chance to protect what we have left in this country," he said. "And it is the right thing to do. But it is not easy."

Given what I had heard about attempts by high officials to enrich themselves, I made my own inference about his last statement. He saw it on my face.

"Everyone does not want the same thing," he said. "Some have to be convinced more than others."

He spoke almost in a whisper now, as if revealing such thoughts was difficult and he wanted only me to hear them. Soon we were engulfed in a candid exchange of ideas as if none of the dozen or so officials sitting around us were present.

There was something disarming about this man that drew me in. I sensed unresolved turmoil, and a need for honesty from someone who didn't fear him. He was a man of strong passions who, whatever his past actions may have been, seemed to care deeply about what was happening to the natural resources of his country, but needed someone to believe in his good intentions.

General Chit Swe had checked out WCS long before our meeting, I learned, and he had read many of the documents I had previously sent to the Forest Department about my work. Still, I felt the need to emphasize that the Wildlife Conservation Society was not a funding agency but a science-based wildlife conservation organization. Originally set up to run the Bronx Zoo, and still active in zoo-based conservation and education, WCS had as its present mission to save wildlife in their natural habitats and to find ways in which people and wildlife could live together. Toward this end, the international division of WCS sent biologists all over the world to do wildlife research and conservation in the field. Although we often couldn't match the money spent by other organizations, I told him, we offered a level of commitment, experience, and intellectual currency that was unmatched by any conservation group in the world.

General Chit Swe smiled and then held up his hand to cut short my fervent discourse.

"I already know of the reputation of your society," he said. "And as for your commitment, I can see that myself."

By the close of the meeting, the minister had given his blessing to a written agreement allowing WCS to act as unofficial advisor to the Forest Department on wildlife research and conservation issues. Neither of us was exactly sure what that meant yet, but he stipulated that I alone remain in charge of the program. The minister, like me, seemed still a bit uneasy with the arrangement. This was to be the first official "memorandum of understanding" between the Forest Department and a foreign conservation organization under the current military regime. I was an untested entity and somewhat of a puzzle to him. To me, General Chit Swe seemed to have a genuine commitment to conservation but, at the time, I questioned how far he would go toward acting on it. Was I justified in committing WCS to a program that might never get off the ground, I wondered. Yet despite my doubts, I was heartened by the sense of commitment I perceived among the Forest Department staff. I just didn't realize that it would take much longer than I expected to get to the places I most wanted to go in this country.

## CHAPTER 3

# Of Rhinos and Sea-Gypsies

If one advances confidently in the direction of his
dreams, and endeavors to live the life which he has
imagined, he will meet with a success unexpected in
common hours.

—Henry David Thoreau

DURING THE NEXT TWO YEARS I returned to
Myanmar more than half a dozen times, organizing training courses
for Forest Department staff and working with individuals who
wanted to get into the field and do wildlife research. While I was
allowed to go farther afield than any foreigner in recent years, my
trips were still restricted to the secure, central region of the country. Forest Department staff always accompanied me, and we stuck
to a strict itinerary. Side trips were out of the question. Meanwhile,
I persisted in my efforts to visit the more remote northern parts of
the country, which included some of the wildest areas.

It was clear from the outset that the country's forests were under
increasing threat, and that wildlife populations were not doing as
well as many believed. Much of Myanmar's natural resources were
free for the taking as far as the local people and the local military

were concerned. But reliable data were needed before we could convince the government to better manage their forests and to crack down on the seemingly omnipresent hunting and trade in wildlife.

General Chit Swe, for his part, seemed to be surprisingly active in putting into practice the beliefs that he had expounded during that first meeting. In 1994, the government wrote a National Forestry Policy that complemented the Forest Law of two years previous. As part of this policy, the Forest Department declared its intent to increase the country's system of protected areas to at least 5 percent of the land area, increase forest reserve areas to at least 30 percent of the land area, and protect all the country's critical watersheds. At the same time, a new, stricter Wild Life, Natural Forests and Nature Preservation Law was enacted, prohibiting hunting and trade of thirty-nine rare mammal species, fifty bird species, and nine reptile species. That same year, General Chit Swe attended the Global Forum on the Conservation of the Tiger in India, and declared his intent to push for forestry practices that would promote wildlife conservation.

That year I was also granted permission by General Chit Swe to journey up the Chindwinn River, the main branch of the Ayeyarwady River, to Htamanthi Wildlife Sanctuary, situated more than 1,500 miles north as the crow flies from Yangon. George Schaller, the director of science for WCS and my mentor, was allowed to accompany me. This was the largest and most remote protected area in the country at the time, initially set up by the British when the upper Chindwinn was prime hunting grounds for sportsmen. Now Htamanthi was home to tigers, elephants, and possibly the last viable population of Sumatran rhinos outside of Malaysia and Sumatra. We were to be the first Westerners to visit this site in anyone's recent memory; in fact, no one from the Forest Department had been there in twenty-five years.

Although I'd spent most of my professional life working on carnivores, my interest in Sumatran rhinos began while I was conducting surveys of these animals in Borneo during the 1980s. By chance, I was on hand after an adult male rhino had been brought out of the forest and placed in captivity, as part of an unsuccessful breeding program in the Malaysian state of Sabah. Expecting something big and dangerous-looking, I found myself besides a diminutive, seemingly gentle beast standing about four feet at the shoulders with long, black, bristly hair along its back. When I put my hand atop the rough hardened skin on his neck, he turned his head, as if only just noting my presence, and stared back at me with empty eyes.

It seems a miracle to me that rhinos still walk the face of the earth. No other group of animals has been so highly prized for so long. Our obsession with this species revolves almost solely around a single body part, the horn, a protuberance of hardened hair that has played an important role in traditional Chinese medicine for nearly 5,000 years. Commonly thought to have been used as an aphrodisiac, rhino horn was actually valued more by the Chinese as an antidote to poisons as well as a remedy for headaches, fevers, and colds. Regular consumption of powdered rhino horn, according to a 1597 medical text, *Pen Ts'ao Kang Mu* by Li Shih-Chen, "lightens the body and makes one very robust." Predictably, as numbers of rhinos have steadily declined, the demand for their horn and the price people pay for it has increased.

Of the five living rhino species, the Sumatran rhino is perhaps the most endangered and the most intriguing. A living fossil whose origin makes it the oldest surviving mammal walking the earth, the Sumatran rhino's closest relative is the extinct woolly rhino of Europe. Most of my efforts to find firsthand accounts of this species' behavior in the wild had proven fruitless, perhaps because, as one author put it, the Sumatran rhino was "already considered a rarity by the time of the ages illuminated by books." Yet I was intrigued by one hunter's 1905 report claiming these rhinos to be ferocious animals, sometimes attacking humans without provocation and "vindictive and persevering in pursuit of the object of their anger."

I looked back into the eyes that were still glued to my face, and stroked his head again. What was the true nature of this beast, I wondered.

⌒⋇⌒

Poring over maps with U Uga, a deputy director of the Wildlife Division, who would accompany us to Htamanthi, Schaller and I decided that we should hike the length of one of the major waterways through the center of the sanctuary to search for signs of rhinos and other wildlife. Surveying along a waterway was the best strategy during the dry months, since any large mammals in the area would come to the river to drink or to use it as a travel corridor. Even species not easily seen would leave evidence of their presence in the form of tracks, scratches, or feces in the soft mud along the river. We just had to figure out how to work around the twenty-one soldiers who were being sent along to protect us.

U Uga and his staff arranged all the logistics of our trip. After flying to the town of Khamti in the Sagaing State of northern Myanmar, we traveled more than 100 miles down the Chindwinn River in small motorized boats to reach the village of Homalin. There we switched to small motorized dugouts and traveled up the Uyu River to Yebawmi, a village on the east side of Htamanthi Wildlife Sanctuary. We then hiked inland, westward across the sanctuary.

The forest inside the sanctuary was beautiful, with a high, closed canopy that showed few signs of human disturbance. But despite reports of fresh rhino tracks in this area three years earlier, we found no sign of them. Even more disturbing, within this seemingly intact forest, there were few or no signs of tigers, elephants, or the other large mammal species that reportedly had once been here in abundance. The reason became obvious not long after we began the survey.

While we were camping along the Uyu River, three Lisu

hunters appeared at our fire just before dark one day. Because most of the soldiers in our party were out of uniform, the Lisu thought they were walking into an encampment of local villagers. I don't know what surprised them more—seeing two Western faces among the group or finding out that they were being arrested. Their packs were filled with metal cables for use in making animal snares, along with the skins, penises, and gall bladders of river otters. But their primary quarry, they explained, was tigers.

In the days that followed, I took every opportunity to talk with these Lisu through a translator. They answered my questions readily, still not quite sure why they were being detained. They had been coming to hunt in this area every year for nearly a decade, and no one had ever stopped them before or told them they were doing anything wrong. They came from the district of Putao, an area where most of the more than 35,000 Lisu in the country lived, more than a week's walk north from where we were. Such distances meant little to these tough, sturdily built men whose nomadic wanderings and hunting abilities were legendary among the Myanmar people and whose talents had made them prized by the British as foot soldiers.

The Lisu I spoke with were not out to stalk game with their traditional crossbows for the cooking pot. They came to Htamanthi for body parts—particularly the highly valued rhino horns, bear gall bladders, otter skins, and tiger bones, which they sold across the border in China, where the majority of their tribe still lived. Unfortunately, the rhinos were all gone from this area, they said, and the otters were scarce now. Both were easy to kill. The men were still getting at least one tiger a year and an occasional bear from Htamanthi, usually with snares, sometimes by setting out a poisoned carcass of a wild animal for other carnivores to feed on. When we told them to show us their trap sets so that we could dismantle them, they readily agreed.

Game trails leading downhill to the river were favored trapping locations for tigers. The snare was made from metal cable and attached to a sturdy tree that was bent over and fastened, ready to spring back into place when the animal stepped on a trigger mechanism under the snare. To ensure that the tiger wouldn't escape, the hunters placed bamboo spikes under the tree where the tiger would dangle. As he fought the snare, his body would be punctured repeatedly by the spikes until the loss of blood weakened or killed him.

After hiking for twelve days across the sanctuary, we met up with our boats at the village of Htamanthi, about 30 air miles from the border with India. The village was populated by a people called the Taman, a tribe considered to have characteristics of both the Bamar and the Naga ethnic groups. In the past, other villages feared these people because of their reported ability to transform themselves into the infamous "Htamanthi tigers," mythical were-creatures with five toes on their front paws. No one in the village claimed such powers now, though.

When we mentioned the lack of any rhino sign on our journey, the villagers weren't surprised. Most of the remaining rhinos were killed during the politically turbulent period of the 1980s, they said. If any still lived in the sanctuary, they were the last of their kind.

When Marco Polo visited Burma in the thirteenth century, he described a vast jungle teeming with wild beasts and unicorns. The "unicorns" he was talking about were rhinos. Five hundred years later, when the Swedish naturalist Linnaeus developed what is still the accepted taxonomic classification for distinguishing different animals and plants, Myanmar gained the distinction of having more rhino species (the Indian rhino, the Javan rhino, and the Sumatran rhino) than any other country in the world. Now, less than 300 years after Linnaeus, nearly every rhino of all three species in the country was gone.

There is ample literature decrying the decline of Sumatran rhino numbers throughout the twentieth and into the twenty-first century. Sadder, however, is the fact that the international conservation community, while paying lip service to the need for strong action to save the species, continues to put most of its efforts into politically expedient strategies that have little to do with the real reasons behind the rhino's decline. Captive breeding, which has repeatedly proven unsuccessful in the past but is a high-profile and easily funded activity, has often been a higher priority than habitat protection and the control of hunting and trade activities.

I returned to Yangon, depressed by the plight of the Sumatran rhino but encouraged by the almost pristine nature of Htamanthi's forests and the potential for protecting the rest of the wildlife there. When the minister read my report and saw my photographs, he authorized the building of a ranger station for Htamanthi Wildlife Sanctuary and named U Thein Aung, a senior wildlife officer and an ornithologist who was with us on the survey, as the first park chief. U Thein Aung was instructed to hire forest guards and to work with the local people in protecting the sanctuary. It was an important start. But it wouldn't be enough to stop the lucrative trade in animal parts that was spreading like a cancer across much of Asia. The Lisu would just be more careful now, entering and leaving the forest like ghosts. Nothing short of the Htamanthi tigers would stand a chance against these hunters.

Several months after I returned from Htamanthi Wildlife Sanctuary, General Chit Swe summoned me again. He had just returned from a reconnaissance flight over the Mergui Archipelago, a group of more than 800 islands off the coast of southern Myanmar. One island in particular, Lampi, had caught his attention because it was the largest and most pristine piece of real estate in the archipelago. He was almost childlike in his enthusiasm, extolling the beauty of its undisturbed beaches and the teeming life beneath its waters. There were no protected areas off the mainland, he commented;

this could be Myanmar's first marine park. If it were worth conserving, he would spearhead the effort.

Pleased with my work in Htamanthi, the minister asked me to join a survey team and make a candid appraisal of Lampi. The team consisted mostly of Myanmar marine biologists, but General Chit Swe wanted me along as the advisor. He trusted me to be honest with him, he said.

⌘

I kept telling myself that this was a unique opportunity as I paced the decks of a retired Navy minesweeper moving at a snail's pace through the Andaman Sea. Looking as if it could have been built in the same era as the *Monitor* and the *Merrimack,* this was the only military vessel that General Chit Swe could arrange, due to my presence aboard. Four long, monotonous days on the boat, which sailed from Yangon, were made much worse by my sleepless nights in a tiny, sardinelike bunk bed, trying to keep scurrying rodents and cockroaches off my sweat-drenched body. The most exciting event was when the crew manned the big gun on the top deck in order to pull over an unlicensed Myanmar fishing trawler that, somehow, was moving slower than we were.

On the morning of the fifth day, I woke to the sight of mist-enshrouded rock walls rising straight up from the sea, interspersed by forested coves and long, unbroken stretches of white sand beaches. Through my binoculars, I could see thick stands of mangroves shielding the mouth of a large freshwater river flowing out from the forested interior. It looked like something out of the television series *Fantasy Island.* The boredom and inconveniences of the previous days were immediately forgotten. We had arrived at Lampi.

We spent a week surveying the island. While it was mostly uninhabited, as the minister believed, there were two small villages on the western side occupied by a dark-skinned people of medium height. Called Sea-gypsies by the British and Salon by the Myanmar people, they referred to themselves as Maw Khen (often written Moken). W. J. S. Carrapiett, in his 1909 book about the Salon, claimed that the term *Maw Khen* means "submerged people," a pathetic but seemingly appropriate term for a group thought to be of Khmer origin with a history of being persecuted and enslaved by other ethnic groups. According to Thai legend, the Maw Khen once lived on the mainland of the Malay Peninsula, but after refusing to ferry a monk across a river, the tribe was cursed forever, becoming homeless wanderers on the sea.

The British discovered the Salon in 1826, two years after the first Anglo-Burmese War provided them with territory in the Bay of Bengal and the Andaman Sea. They stated that all attempts to "civilize" them were complete failures. While a 1901 Burma census listed 1,325 Salon within the country's borders, only small remnants of these people still survived at the time of our trip. Lampi Island, they claimed, had always been one of their favored retreats, where they kept semipermanent habitations during the rainy season.

Although the Salon once fished only to feed their families, and were said to reject any accumulation of wealth, these Lampi inhabitants now scoured the coastal waters for increasingly rare and endangered species such as marine turtles, sea cucumbers, and sea urchins. Valued as Asian culinary delicacies, the species were sought after by Thai merchants, who exchanged cheap kitchenware and gold necklaces for these biological treasures.

The activities of the Salon were not the only disturbance we found on the island. Timber poachers from the mainland and nearby islands had already cut down the largest trees on Lampi. Many of the surrounding coral reefs had been destroyed by people using explosives to kill fish, and by passing boats anchoring in the area. Still, there was much to be said for what remained on Lampi. In time, if protected and undisturbed, the coral reefs could reestablish themselves and the smaller trees would become big ones. General Chit Swe was right. The beauty of Lampi and its potential as a national park were undeniable.

On returning to Yangon, I worked with the survey team to design a plan that would protect Lampi Island and the surrounding waters. The Salon could continue to live on the island, we believed, but neither they nor anyone else should be allowed to harvest marine resources within the boundaries of the protected area. The minister was pleased with the survey and supported our recommendations. Almost eleven months later, on February 28, 1996, the cabinet would approve Lampi Island as Myanmar's first marine national park.

I waited in the departure lounge of the Yangon airport for a flight to Bangkok. It was April 1995 and my emotions were in turmoil. The last two years in Myanmar had been some of the most productive of my career, and I felt I was only just beginning here. I had hired a young, dynamic forestry graduate, U Tint Lwin Thaung, to coordinate our efforts with the Forest Department in Yangon. Forest staff were getting trained, new research projects were starting up, and General Chit Swe was starting to trust my judgment more and more. Recently he had even asked me to move to Yangon.

But I was no longer a full-time field scientist, nor was I a bachelor, as I had been less than five years earlier. My home now was in New York, where I had to return in order to resume my administrative duties as director of Asia programs, a job I was finding increasingly unsatisfying. I also needed to spend more time with my wife, Salisa. We had been married for less than three years, after having met when she was a university student in her homeland of Thailand. She now worked with me at WCS as a geneticist, but much of the time we had known each other I had been in the field, far from our home. I loved her deeply and wanted our marriage to work, yet the thought of tearing up my plane ticket to New York and not going back at all kept popping into my mind ever since I had returned from Lampi.

Thus conflicted, I picked up a copy of the local English-language newspaper, *The New Light of Myanmar,* which had been left on the seat next to mine. The first article I read was to change the course of the next few years of my life. A few months earlier the Japanese mountain climber Takashi Ozaki, after a thirty-day walk, had nearly reached the north face of Mount Hkakabo Razi, more than 19,000 feet high, before unstable snow and poor weather conditions forced him back. Deep in the farthest reaches of northern Myanmar, Ozaki, who had raced against the famous climber Reinhold Messner to scale all fourteen Himalayan peaks higher than 26,000 feet, had stood before a mountain that had long been off-limits to foreigners and remained one of the highest unclimbed peaks in the eastern Himalayas. That had been only a reconnaissance trip, however; he was planning his first real assault on the peak in the next few months.

I lowered the newspaper to my lap, no longer concerned about other news. All that mattered to me now was that Ozaki was the first outsider I knew of in nearly half a century to penetrate the heart of Myanmar's most remote, unexplored wilderness. His trip had set a precedent that perhaps could help me get permission to travel to the place I had most wanted to go since my arrival in this country. Ozaki had gone to conquer a mountain. I wanted to probe the region's biological mysteries.

I hadn't dared to ask permission to attempt such a trip before. Only in 1994 had a cease-fire agreement finally been signed between the government in Yangon and the Kachins, who controlled the area I sought to visit. But the news about Ozaki could change everything. Riding on my successful trips to Htamanthi and Lampi, and all the work I had done with the Forest Department up to this point, I decided it was time to call in my chips. On the plane to Thailand, I drafted an urgent request to General Chit Swe.

## CHAPTER 4

# Gateway to the North

We all naturally move on the edges of eternity, and are
sometimes granted vistas through the fabric of illusion.

—Ansel Adams

THE FAX WAS WAITING FOR ME when I arrived
at my office at the Bronx Zoo. It was good news. General Chit Swe
had given me permission to fly to Putao, the northernmost accessible town, where I could visit nearby villages and ask about tigers
and other wildlife. The area was not considered completely secure,
so I would again be accompanied by military personnel. The minister of defense, who also had to sign off on the trip, restricted us to
Putao township, encompassing about a 30-mile radius around Putao
itself. In the fax it stated pointedly that the Japanese climber Ozaki
had paid a large permit fee to climb Mount Hkakabo Razi. I was
asking to go for free.

I leaned back in my chair and smiled. This was a start. Looking
up at the map tacked to my office wall, I could easily find Myanmar. I had blackened its nearly 4,000 miles of border with a felt-tip
marker. Areas I had already visited were circled in green, and areas

I still wanted to explore were circled in yellow. Only one area was circled in bright red, so that it would catch my eye whenever I looked at the map—the farthest northern reaches of the country, from the town of Putao to the borders with India, Tibet, and western China.

I followed the little blue river lines as they emerged from the Himalayas and came together as a bigger blue line bisecting the country, the Ayeyarwady River, flowing more than 2,100 miles southward. This was Myanmar's lifeline; its waters carried barges of cargo, boatloads of passengers, and rafts of bamboo and teak, all passing each other on a daily basis. Along its banks, historic capitals had risen and fallen, cities with names like Mandalay, Ava, Amarapura, Prome, and Pagan. The river was navigable by steamer only as far as the city of Bhamo, 900 miles from its mouth. Beyond that, smaller boats were needed to go farther upstream. At its southern end, almost as if tired from carrying its burden, the thick blue line broke into eight branches, creating the 13,000-square-mile delta, the country's "rice bowl." This was where the glacial water molecules of the far north finally made their way through the mangrove-filled estuaries and passed into the Andaman Sea.

I got up out of my chair and walked into the office of John Robinson, a senior vice president of WCS and head of our international division. John and I were friends, but the smile on his face disappeared when I told him that I wanted to resign as director of Asia programs. I felt like a caged animal in the office, I told him. I needed to get back into the field and do what I did best. After a long discussion that took us from the office to his house, Robinson reluctantly agreed to my request. I would stay in the job until we could find someone else to take it over. Then I would become director of science for Asia, a position that would allow me freedom to come and go as I pleased.

Salisa was not entirely surprised when I told her that evening what had transpired. We had already talked about the possibility of my stepping down as Asia director. She was supportive but less than enthusiastic. Though I claimed to be making this move partly for us, she had a better sense of what might occur than I did. She feared we would see each other even less in the future.

In March 1996 I landed in Yangon for the fourth time and was met by U Saw Tun Khaing, a man I had recently hired to replace U Tint Lwin Thaung as coordinator of WCS's conservation program in the country. U Tint Lwin Thaung had been accepted to a forestry Ph.D. program in Australia. Khaing, as he said to call him, was a fit, 53-year-old former deputy director of the Forest Department with a master's degree in forestry from Aberdeen, Scotland. In the mid-1980s he had been in charge of Ahlaungdaw Kathapa National Park, one of the only protected areas in the country that was actively managed. But the limitations the military regime placed on him left him feeling unable to do his job properly. In 1991 he left the Forest Department and worked as a consultant for the United Nations Development Program and the Food and Agriculture Organization, trying to help raise the living standards of the Myanmar people in remote areas.

Along with his contacts in the government, Khaing's gentle manner and quick smile made him an ideal candidate for a job that both was demanding and required sensitivity. He had proved himself a good administrator already by helping me set up a small office in Yangon where we could coordinate the expanding WCS activities. New York had agreed to appropriate more money for the Myanmar program, and I had set aside a few thousand dollars so that the Forest Department staff, whom I had trained for the last two years, could continue to pursue research and protection efforts in the field. Now I was also able to designate $5,000 more toward a small grants program for wildlife conservation that would be open to students from the universities as well as to Forest Department staff. Khaing would be in charge of these programs.

I knew nothing of Khaing's personal life and, as a foreigner, I was not allowed to visit his home at the time without government permission. While I admired his commitment to his country and his people, I had yet to see him perform in the field where, he said, he was most at home. He was coming with me to Putao, and I was anxious to get to know the man in whom I was placing so much trust.

For the first few days, I made the rounds of Yangon government offices to meet new officials and reestablish ties with people who had helped me on previous trips. This was always required before a trip, both as an official courtesy and as an important means of giving "face," or creating an air of importance concerning the position of particular officials. But there was such a rapid turnover among the middle- and upper-level civil servants that it was difficult to know who would be in power each time I arrived. This time there were two new director-generals I had to meet. As I had done many times before, I waited patiently in the official meeting room of the Forest Department for our formal introductions.

I was used to waiting by now. So much of my work involved putting up with the boredom and frustration of endless delays and last-minute setbacks, most of which had no apparent logic to them. This was the reality behind the perceived "glamour" of fieldwork. In Myanmar, it seemed worse than in other countries where I had worked. Still, it was a small price to pay to get to the places I wanted to go, and to make sure that my work had meaning long after I was gone. I sank down further into the overstuffed orange velvet chair in which I had been told to sit, a chair that was stained and worn from the many previous visitors it had hosted.

❧

Once the necessary protocol was completed, Khaing made arrangements for our flight. Internal flights could be booked only the day before travel. There were no such things as computer reservations or strict timetables. We arrived two hours early at the airport the next morning to make sure that we would be able to get on the plane and would not be bumped by some government or military VIP at the last minute. It was a chance for me to catch up on some reading, unlike the previous days, when I had spent long hours staring at the walls as I waited to make small talk with government officials. I was guaranteed a seat on the plane since my ticket was paid for in U.S. currency at the official exchange rate. Khaing's seat, however, was paid for in kyats, the local currency, so he could be bumped from the flight at the whim of higher authorities.

Fortunately, the plane was only two-thirds full and only ninety minutes late. I checked a large duffel bag at the counter and hand-carried a small day pack containing my cameras. Khaing had said that luggage space might be limited, so I spent part of the previous evening repacking my bags and deciding what could be left behind. A week's supply of underwear, an extra can of shaving cream, a half-dozen trashy paperbacks—things that were so important in New York now appeared superfluous. Converting three bags into one was easy.

Getting from Yangon to Putao took three planes and three days. I considered us lucky. Not so many years before, a similar trip took at least a month, with the last stretch traveled by oxcart. The plane from Yangon was an old Fokker F-28 with discarded food wrappers still stuffed in the magazine slot in front of me and a musty, almost decaying smell emanating from the upholstery. None of that bothered me. It was only when the flight was further delayed because of engine problems that I got nervous. A warning from the 1993 edition of the Lonely Planet's guide to Myanmar was still fresh in my mind: "Considering Myanmar Air's recent safety record, we wouldn't recommend taking a domestic flight even if you could get a ticket."

After a night in Mandalay, we flew the next day to Myitkyina, the real entry into north Burma and the capital of the Kachin State. This was still a restricted area for tourists because much of the region was under the nominal control of the Kachin Independent Army (KIA). Formed in 1961 with only a few World War II rifles and the dream of establishing a free Kachin republic, this fledgling army soon became a force to be reckoned with, using jade and opium to barter for guns, ammunition, medicine, and other necessities from neighboring countries. During the 1970s, the KIA's influence grew so substantially that a political wing was formed, the Kachin Independent Organization (KIO). Over the next decade the KIO administered an area of more than 15,000 square miles containing more than 300,000 people. The central government couldn't control this growing insurgency, which reached its high point in 1986 when a Myanmar regional military commander was gunned down in the middle of Myitkyina. A cease-fire agreement was finally signed in 1994, but the reality of peaceful coexistence between the Myanmar military and the KIA was still being tested amid discernable tension.

For "security reasons," we couldn't get our luggage until the plane took off again, and then there was a lengthy wait while officials at the airport examined my passport and verified that I had permission to be there. Finally, we made it into town and checked into the Popa Hotel, built over the railroad station. For $12 a night I shared a bathroom with the rest of the floor, and my bed shook whenever a train came through. I could have slept regardless, had trains not blasted their horns at intervals through the night, like elephants trumpeting their arrival. The only other occupants of the hotel were a group of elderly Japanese who had also received special permission from the government to be here. They were visiting sites where friends or family members had died fighting the British during World War II.

The next morning, a local Forest Department official took Khaing and me on an excursion 30 miles north of Myitkyina. My stomach was upset, but I was adept by now at taking care of indigestion and diarrhea in the country. Myanmar food was tasty but far too oily for my liking, and the sanitary conditions in many of the places I found myself left much to be desired. But as long as I kept a stock of Pepto-Bismol and Imodium close at hand, I felt I could deal with almost anything that wanted to slide through me.

We parked in an area cleared for visitors and walked down onto a rocky beach where the water from two tributaries came boiling and surging over huge boulders to join forces. This was one of the places I had wanted to visit on this trip, the beginning of the main body of the Ayeyarwady River. I stood below the confluence and looked across almost 1,000 feet of water to the unbroken forest on the other side.

In its journey to the sea, the Ayeyarwady River, which remains free-flowing throughout its length, narrows in places to as little as 150 feet across, and then widens again to as much as 3,000 feet. It was March now, and the water was 40 feet below the banks, the river's lowest level for the year. During April and May, as the snow melted in the mountains, the river would begin a steady rise, peaking around September. Then the great Ayeyarwady, carrying vast supplies of fertile alluvium downstream, would spill itself onto the floodplains and revitalize the soil for a new round of crops the following year.

Much of the forest looked wild and intact here, but the owner of a food stall nearby told us that Lisu hunters had killed off all the tigers long ago. Elephants still came around occasionally, he said, but most of the wildlife had become scarce. Then he offered us the day's special: barking deer, a small 50-pound deer species that made dog-like barking sounds when frightened. It was still relatively common throughout many of the tropical forests of southeast Asia and was easily hunted when it fed along the edges of open plantation areas.

While Khaing watched the Ayeyarwady River on its course southward, I turned to the north, to where the tributaries that formed this famous river disappeared into forest, and unfolded a topographic map of the region. The western branch, the Mali Hka, appeared almost a continuation of the Ayeyarwady, flowing through a relatively flat valley south from Putao, several hundred miles from here. The other tributary, called the Nmai Hka, literally translated as the "bad waters," bent sharply to the east and flowed down through country that, earlier in the century, was described as so "wild and savage" that even the Kachin avoided it for fear of attack by less civilized tribes. Between these wild rivers, spawned from the snow-covered mountains of the far north, lay the rugged Shan-ngaw Mountain Range, part of an area known to early explorers as the Triangle. Until the 1930s, much of this terrain was unexplored, and the source of these larger tributaries, far to the north, was regarded as one of the great unsolved geographical mysteries of its time.

Before leaving for Putao, we also visited Pidaung Wildlife Sanctuary, an hour west of Myitkyina, accompanied by seven soldiers and a captain. Pidaung was the first protected area established in the country, set up in 1911 to encompass pristine forest, salt licks, and open grasslands and containing substantial populations of rhinos, tigers, elephants, and wild cattle species. Expanded several times until it was nearly 300 square miles in area, Pidaung was touted in the 1930s as "one of the most rewarding places in Burma for viewing big game," a model park that would one day rival South Africa's famed Kruger National Park. Instead, it became an example of the desecration and abuse that could be perpetrated on even the best and most prominent of a country's protected areas. A wildlife survey in 1960 by two American scientists found the wildlife in Pidaung to be "a forlorn remnant" of what had once been there, finding evidence of only two tigers, two leopards, two bears, two wild dogs, and forty-nine elephants. All the rhinos were dead.

Now, in 1996, I stood atop a rise looking over an open, empty plain, much of it recently cleared, within the heart of the Pidaung Sanctuary. Having talked with the park's chief, I already knew that within the sanctuary's boundaries there were two villages containing 640 people, 5,000 acres of illegal rice fields, a train station, a major through road, and a military compound with a shooting range that occupied more than 1,400 acres. Much of the former open grasslands were gone, and 6,000 additional acres of grassland

were scheduled for conversion by the military to rubber plantations. Every species bigger than a barking deer was gone. Anything
smaller, such as macaques, civets, and porcupines, were openly
hunted by the local people using steel or rope snares. I watched a
villager proudly tack a fresh leopard cat skin to the outside wall of
his house while, behind him, military trucks lumbered by, filled
with newly felled trees from within the sanctuary, to be used for
fuel wood.

Ironically, the Forest Department still had staff assigned to protect and manage Pidaung Wildlife Sanctuary. But they had no vehicles with which to get around, and they needed permission from
the military to go anywhere or do anything within the sanctuary.
Already at least 10,000 acres of wildlife habitat had been lost or
degraded in Pidaung, I was told. Forest Department staff were well
aware of the continuing devastation, and any remarks I made on the
forlorn state of this once magnificent area were met with sad smiles
and polite shrugs. The last forester to complain about unauthorized
cutting of wood in the sanctuary, I was told, had been quickly trans-
ferred.

That night we had dinner with a senior forest officer based in
Myitkyina, an old friend of Khaing. He drank his beer far too
quickly as he and Khaing reminisced about their early days in the
Forest Department. Although I couldn't understand what was being
said, I could tell when the conversation turned maudlin. Khaing
explained that his friend was embarrassed that a foreigner like me
could see how ineffective he was. He had always been proud of
working for the Forest Department. It had been a noble career at
one time. Now he was a puppet, controlled by a military regime
that rendered him and all the other forest officers fearful, ineffective, and mute. And the worst of it all, he told Khaing as he finished
off another bottle of beer, was that some of the once proud forest
officers now had to take other jobs or engage in illegal activities in
order to support their families.

I left Khaing and his friend at the restaurant and walked back alone to the hotel. We had to get to the airport early the next morning in order to get seats on the flight to Putao. The streets outside were dark, lit only by the flickering candles and oil lamps shining from the small stalls selling food and sundry goods along the road. A horse-drawn buggy passed in the distance. The only other sounds were of the soft voices of people at the stalls. Smoke from a cooking fire floated across my line of vision, creating an almost otherworldly view of the scene. Wherever I turned, I was met with smiling faces that watched me pass. This was probably not unlike a scene from Myanmar a century ago, I thought.

Dinner with the forest officer had depressed me, although it revealed nothing new. Pidaung was dead as a wildlife sanctuary. Even the more intact, remote protected areas such as Htamanthi Wildlife Sanctuary, which I'd surveyed two years earlier with George Schaller, were in trouble. But there was an "oldness" here, a wildness predicated on major geologic changes that long predated human presence in this northern region. What I sought, I knew, was not to be found in the few, small protected areas set up under British rule and scattered throughout the country. I wanted a chance to explore and try to protect some of the larger, lesser-known forest areas farther north that had been rarely visited by outsiders. I could feel the urgency more than ever now. After what I had seen of the wildlife situation in Htamanthi, Lampi, and now Pidaung, I knew we were racing against the clock.

❧

Even from the air, Putao, at 1,342 feet in elevation and with a population of a little under 60,000 people, had the look of a frontier outpost. Clusters of simple wooden homes were dwarfed by the vast, open countryside stretching to the foothills of the mountains. On the highest point of the town, I could still see a piece of the wall from the original fort built here by British Deputy Commissioner W. A. Hertz in 1918, when he made Putao his district head-quarters and established firm control over this far northern region.

We were met at the airport by a military officer in one of only three cars in the town. There were few roads to speak of, and only the main street was paved. A road connecting Myitkyina to Putao had been built by the British before World War II, but after independence it had fallen into disrepair and become virtually unusable. Now, essential cargo into Putao arrived by plane, and only when the weather was clear. The officer informed us that the regional commander from Myitkyina was prohibiting us from visiting some of the villages north of Putao because of "problems" there. Despite the restrictions, there was still plenty for us to do in the areas that we could explore.

From Putao, which was surrounded by distant snow-covered mountains that could be seen on clear mornings, there was no place to go except into wilderness. By early afternoon, the higher peaks in the distance started fading into a hazy blur before disappearing from view. The people in Putao said that this was because the icy mountains were "shy"; you could get to know them only slowly.

Putao had a quiet, settled feeling, although there was a constant ebb and flow of people on foot or bicycle, dressed in the colorful garb of different ethnic groups and loaded down with baskets of goods. Some had traveled more than a week from the "wild and savage" lands to the north where, it was rumored among the townspeople, slavery and banditry were still practiced. Travel from Putao northward had to be mostly on foot, with distances measured in "marches" rather than miles, between villages that were not on any maps.

I'd already been gone more than a month on this trip. I missed Salisa. I'd promised her that after I'd resigned as director of Asia programs, we would be together more. Yet there was always something new to do here, another opportunity I felt I couldn't pass up. If I could just share these scenes and feelings with her, I knew she'd understand. But whenever I arrived back home, it would always take awhile before we felt comfortable with each other again. The sharing of feelings occurred less and less between us lately.

I took out the picture in my wallet, the one of Salisa in cap and gown graduating with her master's degree from Mahidol University in Bangkok. The fresh, hopeful look on her face saddened me. What were her hopes now, I wondered, after five years of a marriage that had displaced her from her family and her country? How often did she think about what her life might have been like otherwise?

The next morning, I was up at 5 A.M. to visit Putao's main open-air market with Khaing. By 7 A.M. most of the stalls selling fresh meat and vegetables would already have closed for the day. Only the more permanent stalls, sheltered from the rain and selling medicines, clothes, and sundry household items, remained open all the time.

The Putao market was similar to many markets I had visited in the Asian countryside—women squatting in the dirt or standing over tables displaying their live chickens, fresh meats, and assorted vegetables. Most of the women had infants attached to their breast or young daughters by their side, learning the family business. Wealthier merchants on the perimeter had luxury items for sale: kitchen utensils, flashlights, makeup, bicycles, and anything else that could be easily, or not so easily, brought over on one's back from China.

Khaing tugged at my shirt and motioned me over to one of the stalls. In front of a selection of rattan baskets lay four animal heads with red hair and small horns. I'd never seen the animal before, but I knew what it was immediately, having studied all the mammal field guides and reference books for this region that I could lay my hands on before this trip. It was a red goral, a rare Himalayan species restricted to a small area mostly along the Tibetan–Myanmar border. Few people, even from here, had ever seen this animal alive in the wild, yet I counted ten heads for sale in the market that morning.

At another stall, we found the head of a Hoolock's gibbon alongside a shoulder bag made from the animal's torso and arms. Its brain was good for headaches, the owner said. Then he showed us more animal parts and pointed me in the direction of other stalls selling wildlife. Within the first hour I had a species list that included parts ranging from Himalayan black bear, black serow, wild dog, and leopard cats to some of the rarest, most unusual Himalayan species in the world—takin, musk deer, red goral, and red panda.

The diversity and abundance of wildlife for sale in Putao varied with the season, I was told. During the winter months, when the high mountain passes to China were closed by snow, people in the surrounding region would bring their goods to Putao to sell. From there, the more valuable wildlife parts were sent to Myitkyina or Mandalay, where they fetched a higher price. In April or May, when the snow melted and the passes opened, most of the wildlife parts were bought by traders coming over from China.

On our second day in Putao, we went to purchase supplies for a three-day trip to surrounding villages that were not off-limits to us. I let Khaing finish the shopping while I wandered back to some of the stalls we had visited the day before. I was bothered by the fact that, while I recognized many of the heads and skins we had seen, some of the shapes, sizes, and colors of the animals were different from their pictures in the books.

I returned to a stall that had a pile of deer heads, set back behind a pair of takin horns, which the owner was trying to sell. The dozens of deer parts I'd examined the day before had all belonged to two species—the large sambar deer and the smaller common barking deer. But there were two tiny heads in this pile that looked different. They were barking deer heads, but they looked darker, with a slightly different shape than the common red variety I was familiar with. The owner had been dismissive of my interest, indicating that they were worth nothing. When I returned this time, he pushed the two heads into my hands and said I could have them.

I met up with Khaing and he took me over to an animal skin that we hadn't seen on the previous day. The shopkeeper said it was from a "jungle dog" killed in the forest nearby, but the skin had been cut up and sewn into a vest for the cold weather. The skin looked familiar, but I didn't recognize the animal it came from until I bought the vest and had the owner remove the stitching. As I laid out and then rearranged the pieces of skin, it came to me. These were pieces of an Asiatic jackal, a small, doglike forest animal that was still considered abundant throughout much of its range. The odd thing was, we were more than 100 miles north of where it was supposed to occur.

By late morning most of the market had shut down. We were heading back to our sleeping quarters when I made what later would turn out to be the most important discovery of the trip. I almost missed it, as I stood waiting for Khaing to buy stomach medicine for a bout of diarrhea that had just hit both of us. Khaing refused my Western drugs, insisting that only Myanmar traditional medicine would work on a Myanmar person's stomach. I was convinced that soon he would come begging for my Imodium.

A child was playing in the corner of one of the stalls, and I walked over to take a picture. While looking through the camera lens, I noticed the snakelike curvature of a large horn sticking out from under some clothes. I went over and moved the clothes aside. Hidden underneath were a set of heavy horns, tips curving upward and back, each horn nearly two feet long and with a spread between the tips of the horns of more than two feet. I recognized them immediately as horns from the blue sheep, a magnificent antelope-like species from the high mountain regions of the Himalayas. Its main predator was the snow leopard. But neither the blue sheep nor the snow leopard had ever been documented in Myanmar.

The horns came from the "icy mountains," the shop owner said, indicating the permanently snow-covered peaks near the border with Tibet. They were not for sale because they were rare and didn't often show up in Putao. I assumed that they had been brought in from China along with other trade goods.

Over the next week, on foot and bicycle, Khaing and I visited the villages and forests around Putao, talking with hunters and examining animal parts. It rained every day, and we spent most of our time in village huts huddled around the open fire pits. It seemed as if the local people were unaffected by the weather, but I realized that was not the case after I found the village cemeteries and saw the freshly dug graves of children. Bronchitis, pneumonia, dysentery, and malaria were common ailments here, with the latter two taking the greatest toll on young lives.

In the more remote villages still surrounded by forest, virtually all of the able-bodied adult males hunted or trapped animals whenever they weren't working their plantations of rice and maize to ensure the year's food crop. There was no shortage of people seemingly knowledgeable about wildlife, and there were lots of animal parts to examine. The forests of the area were still rich in wildlife. What I noticed immediately, however, was not the abundance but the diversity of species found in the same place, some of which, such as the forest-dwelling Chinese pangolin and the higher-elevation, mountain-dwelling serow, occupied very different habitats.

During the course of a few days, I confirmed my suspicions that the forests north of Putao comprised a biological transition zone between lowland tropical Indo-Malayan species and upland Sino-Himalayan species. There appeared to be a region of overlap between species coming up from the south, such as the Chinese pangolin, Asiatic jackal, yellow-throated marten, and small-toothed palm civet, and those from the cold, mountainous north, such as the takin, goral, Asiatic black bear, and red panda. This explained the strange mix of animal parts I was seeing in the marketplace. Some of these species, adapting to a changing set of environmental pressures over the course of many generations in this transition zone, were different in size and appearance from their relatives elsewhere. Unfortunately, some of the larger species, which reached the northern limit of their range here—tigers, elephants, and Sumatran rhinos—were already gone from the area, having been hunted to extinction long ago. One large mammal, the gaur, a 2,000-pound wild cattle species, was still around but extremely rare.

But something else intrigued me about this place. Frank Kingdon Ward, the renowned British botanist who collected plants here in the 1930s, called northern Myanmar (the region north of 24° latitude) one of the most biologically diverse regions in Indochina. He documented plant communities of Miocene origin (dating back between 5 to 24 million years ago), along with new plant species, which he believed had evolved since the last Pleistocene glaciation (approximately 100,000 years ago). If he was right, it was likely that certain animals here had also become isolated and survived, perhaps becoming new races or even evolving into new species. Already I had heard consistent reports of at least two different kinds of deer in this region, when only one deer species from here was known.

The biggest coup of our excursion to the villages was the finding of five more sets of blue sheep horns. I was now certain that these specimens came from the southeast edge of the Himalayan Mountains, in Myanmar rather than China. A Rawang hunter, who had married a Tibetan woman and moved down from the mountains into Putao, gave me a leg piece from a blue sheep that he had killed while hunting at the base of Mount Hkakabo Razi. There were lots of villages up there, he said, and plenty of hunters. All the different tribal groups in that region even had special names for the blue sheep, some calling it "the goat from ice mountain." This clearly signified a new species for the country as well as an expansion of the animal's known range.

The people living in the region of Mount Hkakabo Razi rarely ventured down from the mountains, the Rawang hunter told us. They believed that the climate of the lower elevations was unhealthy and could kill them. There were trails though this area, mostly in the valleys but sometimes crossing over high mountain passes, all the way to Tahundan, the last village. He sketched a rough map of the villages and the trails he knew. Two hours later, as we prepared to leave, his final comment came almost offhandedly.

"There is a Burmese monk who lives with the Tibetans in Tahundan, at the base of the farthest icy mountains. He teaches the people about Buddhism. He's in Putao now, staying at the monastery. I heard he wants to go back."

⚜

The name given to him when he was ordained was U Tilawka, meaning master of three worlds, the monk said when Khaing and I visited him at the monastery the next morning. He belonged to a small, select group of missionary monks who, under the auspices of the government, traveled to live in remote areas to bring Theravada Buddhism to different ethnic groups. I sat cross-legged next to him as Khaing translated our conversation.

"I heard there was a foreigner asking about animals in the icy mountains," he said, pouring a cup of tea and handing it to me. His face was unlined, almost childlike, and his movements were deliberately unhurried. He looked young, maybe in his early 30s. I was surprised to learn he was 40 years old, nearly my age.

"There are many kinds of animals up there. Many different people too. They kill the animals for their skins, but there are still many. It is very cold there, even after winter, but the mountains are beautiful." He smiled.

"I want to go back," he said, looking directly into my face now. "But there is no one to accompany me on the trip. I cannot make the trip alone, and it is too late in the season. I know the way. You have a strong body. Will you go with me?"

I watched the monk as Khaing translated. I had come to Putao not knowing what I'd find, hoping only for a good reason to convince the government to allow me to travel farther north. Now I thought I had that reason. I had discovered that the magnificent blue sheep had found its way into Myanmar's farthest northern mountains, and that much of the wildlife from this region was probably all but unknown. The little we had uncovered in Putao could be just the beginning of our discoveries.

I shifted my focus and looked through the unshuttered windows behind the monk. It was late afternoon and the view of the icy mountains was just now being lost to the clouds. Few Westerners had ever visited even this far north in Myanmar. Beyond here, the number was less than a handful, of which none had been wildlife biologists. I was on the edge of something wondrous.

I looked back to the monk. There was no hint of pretense or duplicity on the face of this gentle man, yet something about him troubled me. I couldn't put my finger on it, but I had learned not to ignore such feelings.

"I'll go with you," I said.

Khaing looked at me, like a parent waiting to scold his child as soon as he got him alone. We both knew that getting permission for such a trip would be difficult, perhaps impossible, despite our findings. I knew he was thinking that I shouldn't make such a promise. But I was counting again on the help of General Chit Swe and on my own perseverance.

"Will you be here next year?" I asked.

"If you say you will return, I will be here," the monk said.

"I'll be back," I said, standing to leave. "You can count on it."

## CHAPTER 5

# Last Prayers at Shwedagon

Then, a golden mystery upheaved itself on the horizon—a beautiful, winking wonder that blazed in the sun. . . . The golden dome said, "This is Burma, and it will be quite unlike any land you know about."

—Rudyard Kipling

WITHIN A MONTH OF RETURNING to New York after the trip to Putao, I learned that General Chit Swe was pleased with the results of our expedition and was willing to consider permission for me to travel farther north. The Forest Department, prompted both by the attention that Ozaki's climb had brought to the area and by our own findings, had in the meantime submitted a proposal to declare the far northern region around Mount Hkakabo Razi a "protected area." But they had no idea where the boundaries should be drawn, and there was no substantive data on the animals or the people of the region to determine the best arrangement. Should the area be protected as a national park, allowing for tourism and other activities, or as a wildlife sanctuary, where protection of wildlife would be the top priority? I proposed an expedition that would help answer these questions by mapping trails and village sites and by obtaining information on the state of the forests and wildlife.

To get permission and security clearance from the Ministry of Defense, we had to submit a detailed itinerary, starting from Yangon, along with a map of our proposed hiking route north from Putao. Although there were no border tensions or insurgent problems at the time, no one from the present government had ever been to this remote area, so it was considered "terra incognita." As with all my previous trips, a contingent of soldiers would have to be sent along to guarantee my safety.

Defining our objective as the foothills of Mount Hkakabo Razi, I proposed a hike along the major river valleys that would depart in March of the following year and take three to four weeks to cover nearly 250 miles in one direction. Our goal was to eventually reach and set up base camp at the village of Tahundan, the last known northern settlement in the country. From there we would go as far north toward the border with Tibet as time and weather would allow. The map we'd sketched was based on information from the monk U Tilawka, from Ozaki's trip, and from the few hunters in Putao who had been that far north. Again, I would be the only foreigner going. Otherwise it would be a Myanmar expedition, made up of a scientific team from the University of Yangon and staff from the Forest Department.

In September, permission from both the Ministry of Forestry and the Ministry of Defense was granted, conditional on final approval from the regional military commander of the Kachin State. The latter was a formality since the higher authorities had already given the go-ahead. This gave us at least five months to prepare. Khaing's job was to select the team, coordinate with the Forest Department, and travel to Putao to make arrangements with local officials beforehand. My job was to raise money for the trip. This was the first biological expedition into this area ever sanctioned by the government, and I would be the first foreign scientist to go there in at least fifty years.

When I told Salisa about the expedition and explained that I might be gone for three to four months this time, she said nothing. It was clear she was upset. But instead of discussing it, we just stopped talking to one another. She listened to more Thai music than usual, a clear signal that she was retreating into her own, more familiar world, and I focused on preparing for the trip.

While I had always exercised regularly, I began a tougher regime to ensure that I would be in top shape for a 500-mile hike. I had converted a 300-square-foot cabin on my property into a gym, including a small area set aside for boxing. Boxing and martial arts were both passions of mine, but it had always been difficult for me to find sparring partners who enjoyed a friendly bout now and then and who understood that sparring did not mean fighting. I had already worked through my neighbors and some of the staff at WCS. The only reliable partner I had now was Salisa. She enjoyed boxing as aerobic exercise, as long as I stuck by our agreement that I could only defend myself and not hit back.

The automated bell system rang, signaling the start of round one. Salisa came out swinging. It always made me smile, seeing this slim, attractive Thai woman coming at me with her fists up, ready for battle. She was fit and well coordinated, but today her punches seemed more powerful and directed. It took intense concentration to just block her punches without swinging back, and within the first 30 seconds I knew this session would be a real workout for me. After five two-minute rounds, normally her limit, she was breathing hard but showed no sign of letting up. If this was the way she wanted to express her feelings, fine, I thought.

My love of boxing had begun in the basement gym of my parents' home. My father was a physical education teacher in the rough-and-tumble New York City public schools. The problem was that, when he came home at night, he was unable to shed the disciplinarian persona that had earned him a reputation for being able to handle even the toughest kids. Throughout my childhood and teens, he was an indomitable presence in my life. I was in awe of him, and I feared him. In his mind I could overcome anything I set my mind to, including my stuttering. In my mind I was damaged goods, a disappointment to him and to myself. Consequently, the frustration and anger that resulted from my stuttering was all directed at him.

"It's all your fault I'm broken inside!" I'd scream at him repeatedly during our many verbal battles. "You did this to me. I hate you for this!" The louder I raised my voice, the better my chances of getting all the words out before the next inevitable stuttering block.

He'd fall silent at such outbursts. Often my mother would cry. Our house seemed filled with continual tension and anger. I learned only much later that my accusations ate away at my father like a festering wound. He wondered his entire life whether he was indeed the cause of my stuttering.

Since I wouldn't open up to him in any other way, my father decided to teach me to box when I was 10 years old. He would let me pummel his rock-hard body before throwing a half-punch that made just enough contact to stop me cold.

"You want to let your anger out. Good!" he'd say to me. "But focus it properly so you make it count. Then nobody can stop you."

I was thinking about my father when Salisa threw a left hook that made solid contact with my right eye. My head spun and I grabbed the wall to keep from falling. My eye starting swelling almost immediately. I started laughing and looked up to tell her what a great punch it was. The words froze in my throat. She was huddled in the corner, arms at her sides, tears streaming down her cheeks. She ran to me and threw her arms around my head.

"I'm sorry, I'm so, so sorry," she cried.

"It's okay," I said. "It was a good hit. It was my fault for not concentrating."

"No," she said. "You don't understand. I wanted to hurt you. It's the only way to get through to you. But you're so hard to hurt. I never thought I could do it." She began sobbing uncontrollably. "I never really wanted to hurt you. I just don't know what else to do."

That night I lay awake staring into the darkness with my one good eye, long after Salisa had cried herself to sleep. It had all finally come out—my reluctance about having a child, the heated arguments that flared up over nothing, the long periods I spent away in the field. She felt inadequate as a woman and a wife and was certain that our marriage was doomed. We talked and I held her tightly till she slept.

I was attracted to Salisa the first time I saw her in the audience during a lecture I was giving at Mahidol University in Bangkok. I asked the professor sponsoring the lecture about her afterward, and he helped arrange a meeting. Within the first two weeks of dating, I had fallen hard for her. But the circumstances were difficult. I was seeing someone else at the time, and I was still doing research on leopards and tigers in a remote wildlife sanctuary in northwest Thailand. She was completely occupied with finishing her master's degree in genetics.

We saw each other as much as we both could manage it. By the end of my field project, I had ended my other relationship and moved to Bangkok to write a book. Salisa moved in with me. We never discussed the future. She told me later that she was convinced that I would leave her eventually, as I had done with every other woman in my life.

We were in an Akha tribal village in a national park in northern Thailand, surveying for tigers, when I proposed marriage. We had bunked down in an abandoned hut and were unsuccessfully trying to sleep in the sweltering heat. I began killing time by telling her of all the places and all the animals I still wanted to see in my life. Only when I stopped talking did I hear her sobbing quietly. For the first time, we talked of my time in Thailand coming to an end.

Sometime in the early morning hours, unable to sleep, I woke her. There was no getting around it. The thought of packing up and walking away from this woman was too much for me to bear. I placed my lips so that they were barely touching hers. "I love you," I whispered for the first time.

The next day we drove into Chiang Mai. I bought her a little brass ring for 25 cents and then put it on her finger in the middle of the street. There would be a better ring later, I promised. This one was just fine, she said.

Memories flooding back, I turned to look at Salisa's face. Still asleep, she snuggled closer and lay her hand against my face. I still loved this woman. Why was I so afraid of having a child with her? Why was it so easy for me to entertain thoughts of leaving her and of being alone again?

---

In January 1997, I received a letter in the mail that was addressed to me in English but with an odd-looking script. The letter inside was written in Burmese, and I immediately faxed it to Khaing for translation. It was from the missionary monk whom I had promised to accompany to the mountains.

> To Dagagyi [meaning "disciple" in Burmese],
>
> I am writing in great remembrance. I pray for you to be healthy. Even we are different race, since we meet each other I remember you almost every day. When we meet again, we will talk various things and about the place which you are interested in. I would like to go with you to Hkakabo Razi. So it is important to meet with you first. I am always longing for you. I wish you good luck and happiness and wish you will come to me as soon as possible. I wish every human being to find the truth and be peaceful.

Buddanta Tilawka
Theravada Buddhist Missionary
Tahundan Village, Putao District, Naungmung Township

The letter had been written months before, but it had taken that long to find its way to me.

※

By February I was back in Yangon, sitting outside General Chit Swe's office, waiting to see the minister for the first time in almost a year and a half. He asked after me often, I was told, but we had had no opportunity to meet again until now. Unfortunately, instead of the small, personal meeting I would have preferred, we were having a press conference and television event to officially kick off the Hkakabo Razi Biological Expedition. The room was filled to capacity and included the entire scientific team that Khaing had selected, most of whom I was meeting for the first time.

I sat at the head of the room with the minister. General Chit Swe looked as stiff and uncomfortable as I felt in my sports coat and tie. When I was given the signal that the cameras were rolling, I formally thanked the minister for granting permission for the expedition and assured him that the survey would be a major achievement for the country's conservation program. The minister's gaze went to the top of my head.

"Why is your hair so short?" he asked. "You look different, younger."

I had gotten a crew cut in Bangkok a week earlier. The cameras were still rolling. Leave it to General Chit Swe to break protocol!

"You've not been watching enough MTV." I smiled. "This is the style now."

He smiled back and then signaled the cameras to turn away from us so that we could talk freely. He warned me of the difficulties I'd likely encounter on the trip north, such as the rough terrain and the possibilities of disease. He told me that the remote tribal groups were very unpredictable. I leaned in closer toward him.

"That's part of the reason I want to go there so badly," I said quietly.

He shook his head in agreement. We understood each other.

After the meeting Khaing and I changed clothes and spent the rest of the afternoon getting money for the trip. Among a plethora of illogical government practices, one of the most absurd was the insistence on maintaining an official exchange rate of U.S.$1 = 6 kyats, when the unofficial street rate when I first arrived was at least twenty times higher than that. Within two years, as the country's economy worsened, the unofficial exchange rate would jump to thirty and then fifty times this same official rate.

Since the prices of everything sold on the street were based on the unofficial exchange rate, an unknowing tourist, changing foreign currency at the official rate, would pay exorbitant prices for anything from a taxi ride to a piece of fruit at the market. Yet I learned during my early visits that changing money at the unofficial rate, while technically illegal, was a service offered by numerous government officials. Finally the government wised up and sanctioned a central money-changing office in downtown Yangon where anyone could officially get the unofficial rate, at a slight cost.

It was at the central money-changing office that we changed U.S.$16,000 at the rate of 164.65 kyats to the dollar. There were no bank notes larger than 200 kyats, and we wanted even smaller denominations than this for use in the backcountry. After two hours of counting money, we walked out carrying 40 pounds of Myanmar kyats filling several shopping bags.

We returned to our office to meet with the other team members and to give them money to buy last-minute personal items. In addition to Khaing and me, representing WCS, the rest of the team included three lecturers from the University of Yangon's geography, botany, and zoology departments, respectively; a medical officer; a cook; an orchid specialist; and seven Forest Department staff, one of whom was a deputy director of the Wildlife Division. Two of the foresters were from the Survey Department; they, along with the geographer, would help us map our route and accurately record the village locations. The deputy director was assigned the task of looking at the area's possibilities for tourism. Several other foresters were to be trained by Khaing and me as a social ecology team, gathering information on the people we met and their activities.

Dozens of boxes of food and gear were already piled up against the walls waiting to be packed. Sorting through one of the piles was a thin, gray-haired man introduced to me as U Win Kyi, whom I was told to call Hpa-hti, meaning "uncle" in Kayin (or Karen), one of the indigenous languages of native minorities living along the border with Thailand or in the Ayeyarwady Delta region. Hpa-hti was our cook and, at 60, the oldest member of our team. Khaing had first met him when they worked together at the Forest Department, and he assured me that Hpa-hti would have no trouble making the trip. Frankly, since neither of them looked to be in the best of shape, I worried about them both.

Our medical officer was an army major, trained as a dentist and currently stationed at the military hospital in Pyin-Oo-Lwin (formerly Maymyo). He had accompanied Ozaki on both trips to climb Mount Hkakabo Razi and presumably knew what medical supplies we might need for such a trip. I was examining a vial of morphine, long past its expiration date, when he came up behind me.

"All the drugs come from Thailand and the Middle East. It's not easy to get such things in our country," he said in excellent English.

"But why is almost everything injectable?" I asked, picking up another vial labeled ampicillin. I saw almost nothing in the way of creams or pills.

"This trip is difficult," he answered. "Either you stay healthy or you get very sick. Anything in between won't matter."

Over by another wall, U Saw Lwin, the orchid specialist, who had also been on the Ozaki trip, was helping to sort through more than 100 pounds of used clothing that we planned to give out to villagers along the way. He had shopped that morning for monk robes, packets of incense, and a small gold Buddha that we would give to U Tilawka for his monastery in the mountains.

We planned to leave Yangon in two teams, the first starting on March 2 with most of the supplies, and then Khaing, myself, and a few others following a few days afterward to meet them in Putao. I still had several appointments with government officials that Khaing insisted had to be kept if we were to ensure that nothing interfered with our plans at the last minute. Our anticipated return date to Yangon was early to mid-May, more than two and a half months away.

This was the biggest and most complicated trip I had ever attempted and, despite the excitement and anticipation, I was worried. With so many people and so many unknowns, anything could go wrong. The university lecturers and at least one person from the Forest Department didn't look very healthy, and our oldest members, though hardened by years in the forest, had never been on a walk like this before. And while the major seemed very knowledgeable and competent, the fact remained that our health was in the hands of a dentist.

I thought of the botanist Farrer who, in 1921, died from diphtheria in the mountains east of Putao. It wasn't the thought of death or illness that bothered me. It was the thought of failing that kept me awake nights. Of not being able to finish what I'd started. I'd never failed at anything truly important in my life, yet right now I was tormented by the thought that both my marriage and the success of this trip were in doubt. When Salisa saw me off at John F. Kennedy International Airport in New York this last time, her eyes were sad and her lips were cold.

Khaing called a meeting of the entire team two days before we planned to leave. When everyone was assembled, he reviewed the itinerary and handed out waterproof notebooks so that everyone could keep a journal. I reiterated our goal of conducting a biological reconnaissance of the Hkakabo Razi region and determining how it should be protected and managed. This could be a dangerous trip, I reminded everyone. If anyone got hurt or sick, there would be no immediate help available, and our success could be jeopardized. I chose my next words carefully:

"If for any reason someone cannot keep up with the team, we'll do everything we can to help the person. But we may have to leave someone behind at a village, to catch up later or wait for our return." No one spoke.

"We have to try to stick to our schedule, and this trip must be a success. If we fail, it could jeopardize everything else WCS wants to do in this country. So if anyone has doubts about going, they should drop out now." No one moved. Perhaps I was being overly dramatic, I thought.

Khaing sensed my uneasiness. He suggested that we go the next morning to the Shwedagon Pagoda, the spiritual heart of Myanmar and one of the wonders of the Buddhist world. It is a long-practiced custom of the Myanmar people, he said, to visit Shwedegon before an important undertaking.

The Shwedagon Pagoda dominates Yangon physically and spiritually. Dating back more than 2,500 years, the original pagoda, only nine meters high, was built on Singuttara Hill to house the eight sacred hairs of the last Buddha as well as the staff, water filter, and bathing robe, respectively, of three previous Buddhas. Enlarged and rebuilt over the years, the current pagoda is a bell-shaped structure atop a three-tiered terrace rising to a height of 321 feet and covered with an estimated 60 tons of gold leaf. The *chedi* is topped with a one-and-a-quarter ton, seven-tiered umbrella-like structure called a *hti,* in the shape of a sovereign's crown. On top of the hti sit a pennant-shaped weather vane and a diamond orb shaped like a flower bud. These last three structures are encrusted with thousands of precious and semiprecious stones of all shapes and sizes.

During the first Anglo-Burmese War in 1824, the Shwedagon Pagoda, because of its commanding location, was used as a barracks and artillery station by British troops. When fighting resumed in 1852, Shwedagon was again controlled and fortified by the British who, for the next seventy-seven years, continued to occupy parts of the structure. It was during this period, the Myanmar people claimed, that many of its precious treasures were pillaged.

We entered the southern entrance, passing between two huge lion figures. After removing my shoes, I followed Khaing up the seemingly endless stairs, ascending the hill toward the golden pagoda. On both sides of us were little shops and vendors selling prayer beads, flowers, and incense for offerings, papier-mâché toys for children, and wooden Buddhas, bronze temple bells, and Myanmar puppets for tourists.

This was my fourth trip to Shwedagon, but I had the same reaction every time I reached the top of the stairs and stepped out onto the main terrace. My visual senses were bombarded. I felt disoriented. The gold surface of the huge chedi was a massive reflector of sunlight and, at first sight, seemed almost otherworldly.

People in various modes of dress were walking, sitting, bowing, or prostrating themselves before the scores of mini-pagodas and temples surrounding the chedi. Some people swept the ground before them as they walked, as a way of gaining merit. Others were offering libations of clear, cool water at a particular shrine, pouring it over their hand first so that their spirit might be as cool as the water they offered. A ceremony was taking place for a little boy, dressed in princely garb and carried on the shoulders of his family. He was a young novitiate celebrating his entrance into the religious order. The orange robes of the monks and the pink flowing garments of the nuns contrasted sharply with the red and gold of the devotion hall pillars. I didn't know where to rest my eyes.

I followed Khaing onto the tiled path in the open plaza and began the requisite three circles around the chedi to pay respect to the Buddha, the dharma (his teachings), and the Sangha (the order of monks). Some people circled five times to include parents and teachers, both of which were also highly respected in this society.

But instead of focusing inward as was the practice, I continued to look around me, entranced with what Aldous Huxley described as the "merry-go-round style of architecture" that made up the Shwedagon.

I passed white cement figures of guardian ogres, serene-faced bronze Buddhas, intricate paintings on lacquer, figures of celestial beings, and planetary posts representing the different days on which people were born. There were the many representations of Kinnaya, a mythical bird-man who supposedly danced at the celebrations following the Buddha's enlightenment. I was mesmerized by the intricate teak carvings of Manaukthiha, a supernatural creature with a man's torso and a lion's hindquarters. The creature is said to have been brought to life by Buddhist monks in the third century B.C. in order to protect the Mon people from an ogre and ogress that were terrorizing the countryside by eating small children.

The Shwedagon in its entirety was an incredible and fascinating work of art. But what appeared beautiful and awesome on the surface became strangely confusing, even disturbing, upon closer scrutiny. Something bothered me about this place. As much as I wanted to experience and absorb the spiritual energy and peacefulness that should have been here, I felt quiet desperation and an almost overwhelming sense of suffering.

I'm not sure what affected me most that day. There was the old woman in brown robes sitting and risking blindness by staring directly into the sun, part of a meditative practice called samatha that is believed to enhance mental powers. There was the gaunt, sallow-faced man dressed like an itinerant, prostrating before the Buddha, up and down, up and down, reminding me of a caged animal pacing off the limited boundaries of his life. But it was the sight of money everywhere that I kept focusing on. Money stuck on the end of bamboo sticks or folded into lotus flowers as offerings to the Buddha. The names of the givers were attached so that everyone would know who the money had come from. Boxes and boxes of money, big boxes, small boxes, scattered among the various temples and shrines, filled with mostly low-denomination kyat notes from the poorest members of society. People giving what little they had to buy themselves a better place on the wheel of death and rebirth.

Shwedagon, it struck me, was just another grand cathedral, a self-indulgent monument to man. This architectural wonder relegated Buddhism to the same level as every other major religious order in the world, conveying a message to the people that merit or salvation came from supporting a structure and a hierarchy that, in reality, were superfluous to the basic teachings of the religion itself. I thought of how my father had not been allowed to attend a high holy day prayer ceremony at a Jewish temple in New York City because he didn't have the money to pay the special holiday fee. Credit was not accepted among the sanctimonious. You needed chips to play at the Las Vegas of the soul. I couldn't help but feel that Buddha might have turned his back on Shwedagon, just as Jesus might have been thrown out of many churches for inappropriate dress.

I didn't tell Khaing my thoughts for fear of offending him. He was a devout Buddhist and a good man. I was a guest in his country. At best, he might think that, as a foreigner, I just didn't understand what I was seeing. Perhaps he'd be right. But I understood what I was feeling.

The first of our group took off on a direct flight for Putao, accompanied by forty-four boxes of food and equipment. It cost us 30,000 kyats (less than U.S.$200) for more than 2,100 pounds in excess luggage. We followed a few days afterward as planned, overnighting in Myitkyina on the way to review the details of our trip with the chairman of the District Law and Order Restoration Council (DLORC). This was also the last place we could purchase the sixty bamboo baskets and extra blankets that we would need for the porters to be hired in Putao.

The sight of other Westerners on their way to the restricted regions of northern Myanmar was rare, so I was more than a little surprised to see the flight to Myitkyina filled with white male faces, none of whom looked younger than 75. After querying their Myanmar guide, Khaing explained that this was a special tour group making a pilgrimage to war graves, composed entirely of a group of men once known as the Chindits.

The Chindits were legendary. Named after the fierce sculptured lions guarding Myanmar's temples, they were some of the bravest British soldiers of World War II. Their commander, Charles Wingate, in one of the most daring adventures of the war, dropped these men into the jungle behind Japanese lines to "wreak havoc out of all proportion." More than a third of the Chindits never made it out of the jungle, and those who did suffered greatly to do so. I looked at these old, lined faces around me, one man in a wheelchair, several with canes. I couldn't even begin to fathom what was going on in each of their minds. They were going into the forest to revisit a past that had changed their lives forever. I was entering the same forest to try to change my future.

We spent the night at the YMCA in Myitkyina, a huge improvement over the Popa Hotel above the railroad station. Yet I still couldn't sleep. I was restless and excited. We had already met with the DLORC chairman, and I was done with the seemingly endless protocol. And seeing the former Chindits on the plane had, in a strange way, eased some of my fears about this trip. I was ready for whatever lay ahead, and I just wanted to get going.

Pouring a dram out of one of the two bottles of single malt scotch I had packed, I took out my cassette player and slipped in an old Cat Stevens tape. I fast-forwarded the tape until the song "Father and Son" came on and then closed my eyes to let memories take over my thoughts. This was the song I'd listened to more

than twenty years earlier as I sat in my dormitory room writing a
letter to my parents explaining why I had to drop out of college in
my junior year and hitchhike across the country. I had tried to
explain to my father that I just didn't fit into this world. I couldn't
fight my way through everything. I had to figure out where my life
was going, and I had to try to put the broken pieces of myself back
together again.

At 19, I'd never had a girlfriend or been on a date. The only living beings I'd ever been able to talk to at length without stuttering
incomprehensively were the various green turtles, gerbils, or gold-
fish I'd had throughout my life. In grade school, I had been placed
in special classes for slow learners. Of the two friends I had from
high school, social misfits like me, one had driven off a cliff while
at college in Kentucky and the other had killed himself on a motorcycle, racing at top speed straight into hell.

I mailed the letter to my parents, although I ended up staying in
school after all: the dean of the college, having gotten word of what
I was doing, talked me out of dropping out. But as soon as I grad-
uated, I took off across the country, moving as fast I could, searching for and running from myself. My parents never mentioned
receiving or reading the letter, and I never brought it up. Now it
seemed that everything had led up to this moment, thousands of
miles away from my birthplace, in some distant corner of the world.
I was still running.

A little past midnight, I started riffling through the dozen or so
books I had brought for the trip. Before leaving Yangon, I had visited the Pagan Book Shop, known by bibliophiles as the place to
pick up hard-to-find literature about Myanmar and other countries
in the region. I pulled out a thin green volume marked *Special
Report Series No. 1: The Tarons in Burma* and remembered having
bought it out of curiosity, because the foreword mentioned a med-

ical expedition in the early 1960s that had investigated reports of a pygmy tribe in northern Myanmar.

I started skimming the first chapter and came upon a double-page sketch map showing the route of the medical team. I hadn't had time to look at the book before. Now, as I spread the map open, I couldn't believe what I saw. The travel route was identical to our own.

I stayed up and read the book cover to cover. Then I went back and read some sections again. It contained mostly technical data about the physical characteristics and health status of a little-known tribe that the medical team was convinced was the world's only known race of what they called Mongoloid pygmies. They had been discovered six years earlier by Colonel Saw Myint, then director-general of the Frontier Areas Administration, who was exploring the region. According to the map, if they were still out there, we would pass right by them.

At first light I knocked on Khaing's door, anxious to talk with him about the book. He was sharing a room with U Saw Lwin, and I woke them both.

"Did you know about these pygmies?" I asked after showing Khaing the map and describing some of the details I had learned from the book.

"No," Khaing replied. "You know more than I do. We've been told that all the people up in that region are different."

"The Taron are different, all right. Look at them." I held up the book and pointed to a black-and-white photograph showing a short, deformed-looking man dressed in what looked like a white sheet. "We have to find these people. I don't think anyone has reported on them for thirty-five years."

"I thought you were only interested in the wildlife." U Saw Lwin came up from behind, smiling.

"I am interested in wildlife," I said. "But this is a mystery we can't pass up."

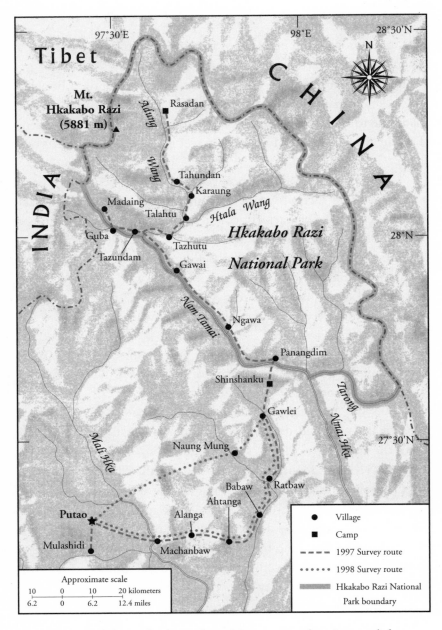

Routes of the author's northern Myanmar explorations and the subsequent boundaries established for the Hkakabo Razi National Park.

## CHAPTER 6

# Into the Triangle

It was as pretty a place as man could wish, a prime place except that the world seemed dying and a man's hankering was cold and foolish in him.

—Arlo Guthrie Jr.

THE PLANE STARTED DOWN THE RUNWAY before we were even strapped into our seats. There were no flight attendants and only six of us aboard. That morning, the week's only scheduled commercial flight to Putao had been canceled due to mechanical trouble. Rather than hold us up, the DLORC chairman arranged space for us on a cargo plane, a forty-four-seat Fokker with all but twelve seats removed. The rest of the plane was filled with large white sacks, forming a wall between us and the cockpit. The sacks were filled with salt.

An air cargo of salt might have seemed strange almost anywhere else in the civilized world, where this condiment is readily available to almost anyone who desires it. But in northern Myanmar, where there are few natural sources of the substance, salt is a highly sought-after commodity. By government regulation, any salt sold or

61

distributed in Myanmar has to be iodized. In the past, endemic goiter, a disease caused by iodine deficiency and characterized by the enlargement of the thyroid gland in the neck, had been widespread. This was particularly true in this mountainous region where natural sources of iodine, such as seafood, were almost nonexistent.

We knew all this before leaving Yangon. The load already taken up by the first team included more than 100 pounds of iodized salt that we planned to barter with and distribute along our route. What I didn't realize at the time was just how much this simple substance affected the lives of not only the people but also the animals in the areas where we were heading. Indeed, salt was to become a central player in my later thinking about how to go about conserving wildlife here.

As soon as we landed, I realized how good it felt to be back in Putao. The air was cool and fresh, life moved at a slower pace, and there was nowhere to go but into the forested mountains that seemed the custodian of the mysterious snowcapped peaks in the distance. We were met at the airport by the rest of our team and taken to a large white colonial house where Khaing and I had stayed on our first trip. There were no restaurants in town, so we took our meals at a little shop where the team had made prior arrangements with the owner. That night, huddled around candles placed on overturned cans and scooping big chunks of curried chicken into bowls of rice, we reviewed what everyone had to do in the days before we headed out on foot from Putao.

At 6:30 A.M. I woke and wandered down to the market. The thermometer I put out during the night read 52°F and 70 percent humidity. I wondered if the clothes I had brought were warm enough for the cool, wet weather that lay ahead. It was now March 1997, almost a year to the day since I'd been in Putao searching for a way to justify a trip farther north. The people, the shops, and the goods being sold looked the same. A quick smile or nod from passing faces showed that some remembered me. The shops selling wildlife still openly displayed their goods, but last year's animal parts had been replaced by more recent kills. At 7:30 I met Khaing and the other team members for our breakfast of noodle soup and fried tofu, always taken at the same little stall beside the market.

In the afternoon, we visited the monastery to meet with U Tilawka. In an unusual display of affection for a monk, he grabbed my shoulders and shook me, smiling and tilting his head as if we hadn't seen each other in years. He'd known of my coming from the advance team, and several boxes stacked neatly nearby indicated that he had already packed and was ready to leave whenever we were. He took one of my hands in both of his and, through Khaing, told me that this was to be a special trip for him. He wanted to get to know me better and share my life, he said. It was a strangely personal comment.

The quantity of people and supplies we brought to Putao didn't go unnoticed. In a town with little else to occupy the time, rumors soon spread about why we were there and where we were going. Some thought we were looking for gold, others believed I was with an American intelligence agency, and still others thought I was a Christian missionary related to the well-remembered Morse family, who had lived and preached here in the 1950s. Few people in Putao had ever been to the area of the icy mountains, and most thought of it as a dangerous, almost mystical place. Seeing a foreigner go into this area, where only isolated tribal groups lived, was unsettling to them.

Over the next two days, while we repacked our food and equipment into bamboo baskets that could be carried by porters, townspeople wandered by to watch and to warn us of the dangers ahead. One old man told of a hunter who had been attacked by a yeti, or "abominable snowman," that "rushed down the hillside with fangs bared and hands raised to attack him." One of the members of the Morse family had written about his brother's encounter with yeti tracks while on a preaching tour east of Putao in the 1950s.

I was both surprised and intrigued that yeti sightings had been reported here, in this remote outpost. Rumors of this legendary man-beast had circulated for years in the Himalayas but first gained prominence in 1951 when mountaineer Eric Shipton published pictures of large unidentified footprints near the base of Mount Everest, far distant from where we were now. It was another indication that, despite the lush green forests and flowing rivers around us, we were truly in the Himalayan realm.

Because we had permission in our hands from both the Ministries of Forestry and Defense, local officials were extremely accommodating to our requests. The soldiers assigned to accompany us came from a local army base and included a signal team with a wireless radio. They were told to report on our daily progress both to their base in Putao and to the Ministry of Defense in Yangon. Unexpectedly, the DLORC chairman of Putao arranged for two trucks to take us as far along on the dirt tracks leading out of town as they could go. This would probably save us several days walking. The problem was that both trucks had been broken down for months.

While the trucks were being repaired, I asked Khaing if we could visit the old Morse family compound in the nearby village of Mulashidi (originally called Muladi). I had heard mention of the Morse family repeatedly since my first trip to Putao, particularly when I inquired about the prevalence of Christianity among the northern tribes. Although its disciples make up only about 6 percent of Myanmar's population, Christianity is the dominant religion among the country's hill tribes, including the Kachin of the north.

Christianity has a long history in Myanmar, dating back to the Portuguese Jesuit missionaries, who arrived in the early seventeenth century. These early arrivals were followed in 1721 by a mission of the Barnabite Fathers, also Portuguese priests. But it was the American Baptists who, by the late 1800s, had exerted the strongest influence over some of the remote tribal groups, because of their greater willingness to live among and try to understand the local people.

Today, three Christian missions dominate Putao District and areas north. The earliest in the area was the Kachin Baptist Mission, which lay claim to most of the Kachin as their followers. This was followed by the Church of Christ, which took in mostly Rawang and Lisu tribal people. Finally, there was the Assembly of God. Of these three, the Church of Christ's mission, begun by the Morse family, had the greatest numbers of converts.

The Morse family, led by Russell and Gertrude Morse, first established their mission in the Yunnan Province of China in the late 1920s, targeting mostly Lisu as their early converts. In 1948, as communism swept through China, their son Robert led an exodus of their Lisu converts across the mountains into newly independent Burma, eventually settling in the Putao area. By the 1960s the Morse family had turned the Putao valley, particularly their own village of Muladi, into what they viewed as a model settlement. Their mission, called the Lisu and Rawang Church of Christ, built numerous schools and churches and established orchards where they experimented with exotic and local fruits, still grown and sold today.

Burma's socialist military government at the time became alarmed by the growing influence of what they considered to be a group of illegal foreigners, and in 1965 they ordered the Morse family out of the country. Instead of leaving, however, the family led another mass exodus—this time of some 5,000 people, a quarter of the population of Putao—to a remote "hidden valley" near the Indian border. Finally, in 1972, the government caught up with the recalcitrant Morses and took them into custody. They were put on a plane to Thailand, where they established a mission in the northern town of Chiang Mai.

Although more than three decades had passed since the Morses' departure from Putao, their house was still intact, albeit in disrepair. The grounds were looked after by a Christian trustee board, and a Bible school still operated in the compound. As we wandered through the old brick home, I felt as though we were in a mausoleum. There were books on agriculture and theology in the library, decaying furniture in the rooms, and old worm-eaten pic-

tures of the Morses and their children still on the wall. There was
no denying that this family of missionaries, through the introduc-
tion of better agricultural and health practices and the establish-
ment of schools, had created a better way of life for the people in
this remote region. Inculcating respect for life forms other than our
own, sadly, was not one of their top priorities. That challenge was
all mine. Seeing how successful the missionaries had been, I wondered how I might use these Christian beliefs to convince the people that all life is sacred, no matter what earthly form it takes.

As soon as the trucks were ready, we packed up and left. The first
day away from Putao was uneventful. We headed southeast, leaving
the grassy plains of the plateau on which the town sat. At the Mali
Hka River, about 14 miles away, the trucks were taken across on a
hand-poled wooden ferry. At the village of Machanbaw, we
arranged for a team of fifteen mules to follow us, for use when the
trucks had to turn back. We next turned northeast into dense tropical evergreen forest and headed toward the village of Alanga, 10
miles away, with hopes of making it there before dark.

I was surprised at how far we could take the trucks out from
Putao. The government, in their recent attempts to make this area
more "civilized," had ordered the villages in the area to construct at
least one additional mile of road each year. But with little other
than a mandate to build these roads, everything from the breaking
and carrying of stones to the clearing or widening of the roads had
to be done by the sweat and toil of the villagers themselves. Consequently, the "road" was little more than a layer of rocks in the
mud, cut into narrow, treacherous slopes that could be used only
during the dry season. Still, it was remarkable that so much of this
jungle track existed at all.

Once the trucks left Machanbaw, they inched along at a

painfully slow pace. Both vehicles had bald tires and worn brakes. The biggest worry were the small log bridges spanning the myriad waterways. Under the weight of the trucks, the logs would sag and the wooden planks would crack. The drivers thought nothing of this. But I was stuck in the passenger seat of a truck whose doors were tied shut, with the only exit route through the glass-less front windshield. By the second day, I had decided to walk.

With the trucks carrying our supplies, and most of the team deciding, like me, that it was safer to walk, we averaged little more than 13 miles a day. The terrain was relatively easy, but because we were not only breaking in new shoes but also walking over the broken rocks of the new roads, it wasn't long before we were all nursing blisters. U Tilawka clearly wanted to walk with me during these early days, but he stayed inside one of the trucks. He was not yet sure of his place among our strange mishmash of people.

After our night in Alanga, we started ascending into subtropical hill forest. We were traveling through the most northern portion of what Myanmar foresters have long referred to as the Triangle, that rugged mountain range running north to south between the Mali Hka and Nmai Hka Rivers, which are never separated by more than 50 miles before they converge at the place I had visited above Myitkyina to form the main body of the Ayeyarwady River. A Myanmar forest ranger accompanying Frank Kingdon Ward on an expedition through the Triangle in 1953 called the trip "an exile from civilization." For us, it was just the first part of a route that would take us into a region far more remote than this.

Entering the Triangle, we were now crossing topography that was part of what Kingdon Ward called the Irrawaddy Plateau, once connected to the Tibetan Plateau to the north and the China Plateau to the east. But the unending panorama of sharp peaks and shadowed valleys that made up this mountainous terrain before us looked nothing like a plateau. What remained of the Irrawaddy Plateau was now a heavily dissected series of north-south mountain ranges and river valleys that had been gouged out of the earth by glacial and interglacial forces during the Pleistocene Epoch, dating back more than a million years ago. That was followed by the gradual but powerful erosive forces of water forming networks of streams and rivers and creating the broken, rugged landscape seen today, aptly described by one visitor as resembling a piece of crumpled paper flung randomly.

To the west, I could see the distant vanguard of the mountains whose name in Sanskrit means "abode of snow"—the towering Himalayas. Here, there was a different story to be told. Geologists attribute the structure of the Himalayan Mountains to tectonic forces, namely the Eurasian plate migrating northward during the Cenozoic Period (65 million years ago) and pushing up against and sliding over the Indian plate. The mountains themselves, stretching 1,600 miles west to east along the fringes of the Indian subcontinent, make up one edge of an ancient shallow sea, formed in stages 30 to 50 million years ago. The Himalayas are nevertheless considered "young" mountains, still actively settling in and establishing their boundaries.

Frank Kingdon Ward believed that the juxtaposition of the west–east running Himalayas and the less jagged but rugged terrain of the former Irrawaddy Plateau, situated north to south, isolated northern Myanmar from the rest of the Sino-Himalayan realm. This isolation became even more pronounced after the end of the last Pleistocene glaciation. As temperatures rose and the glacial ice retreated, the deep cuts in the earth's surface, made more pronounced by the formation and flow of rivers, became narrow valleys colonized by tropical and subtropical plant species moving in from all directions. Steep, towering peaks often isolated these valleys from each other, fragmenting the landscape and producing what Kingdon Ward found to be a unique composition of plant communities in the area. And if the floral communities were so affected, why not also the animals occupying the region, he asked. Thinking back on the wildlife diversity found during our several trips to the Putao market, I had cause to wonder the same thing.

Although our food and accommodations had been simple in Putao, they became even more basic once we ventured farther afield. The village houses we encountered were mostly bamboo or wooden structures with thatched roofs, raised off the ground on thick wooden poles to keep out the domesticated pigs, chickens, and dogs. A notched log served as the stairway that led to a veranda where you removed your shoes before entering the house. This arrangement kept out the pigs but not the chickens or dogs, which, along with their fleas, easily scaled the stairway and got in anyway.

I marveled at the chickens, which provided us with a much-needed protein supplement. As stupid as the chicken looked and acted, it was not domesticated until long after humans were able to domesticate and exploit seemingly more clever animals such as the cow, goat, and sheep. This was because the shy red jungle fowl, first noted by Charles Darwin as the progenitor of the domestic chicken, was smart enough never to associate itself voluntarily with, or scavenge from, humans. It is one of the only domestic animals that has had to be forcibly subjugated by humans.

Every house had at least one, and usually two, hearths for cooking and keeping warm in the cold season. The hearth was a square structure measuring about three feet on each side, filled with dirt and usually set level with the floor. It was made from either clay and rocks, or concrete that was carried in from Putao. Special log posts supported the hearth from below. Every household had at least three items on the hearth: a heavy iron tripod, a metal teapot, and a large wok, all brought over from China.

There were few windows in these huts, and all had shutters that were closed at night. The walls and thatched ceiling were blackened by years of smoke from the fire, creating a dark and stuffy, albeit cozy, interior. Walls were generally bare except for the occasional religious poster or long-outdated calendar from Putao, showing beautiful Myanmar models from Yangon and scenery from other parts of the country that must have looked as foreign to the local inhabitants as I did to them.

Villages were always situated close to a river, which served as the kitchen sink, the laundry room, and the bathtub. Toilet facilities were usually some crude, poorly built outhouse over a shallow hole, sometimes shared by more than one household. Piles of bamboo slivers were placed inside the outhouse for use in scraping one's bottom when finished. Fortunately, we had brought our own supply of toilet paper, and after seeing the bamboo slivers, I made sure to squirrel away extra toilet paper for myself in case we ran out. I could put up with many discomforts in the field, but blindly sticking bamboo slivers up my rear end was not one of them.

In some villages, in lieu of a outhouse, there was simply a stick to hang on to as you squatted on a ledge by the river. As much as I enjoyed communing with nature while my pants were down, it was not a pleasant experience on a slippery ledge in the rain. As we moved farther into the backcountry, a few villages simply had a brushy area that was used as a common toilet. Having experienced these communal toilets in other countries, I didn't need to be told of the connection between the fat pigs running around and the fact that the toilet area was always free of waste. I passed on any pork dishes I was offered during the trip.

# CHAPTER 7

# Savage Land

The voyage of discovery is not in seeking new land-
scapes but in having new eyes.

—Marcel Proust

THE WEATHER WAS DRY and pleasant for the
first week, but the insects, particularly the little bloodsucking sand
flies, were brutal. Once, after several runs into the forest from a bad
stomach, I had so many sand fly bites on my genitals that the
swelling of my penis made urination painful for two days. From
then on I doused myself liberally with insect repellent. The local
people were not immune to such bites either, as the many scars and
fresh oozing wounds on their legs and arms clearly indicated.

Our sleeping arrangements varied daily but always followed the
same protocol. Khaing, U Tilawka, and I would usually be put up
at the house of the preacher or the village headman and given the
best sleeping spots, close to the hearth. The rest of the team would
occupy one or two huts nearby where Hpa-hti could cook and we
would take our dinner. Sometimes we all shared one large room of
the building that was used as a schoolhouse or church.

No one would lay their things down until U Tilawka and I had first picked our sleeping spots. He would inevitably choose a place right beside me, often a bit closer than I liked. Khaing and U Saw Lwin selected their sleeping sites next, and then the others. When this was done, everyone carefully arranged their bedding, so that no one's feet pointed at someone else's head, considered by Buddhists to be the lowest and highest parts of the body, respectively. This made for interesting spatial arrangements when the whole team was forced to sleep together in one large room.

After the first few villages, my sleeping bag was permanently inhabited by fleas from the chickens and dogs that were always finding their way into the huts. Villagers seemed to think it was easier to constantly chase the animals out of their huts than to simply keep the door closed or put up a partition that would keep them out in the first place. Eventually, I learned to ignore the flea bites. Not so the snoring from Khaing and U Saw Lwin, though. I slept with tissue paper stuffed in my ears.

During the first few days we encountered only Kachin and Lisu people. It was soon clear that both of these groups had a major effect on the social dynamics and resource use in this region. Of the one to two million Kachin in Myanmar, all come from five original families of Sino–Tibetan origin. Herman Tegenfeldt, a Baptist missionary who lived with the Kachin from 1941 to 1946, estimated that their arrival into northern Myanmar occurred during the 1500s or 1600s. The numerous tribes of Kachin represent different linguistic groups but are actually related through a complex system of clans. Although they had no written language or literature until the arrival of the missionaries, they had a rich oral tradition.

In Putao I learned that the term *Kachin,* commonly used to refer to nearly all the people in the north, is considered a corruption of the Chinese word *ye-jen,* meaning "wild men." Among these people, the largest group is the Jinghpaw (called Singpho across the border in India), whose name means "man" in their own language. The Jinghpaw we spoke with didn't like to be referred to as Kachin;

they preferred to be called by their tribal affiliation. They believed that the more remote tribes, who lived in the areas where we were heading, were remnants of those "left behind" in the migration from China and thus were socially inferior.

The Jinghpaw we met seemed to be an extremely friendly and hospitable people. I had been warned that they were capable of cruelty and treachery if they didn't like you, but I saw none of this, although we met fewer and fewer Jinghpaw as we traveled farther north. Jinghpaw traditional dress was the most elaborate of any I had yet seen. Women wore black jackets decorated with colored beads along the sleeves and waist, and elaborate three-tiered silver disk necklaces sewn around the neckline. A long, woven, kiltlike red skirt decorated with colorful geometric shapes was set off by silver bangles on the wrist and cane rings around the waist. The more elaborate the dress, I was told, the greater the wealth of the individual.

The Lisu seemed simpler and more standoffish than the Jinghpaw, but they were also considered the best hunters in the region. When they realized I was interested in animals, they grew friendlier and readily produced their most recent kills. One hunter brought me a sack containing a sambar deer head, two barking deer heads, five turtle shells, a hornbill head, and skins from a monkey and a leopard cat. This was just his previous week's take. More than ten years ago, he said, he and his friends could still catch tigers using iron jaw traps from China. Now, only leopards and wild dogs (dholes) were around. All the animal parts were dried and kept until someone made a trip to China or Putao to sell them, or until traders came to their village.

I was surprised at how openly the hunters in every village talked about and showed me their kills, despite the presence of the uniformed soldiers. Clearly, as I had seen with the hunters in Htamanthi Wildlife Sanctuary, they had no idea that they were doing anything wrong, nor that nationwide hunting laws, which covered several of the species they were killing, even existed. I saw no point in trying to tell them otherwise.

I had initially prepared a speech for Khaing to translate for each village headman, explaining that we were not with the government but were scientists trying to find out more about the animals in this area. Khaing tried the speech a few times but gave up when he realized that no one really understood or cared what we were saying. Since we had soldiers accompanying us, the villagers often drew their own conclusions.

"They think you're just a different kind of trader, wanting to take the parts back to your country," Khaing said to me one night, laughing.

"In a way they're right." I scowled at him. "Anyway, it works."

It bothered me at first to be buying animal parts, although I never felt I was supporting the killing by a one-time purchase. In fact, we were lucky that there were so many animal parts available for me to examine. The mountain passes were still closed, and the traders hadn't yet made their yearly sojourn into the area. After they did, everything would be gone until the next season.

I had to buy parts of many of these animals because I needed to examine them in closer detail, and our travel schedule didn't allow for much time in any one village. There was also another reason. No reference collection of these species existed anywhere in the country, and I had agreed to help the Forest Department set up a biodiversity exhibit in Hlawga Park, outside Yangon. I was unwilling to kill or collect animals specifically for that purpose. The parts I was buying from these villagers, while not ideal as museum exhibits, could still be used for educational and research purposes.

I had had this discussion with the director-general of the Forest Department before leaving Yangon. He had asked my opinion about a request by two well-known American museums to collect wildlife from some of the few national parks and wildlife sanctuaries in Myanmar. They proposed to leave a collection of samples in Myanmar, although no assistance or funds were offered to train curatorial staff or to purchase the proper equipment to care for such a collection. The bulk of the collected animals, a number that was never specified, would be taken back to their respective institutions in the United States.

The director-general was surprised by my response. As a scientist, I told him, I understood the important role that museums played as educational and research facilities. But there was no denying the obvious—that museums are biological and cultural mausoleums. Thoreau aptly described them as "the catacombs of nature."

It bothered me, I said, that as we enter the twenty-first century, racing against the clock to save some of the last representative wild places and wild animals that are part of our earth's magnificent biodiversity, scientists and conservationists are not united in their efforts. Instead of promoting field conservation, museums still actively support the killing and collecting of wildlife to fill their shelves. Sadly, these collections are obtained from some of the best remaining wild areas, often with little regard for the population of that animal in the wild and with scant consideration for what the local people might think—people who often are forbidden to kill such animals themselves. Furthermore, thought is seldom given to whether a sufficient representation of that species might already exist in museum collections elsewhere, because each museum wants its own collection.

Nearly sixty years ago, after traveling with the Vernay-Cutting expedition in northeast Myanmar for the American Museum of Natural History, J. K. Stanford described in his book *Far Ridges* his hopes for future collecting expeditions:

> If all goes well it should be a humaner, quieter, surer expedition than ours or any of the present day. Its collectors will not want too many specimens for by then there will be a world museum, a big central clearinghouse of natural history facts, in which picked men will have already worked out exactly the problems needed to be solved, and will have all the relevant material and ref-

erences in the world ready in their hand. There will be no power to shoot haphazardly or collect indiscriminately; they will devote themselves to filling up gaps which are obvious to all.

Unfortunately, none of what Stanford hoped for has come to pass. I worked for a society that ran one of the most prominent zoos in the world, yet I still felt that museums and zoos were mankind's trophy rooms, appealing to our basic desire to dominate and be entertained by a semblance of nature that can't threaten us.

I voiced my thoughts to the director-general, though he had already decided to grant permission for the museums to come and collect, hoping that they could help conservation efforts in Myanmar in some way. In the end I reiterated that he should at least steer them clear of the country's parks and sanctuaries, where we were trying to teach the local people to have more respect for wildlife.

"But you told me that local people kill these animals anyway," the director-general said, now sounding a bit concerned.

"That's true," I said. "But we don't have to help them do it."

Hunting by the Lisu and other tribes in the areas that we were traveling through was done mostly with crossbows and poison arrows. These crossbows were incredibly powerful weapons, much more so than the smaller, less durable ones I'd seen used by the Hmong in the mountains of Thailand. No hunter went anywhere without his crossbow. In the past, when a Lisu died, his crossbow, thought to be imbued with the spirit of the hunter, was hung over the grave.

While the largest crossbows reportedly were five feet across, the ones I examined averaged three to four feet. The beautifully arched bow was made from a species of wild mulberry tree, while the three-foot-long stock was carved from wild plum wood. The bowstring was made from plaited hemp, and the trigger built into the stock was made from animal bone. The arrows were split bamboo, 13 to 15 inches long and coated with a poison from the tuber of a local plant of the genus *Aconitum,* commonly known as monk's hood or wolf's bane. This plant was found only in the temperate zones, between elevations of 8,000 and 10,000 feet.

Arrows were coated with different amounts of poison and had different tips, according to the prey being hunted. Metal barbed tips were for larger species such as bear, while arrows with sharpened bamboo tips were used for deer and smaller animals. Because the poison was both dangerous to humans and water soluble, arrows were kept in bamboo tubes that were strung over the hunter's shoulder. Usually two tubes would be tied together, one containing pieces of split bamboo that had yet to be made into arrows, the other containing poisoned arrows and covered with a bamboo cap coated with deer skin to keep out rain and dampness.

A hunter strung a crossbow by simply placing the end of the stock against his stomach and, in one smooth motion, drawing the bowstring back into the notch on the bone trigger. With an estimated pull of 35 to 40 pounds, this looked easier than it was. Only I and one of the foresters on our team could string the crossbow.

A few hunters had black powder rifles, but they were rare in this region. Bullets came from local lead deposits. Saltpeter, which could be used to make gunpowder by combining it with sulfur and charcoal, was obtained by boiling and sifting the dirt under a house where pigs had been kept for several years. Although gunpowder was first discovered in the ninth century by Chinese alchemists, the hunters I spoke with had no idea where their knowledge of how to make it had come from. Their only concern was that misfires, exploding guns, and consequent loss of fingers occurred regularly with rifles. Most preferred the crossbow.

Although most hunters were able-bodied men, hunting was usually done within one or two days' walk from the village. Some hunters, however, traveled much farther in order to pursue certain species that were more valued by the traders. In the low-lying forests north of Putao, hunting or snaring of wildlife was done year-round but was more prevalent during the rainy season (June to September) and winter months (October to January) than during the summer months (February to May), when plantations had to be cut and planted. As we moved farther north through cooler, more sparsely forested areas, the kinds and numbers of animals available dropped dramatically, and the terrain became much more difficult for hunting. In these higher-elevation regions, the hunting season generally spanned the warmer, wetter months—April to October—and involved a complex system of hunting "territories" that were acknowledged and usually respected by all the villages. These were also the months when traders could cross the high mountain passes and easily move between villages.

Although a few villagers survived by hunting, most village life and sustenance revolved around the plantation, or *taungya*. This was a type of dry agriculture involving the slash-and-burn of hill forest followed by shallow cultivation. The kinds of crops that could be grown (such as rice, corn, wheat, yams, and potatoes) depended on elevation, season, and topography. A newly cut taungya was good for only one or two seasons before it was abandoned and a new area cut and burned. Abandoned taungyas were left fallow for about seven years before being used again.

The problem with this kind of agricultural practice was that much of the land available to the villagers was on some of the steepest terrain. The next rainy season would then sweep away the shallow topsoil on these open slopes. In this region, another 500 to 1,000 years were needed to create an inch of topsoil; thus, many of these steep hillsides never recovered. The attempt to change the destructive practice of shifting cultivation to a practice of maintaining permanent land plots, particularly in the mountains, has been one of the longest and least successful battles of the Myanmar Forest Department. Local people were just never given proper incentives to make such a radical change in their traditional practices.

Visitors to these mountainous regions often called the local inhabitants lazy because they did just enough work to subsist. George Forrest, a botanist who worked in the region in the early 1900s, wrote: "All the rest of their lives is spent eating, sleeping, and squatting round the hearth, varied by a rare expedition to obtain wood for a crossbow, poison for their arrows, or a stock of salt or wild honey." From what I'd seen so far, I concurred with his observations but not with his conclusion that the people were lazy. Mere survival in this landscape was a challenge and a hardship. Staying rested and healthy was not a luxury but a necessity in order to survive until the next season.

In most of the Lisu villages, the best hunters kept what I called a "trophy board," a large square of interlacing bamboo with the skulls of the different animals they had killed attached to it. Once the board was filled with a hundred skulls, one hunter said, they burned the board in its entirety and started over again. Keeping and destroying the skulls in this manner, they believed, guaranteed their success on future hunts for these same species.

The board was mounted on the wall of the hut, and it was considered bad luck for any skull to be detached or for the board to be placed on the ground. On most boards, eggshell halves were placed over the antlers of deer skulls; this was believed to ensure that the hunters would be able to catch more of that same species quickly. These trophy boards were a bonanza for me, providing a rich source of data on what the hunters were killing as well as the number, sex, age, and measurements of many individual species. The problem was that the hunters didn't want me to remove any skull from the board or take the board down from the wall.

It was on one of these boards that I was shown my first evidence of the small mountain barking deer that the hunters called *phet gyi,* or leaf deer, because they could wrap its dead body inside several large leaves of a local plant. I had no idea of the actual size of the deer, but I realized these were the same tiny skulls, six to seven inches long, that I'd seen but not been able to identify in the Putao market. Up here, these skulls were on nearly every trophy board. I had to get some of these skulls if I was ever going to learn more about this animal.

In the end, hard currency and trade goods won out over animistic beliefs, and I started a collection of leaf deer skulls from various villages. Sometimes I had to purchase an entire trophy board so that my removal of all the heads constituted, in the hunter's mind, a burning of the board. Maybe starting my own collection contributed to the stroke of luck that came soon afterward, between the villages of Ahtanga and Babaw.

I almost walked right by the hunter as he stood, watchful and quiet, no more than a few feet off the trail and all but hidden by the jungle foliage. It was the big green eyes reflecting the early morning light that stopped me in my tracks. Not the hunter's eyes, but the eyes of the carcass hanging over his shoulder. He was a Lisu, returning home through the forest from an early morning hunt. He had been about to step out onto the trail when he saw us coming.

When we motioned for him to come toward us, he laid the carcass on the ground. It was a little female orange-colored deer, weighing no more than 25 pounds, with bony protrusions called pedicles forming ridges along the sides of her face. Sticking out of a basket on the hunter's waist was a two-foot-long gray peacock pheasant, a bird of high mountain forests. I knelt down to examine what I'd already concluded was a juvenile common barking deer, as I pried open the animal's mouth to examine her teeth. My heartbeat quickened. The teeth were worn and stained. I rolled her onto her back. The nipples were brown and wrinkled. This little deer was no juvenile. She was an old adult!

This was it. This was the phet gyi, the leaf deer whose head I had been collecting from the trophy boards and which hunters said was found only on distant mountaintops. I hadn't recognized it immediately because females lack the distinctive small spiked antlers on their heads. The hunter seemed puzzled by my intense interest in this common species and by the barrage of questions that followed. But as I looked at the head shape, the long canines, and the rest of the body of this little adult female, I knew that this animal was anything but common. I was sure it was a new species to science. I bought the entire carcass from the hunter, planning to examine it more thoroughly later.

By the fourth day, we had arrived at the village of Ratbaw, having come 67 miles but having climbed only 400 feet in elevation since Putao. This was one of the larger villages in the area, with a population of nearly 300 people and a middle school with 200 students. Now we were mostly among the Rawang, formerly called Nung, one of the country's least-known ethnic groups. The trucks could go no farther, so we spent an extra day here hiring porters and waiting for the mules. With each mule carrying about 50 to 60 pounds, we needed another eighty porters to join our expedition.

The extra day gave us an opportunity to gather data from the area and prepare for the more difficult hike ahead. The soldiers set up their radio, checked in with Putao, and then went off to flirt with the local girls. U Saw Lwin and the other botanist scoured the village perimeter for plants to collect and press. The Forest Department staff collected village and location data, while the zoologist and I interviewed hunters and examined wildlife parts.

Questioning the local people was a slow, tedious process. Khaing was the only member of our team fluent enough in English to translate my questions exactly as I asked them. Then we needed one of our local Forest Department staff to translate from Burmese into Rawang. As we proceeded farther north, dialects changed and we sometimes had to use porters as third translators.

Working through the mouths of so many people multiplied the chances for misunderstanding, so I had to be careful of what I asked and how I asked it if I wanted an accurate response. In anticipation of this, I had put together a book of drawings and photographs of animals before leaving the United States. Some of the pictures were of species from this area, some were animals that looked similar to local species but were not found here, and some were of animals that did not even closely resemble anything here. This allowed me to gauge how accurate people's answers were.

✖

Most of our porters were young boys and girls, between 13 and 21 years of age. Older men and women usually didn't want to leave their homes, but the younger people were anxious to get away from their chores and meet others of their own age in neighboring villages. No one was given more than a 40-pound load to carry. Regardless of age or ability, every porter was paid 300 kyats (about U.S.$3) per day, which pleased them greatly. Each porter's basket was numbered, so we could find what we needed quickly and could record the porter's name in a notebook and know who was responsible for a particular load each day.

Most of the weight and volume of the loads was made up of rice, the basic staple of our team's diet. Khaing had calculated that each member of our permanent group would need at least half a pound of rice per day because of the strenuous hiking. This sounded like a lot to me until the Lisu hunters told me that they could eat three times that amount. Still, with a trip projected to last two months, this meant we had to carry at least 600 pounds in rice alone. Then there were our other foodstuffs, such as noodles, tins of sardines and meat, dried fish, beef jerky, canned fruit, sugar, coffee, condensed milk, and biscuits.

At each village, a number of the porters were replaced. Some wanted to travel only a certain distance from their village so they could get back quickly. Many of the younger people, however, would have liked to make the whole trip with us, but we had to send them back to their homes at certain points along the way. Every village wanted the money and trade goods we provided for porter service, so each village headman usually requested that we take porters from his village. We obliged, even when we didn't want to, in order to foster goodwill and encourage the villagers to be more hospitable to us.

Six permanent porters had come with us from Putao, two of whom were assigned to Khaing and me. My personal porter was a strong, handsome 16-year-old named Zawgan who stayed close to me at all times, carrying my camera equipment as well as his own pack. He was shy and cheerful, and by the end of the trip we joked openly with one another through mime. Occasionally I caught U Tilawka looking a bit glum when I spent too much time with Zawgan.

Our only problem with the porters came early in the trip. All the tribal groups in this area except the Tibetans in the far north were Christian, as a result of the Morse missionary effort. To many, this meant little beyond Sunday social gatherings. But some of our porters, sometimes urged on by their village preacher, refused to carry anything belonging to U Tilawka because he was a Buddhist monk. At first we solved the problem by giving his load to porters who didn't care or by quickly getting rid of the problem porters. But this wasn't good enough for some, and eventually we just split his load among the soldiers. This resolved the stated complaint but didn't ameliorate the underlying animosity toward us for traveling through Christian territory with a Buddhist monk.

The monk was now very comfortable among our group and stayed as close to me as he could. When Khaing wasn't there to translate, my communication with U Tilawka consisted of smiling and miming. Sometimes I'd catch him watching me intently or playing with my belongings in an almost childlike way. If he saw me tiring during the day, he would rush to my side and break off a chunk of cane sugar, which he carried with him all the time. As a Buddhist monk, he was not supposed to eat after midday, but he was allowed to take medicine when needed. Interestingly, stimulants such as sugar and coffee were considered "medicine" by some monks.

We were averaging nine miles a day now along narrow but well-defined trails between villages, moving through beautiful pristine forest as we climbed in elevation rapidly. Only the ever-present patches of old and new taungyas, situated high up on seemingly impossible 60-degree slopes, marred the landscape. Each morning, with the mist rising off the mountains, we would be serenaded by the cacophonous calls of Hoolock's gibbons. On several afternoons, large groups of Oriental pied hornbills flew overhead.

After leaving Ratbaw, we passed through two more Rawang villages and one small cluster of huts in two days, crossing back and forth across fast-flowing tributaries over narrow rattan bridges. No matter how poor or wretched some villages seemed, they were all filled with laughing, noisy children who, with their toys of sticks and rocks, seemed oblivious to their harsh surroundings and mobbed us when we arrived.

Early on in the trip we all fell into our own routines. We broke camp at different times and walked at our own pace. I was always the most impatient to get going in the morning so I left camp first, much to the consternation of the soldiers, who had to send at least one person with me at all times. I wanted to reach the next village as quickly as possible so that I could talk with villagers and write in my journal. Khaing would often start out with me but fall behind quickly. Others intentionally lagged far behind and always saw more than I did. The ornithologist walked quietly, looking skyward for birds, while the botanists were always taking little side trips off the trail to collect plants.

Once we had arrived at a village and decided where we'd spend the night, I'd pick my sleeping area, shed my wet clothes, and have hot tea with the village headman. I liked these moments, when I could huddle by a fire and quietly watch everything around me. There could be no conversation until Khaing arrived to translate for me.

It wasn't long before the members of our team formed four

cliques: the foresters, the soldiers, the university people, and the WCS staff, including U Tilawka, who occasionally wore a WCS baseball cap I gave him and considered himself a WCS monk! Each group chose their own sleeping areas, sometimes arranging themselves side by side in tight groups. Khaing, U Saw Lwin, and I liked a bit more personal space and would stake out little territories around our sleeping bag using canteens, flashlights, teacups, and other gear as boundary markers. Although conversation flowed freely during the day, after we bedded down for the evening, there was little interaction outside one's group. The porters always kept to themselves and rarely interacted with our team members.

Every morning we'd crawl out of our bags and blankets around 6:00, pack our gear, and quietly go about our morning rituals before breakfast. I'd brush my teeth, apply medicine to my athlete's foot, and bandage my blisters. I knew, from many years in the field, that seemingly small problems—a toothache, an infected insect bite, a twisted ankle—could become debilitating if not cared for quickly. The hardest part of the trip was still ahead.

When we reached the village of Gawlei, 85 miles from Putao, the mules could go no farther. Before us loomed a high mountain range that would take two days to cross before reaching the Nam Tamai, the western branch of what would form the Mai Kha River. We needed 30 more porters to replace the mules, bringing our total to 116 porters. Since this would have required about a third of the population of this fourteen-house village, some porters from previous villages were called back. Gawlei looked to be the most impoverished settlement we had yet encountered, so it was here we decided to start distributing some of the extra clothes, salt, and medicine that we had brought.

That evening, I walked along the river to be alone for a while. I had been bothered all day by the thought of having missed another of

Salisa's birthdays. She was 34 years old today and alone in New York. I sat down on a rock and tried writing a letter to her explaining why my work was so important to me and telling her that I loved her. But I just couldn't put the right words together.

Frustrated, I threw the notebook and pencil to the ground and took off my shirt to wash up before dinner. As I squatted beside the river, something caught my eye. It was a footprint, with water starting to seep in around the edges. I stood up and looked around to see whom I had scared away and find out why they hadn't made themselves known. Bushes rustled on the other side of the stream, and a patch of black disappeared among the greenery. Then I looked back at the footprint, and it hit me. This wasn't a human footprint at all. It was the track of a Himalayan black bear.

I plopped back down on the rock and picked up the notebook. Salisa's birthday was forgotten. I had been waiting to see evidence of this more than 200-pound ursid as we moved up into the mountains. After leaving Putao and ascending in elevation, the changes in forest types and vegetation had been obvious. Tropical evergreen tree species with bamboo and palms in the lowlands had given way to subtropical hill species such as rhododendrons and oak. But seeing or finding signs of wildlife that would give me some clues as to the distribution, diversity, and numbers of animal species that lived in these areas was more problematic. I would have had a hard time had not hunting been so prevalent, with the hunters able to show me parts of virtually every species they killed.

The scores of animal parts that I'd already examined, together with my interviews with hunters, clearly indicated what I had started to suspect in Putao—this part of northern Myanmar was a transition area between ecological life zones. Over the last week we'd been climbing out of the tropical Indo-Malayan habitat and moving into areas of cooler subtropical and temperate mountainous habitats. But in just the last couple of days, I had noted further subtle changes in what I was seeing. Certain animal parts, which were abundant in villages near Putao, were scarce here. The parts of some species, such as civets, deer, porcupines, and pangolins, were a bit different in coloration and size than what I had seen earlier and than the descriptions in my reference books.

I had been watching carefully for the place where there was a distinct shift in the dominant vertebrate life forms. This was it. Around me now were Phayre's leaf monkey and Hoolock's gibbon, bridging the tropical rain forest and the subtropical broadleaf evergreen forest habitats. The sun bear, ranging far into the south of the country, still persisted up here in small numbers and, in this area, overlapped with the Himalayan black bear, one of which had just visited me. In the mountains surrounding us, hunters from Gawlei had told me there were black serows and the still mysterious little leaf deer, while up ahead, as we climbed into temperate and alpine habitats, I anticipated a host of new Sino-Himalayan species. Clearly the transition zone was coming to an end.

Earlier that afternoon, while sitting with the headman as he spoke of a huge cave not far from the village, I watched his wife use a piece of brown furry skin to grab the handle of a boiling teapot. When she put it down, I realized that it was not a piece of skin at all but rather an entire animal with an almost indistinct white line running down its back. After jumping up and grabbing one of my reference books, I asked to see the skin and compared it with one of the pictures in my book. There was no doubt about it. It was a back-striped weasel, an animal I had never seen before, which lived mostly in mountainous evergreen forest. As of 1990, there were less than a dozen specimens of this extremely rare weasel in collections worldwide, most of them from the Himalayas. Yet villagers here said that the animal was actually quite common, and the headman's wife was amused when I asked if I could buy her teapot holder.

In 1935, the Vernay-Cutting expedition, exploring the mountains along the border with China southeast of our present location, collected bird data that clearly indicated the elevational gradient from 3,000 to 5,000 feet to be a belt of overlap between the lowland fauna and the Himalayan fauna. This coincided with what we were seeing now. At the village of Gawlei, we were at 2,200 feet, only six days out and nearly 1,000 feet above Putao. The next village up ahead, Panangdim, was two days away and nearly 4,000 feet in elevation. After that, the maps showed we would continue to climb steadily.

Animals that few people had ever heard of outside this region—takin, musk deer, and red goral—were still ahead of us. That was certain. But what excited me most were the still unsubstantiated reports I had been getting from local hunters. The sighting of a black-colored deer in the village of Ngawa, a week's walk north of here; the possibility of snow leopard, called *kanzi* in Rawang; the report of wolf in the high mountains along the borders; a hunter identifying the picture of a lynx, claiming he had killed two of these animals over a thirteen-year period near the border with China. Confirmation of these species would be new records for Myanmar. More than that, it would lend greater credence to my belief that this was a biologically important and unique area for the country. Such knowledge was crucial in addressing the Forest Department's question of how this area should be protected and managed.

## ❧ CHAPTER 8 ❧

# For the Love of Salt

The dangers of life are infinite, and safety is among them.

—Johann Wolfgang von Goethe

WE CROSSED PANANGDIM PASS at nearly 10,000 feet and then dropped steeply down the mountain to 6,000 feet to reach a way station called Shinshanku. There was a single dilapidated cabin for travelers here, along with a watchman's hut occupied by a man who spent most of his time hunting. Two Chinese traders coming from Panangdim already occupied one corner of the cabin. Our team squeezed into the remaining section.

The presence of the traders surprised me, since it was only mid-March and I'd been told that the peak trading season ran from June through September. I asked Khaing to try talking with the traders, but they wouldn't answer any of his questions. Soon afterward, they packed up and left.

A fresh black serow skin was stretched and drying against the watchman's house, the animal having been caught in a snare that morning. We bought the meat and distributed it among the soldiers and porters, while I took the skin for my growing collection of animal parts. The watchman kept the parts of the serow that he valued most: the tongue, which he ate to alleviate the pain of swollen feet; the hooves and bone marrow, which would be made into a liniment for the joints; and the skull, which was boiled to make a tasty curry soup. It was his third serow for the month.

This fresh kill was the closest I'd ever come to a wild serow, one of the more widely distributed high-elevation species in this region. A short-bodied, long-legged goat-antelope, this ungainly-looking beast with coarse, thin hair, often black or gray in color, can weigh up to 300 pounds. Less fond of cliffs or open, arid habitats than the smaller goral, the serow is found at elevations from 3,000 to 9,000 feet on steep forested hillsides, or in thickly wooded gorges. Usually solitary and moving over small areas, serows feed on tender leaves and shoots in late evening or early morning. The serow's curiosity makes it seem fearless of man, and hunters consider it an easy target.

The temperature hovered around 54°F all day, and the skies cleared long enough in the north to give us our first good look at the snowcapped peaks of the icy mountains. But the good weather didn't last: heavy winds and rain battered us through the night. The roof of the way station was riddled with holes, and there were large gaps between the rough-hewn boards that made up the walls. No villager would have let his own house deteriorate to such an extent. I woke in the darkness with water dripping on my head, so I pulled myself up and huddled against a dry piece of wall. I finally dozed off to the sound of our porters singing as they huddled together outside under a plastic sheet.

In the morning we climbed another mountain, crossing a low pass at 6,000 feet, and then descended a very steep, slippery slope of mud and wet rock, straight to the Nam Tamai River. The rain was coming in torrents, and at one point we took shelter under a rock overhang while some of the porters constructed a simple bridge over a stream that was quickly rising above its banks. Several long stems of bamboo were felled and placed atop large boulders that had been rolled into position in the raging water from one bank to the other. A waist-high bamboo railing was attached on one side. It was too risky to try to ford the stream: 20 feet below the crossing, it dropped over a ledge and fell 30 feet to the rocks.

The Nam Tamai itself, which we soon reached, was one of the rivers that formed the Nmai Hka. A long, narrow suspension bridge spanned the river, taking us into the village of Panangdim. Without even thinking about it, I climbed to the platform and stepped out onto the bamboo walkway, crossing with a now familiar cadence that timed my steps with the swaying and bouncing of the bridge. What had made me very nervous only a week before was now rote. We had crossed at least a dozen similar bridges already, and I could now look down without imagining falling to my death into the ice-cold rapids below me.

The building of these bridges was an acquired skill of the people in this region. Bridges on the main trail between villages were the most elaborate and sturdy. The hammocklike structure was firmly anchored on either side of the river by stout scaffolding built from large tree trunks high off the ground. A crude stairway made from a notched pole or tree branches took you up to a platform at the start of the bridge. Spanning the water, on larger bridges such as the one we crossed now into Panangdim, were two pairs of supporting thick-gauge steel cables that had been carried from China. One pair was for the walkway, while the second pair, several feet higher, acted as a stabilizing handrail. On smaller bridges the cables were made from rattan or twisted bamboo strands, which had to be replaced every few years. The floor of the bridge was usually made of strips of bamboo or wood laid widthwise. Cane strands connected the cables underneath the floor to the handrails, creating a shaky but reliable structure.

❧

Panangdim was a tiny Rawang village of only six houses and thirty-four people. Having had no break in the rainfall since the previous night, we decided to spend an extra day here to rest and to find out more about the area. It turned out to be a day well spent.

I took off my boots and crouched down to enter the doorway of the smoke-filled hut. The village headman, his outline barely visible, was comfortably settled beside a small fire burning in the center of the room. He motioned for me to sit beside him on a pile of deer skins and then placed a teapot on the hot coals. A woman came out of the shadows, carefully handing over a little bowl. Turning to me, as if to make sure I watched what he was doing, he reached into the bowl, dropped some of its contents into the teapot, and then sprinkled a little more into my cup. I'd seen this ritual performed many times in the previous week.

The headman was sharing with us one of his most precious possessions and giving me a little extra to acknowledge the value that he placed on my visit. I thought of my flight on the cargo plane to Putao. It still surprised me that one of the most common condiments of the modern world not only was scarce and highly valued in this remote, mountain region, but also was the central object in a bartering system that provided the only regular contact these people had with the outside world. He was giving me salt.

Despite its small size, Panangdim was a major crossroads in the wildlife trade in this part of northern Myanmar. There were two trails that led off from here. One wound along the Nam Tamai River upstream to the north, toward the borders with India and Tibet, and the second curved to the east, first downstream along the Nam Tamai to where it joined the Nmai Hka and then along the Tarong River to the Chinese border.

There were at least five more villages with more than fifty families total along the 35-mile trail that went east to the village of Mahkumkang on the Chinese border. And only 22 miles farther, still in the Tarong Valley, was the Chinese village of Mungdam, with at least thirty more families and itself only a mile from the nearest road traveled by cars. Rawang and Chinese hunters and traders from China routinely crossed over into Myanmar from Mahkumkang, and Mungdam was a major trading center for wildlife parts coming out of Myanmar. While other mountain passes between Myanmar and China could be crossed only a few months before winter each year, usually from July to November, the Mahkumkang crossing was passable and actively used all year round, which didn't bode well for the wildlife of the region. Unfortunately, we didn't have enough time to check out this eastern route. We had to head north.

From what I had already seen so far, there was a thriving trade in animal parts in this region. But I hadn't fully understood the driving force behind the trade, or where the bulk of the animal parts were going. There was a market within Myanmar, with special factories actively purchasing deer skins to use in making leather jackets. But now it was clear that most of the wildlife parts ended up in China, to be used in traditional medicines or, in the case of skins, for leather clothing and fur linings.

The ominous nature of this trade wasn't new to me. I had already seen how the commercial trade in wildlife parts had contributed to the depletion of wildlife populations throughout the rest of southeast Asia, and how it changed the way indigenous cultures viewed their environment. While I knew that the trade occurred elsewhere in Myanmar, I was surprised to see its extent in this remote region. The headman of Panangdim, while not able to remember the age of even his youngest child, could easily recite to me the current prices for the most valued wildlife parts in the region:

Musk deer musk: 8,000–10,000 kyats/tical (1 tical = .036 pound)

Red goral skin: 200–500 kyats

Red goral horn: 50 kyats

Takin horn: 4,000–6,000 kyats

Red panda skin: 200–500 kyats

Serow skin: 1,000–2,000 kyats

Serow horn: 100–300 kyats

Himalayan black bear gall bladder: 5,000–8,000 kyats/tical

Otter skin: 10,000–30,000 kyats for a three-foot length

Barking deer skin: 200 kyats

Barking deer antlers: 50–100 kyats

Pangolin skin: 7,000–8,000 kyats/viss (1 viss = 3.6 pounds)

Sambar deer skin: 800 kyats

Sambar deer antlers: 150–200 kyats

Flying squirrel gall bladder: 500–600 kyats

When I first arrived in Panangdim, as in every other village where we'd stayed so far, I was offered the best and the largest hut; its owner and his family left and moved in with a neighbor for the time I was there. In this case, the house belonged to the headman. Sometimes the best house belonged to the Christian preacher and contained more wildlife parts than any other dwelling in the village. The Christian preachers, with more free time on their hands than the other villagers, were often avid hunters or the village's most fervent wildlife traders. Many of them received skins as part of their tithe from the villagers or acted as the middlemen between the hunters and traders.

Except for the preachers, who knew the dollar value of God's handiwork, most hunters received relatively little for their efforts. In return for animal parts that sometimes fetched hundreds of dollars elsewhere, eventually ending up in the medicinal shops of Asia's largest cities, the people of this region received modest amounts of clothing, tea, and salt. Of these few goods, salt was valued above all else.

There were no natural sources of salt in this part of upper Myanmar, and the people here knew, without quite understanding why, that they needed salt to survive. Without salt, one gets weak and tires easily, they told me. But they also liked salt. Food and tea just didn't taste good without it, everyone said repeatedly. If there were a choice, white salt was the most desired for human consumption, but a type of red salt from China was also in demand for feeding livestock.

This salt–animal parts barter system had been going on as long as anyone could remember. Frank Kingdon Ward, after meeting Chinese traders in this same area more than half a century earlier, wrote: "There is one commodity which all men, of whatever colour, crave. It influences their lives. No hardship is too great to be borne, if only the need be thereby satisfied. This commodity is not bread, nor opium either, but common salt; common, that is, almost anywhere but here." The salt trade had a "civilizing" influence on the people of this region, Kingdon Ward went on, forcing them to interact with their neighbors more than they would have otherwise.

Only later did I come to realize what a pivotal role salt has played in human affairs. Human settlements have flourished or disappeared based on the availability of salt, children have been sold into slavery in exchange for salt, and wars have been fought over control of key salt sources. Over large parts of Africa, people drank the urine of their animals for its salt; in China, the collection of salt as a tribute is recorded as far back as 2000 B.C.; even the word *salary* comes from the Latin *salarium,* referring to the salt allotment given to Roman soldiers. Only as technology developed to the point where salt could be mined from mineral deposits or extracted from natural salt lakes, thus greatly increasing the overall supply, did the influence of control over salt begin to wane, although the demand for it did not.

The greatest mystery behind salt, however, has been the inability to fully understand our strong desire for this substance, which at least one author calls the "primordial narcotic." Medical research indicates that, while our body needs somewhere between one and three grams of salt daily to help regulate internal body fluid levels, much of what we need is obtained from the food we eat (except in the case of strict vegetarian diets). Yet most people across the world consume much more salt than their bodies need. The fact that we actually like the taste of salt has led to conflicting theories about whether salt consumption is influenced more by culture or by nature.

Only recently have we come to more fully understand the phenomenon known as sodium hunger (as opposed to salt hunger), first discovered in 1936. While our need to consume other vitamins and minerals requires some learning, our need for sodium is hormonally generated, and thus is a truly innate mechanism. Yet when an animal is hungry for salt or is sodium deficient, it also experiences a hedonic shift in the perception of salt—that is, salt becomes more pleasurable to the senses. Thus, both innate and behavioral mechanisms work together so that the biological need is reinforced by a pleasurable sensation associated with salt ingestion. This is a self-perpetuating cycle that increases the motivation to obtain salt.

Clearly, some supply of salt was necessary up here if these northern Myanmar tribes were to keep and maintain livestock. But how much they themselves really needed the additional salt in their own diet was open to question.

The roadless, mountainous terrain north of Putao,
as we embark on our 1997 survey. (Alan Rabinowitz)

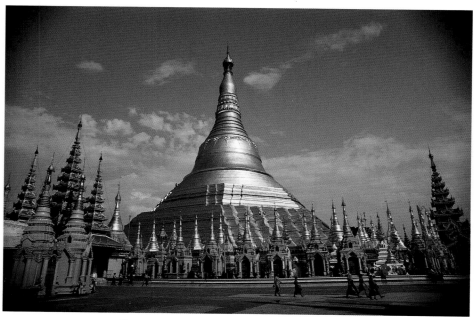

Shwedagon Pagoda in Yangon. Myanmar's
most revered Buddhist site. (Alan Rabinowitz)

Author examining a dead leaf deer a hunter had brought to Naung Maung village during the 1998 survey. (Salisa Rabinowitz)

Skulls of hunted animals hung on a "trophy board" in a Lisu village. The first evidence of leaf deer was found on this board during the 1997 survey. (Alan Rabinowitz)

Hunter in Ngawa Village carrying a freshly killed black barking deer. This carcass confirmed the presence of this species in northern Myanmar. (Alan Rabinowitz)

The village of Karaung nestled between the river and the mountains. This is the last home of the remaining Taron pygmies in Myanmar. (Alan Rabinowitz)

Arriving at the Nam Tamai River after descending through Panangdim Pass. This river acts as a dispersal barrier and was proposed as the southern boundary of the park. North of this river, animals from the Indo-Malayan realm have clearly been replaced by those of the Sino-Himalayan realm. (Alan Rabinowitz)

Crossing a bamboo bridge built by our porters that morning to cross a swollen, icy stream. (Alan Rabinowitz)

Making our own trail along a cliff face en route
from Tazundam to Guba. (Alan Rabinowitz)

Author showing Karaung villagers their own faces on a
video camera. None of them had ever seen anything like
this before. (Courtesy of Steve Winter)

Author questioning a Tibetan family in Madaing Village about wildlife they may have seen. (U Saw Tun Khaing)

Typical log house of Tibetans in northern Myanmar, with wooden shingle roof. (Alan Rabinowitz)

Htawgyi and his cousin watching our arrival in Tahundan during our January 2000 return trip. (Alan Rabinowitz)

The matriarch of Tahundan, Daw Sri Daraemar, with her granddaughter, Ma Phae Darae, who suffered from acute pink eye. Without proper medicine, the little girl died the month after this photograph was taken. (Alan Rabinowitz)

Phet gyi, a live leaf deer, captured and brought to us in Naung Maung village during our 1998 trip. We discovered this new deer species during our 1997 expedition. (Alan Rabinowitz)

Rawang mother preparing to give up her baby to U Saw Tun Khaing so that the baby might survive and have a better life in Yangon. (Alan Rabinowitz)

I finished my tea and reached for the pot, realizing I too had come to enjoy and look forward to the salty taste after a long day's hike. Before I came to Myanmar, I had never given a moment's thought to salt, other than wondering whether or not I should add it to my popcorn at the movies. Now I was faced with a situation in which salt played a key role in the economy of the region. More importantly, this simple substance was closely tied to a cross-border trade in animal parts that threatened the future survival of some of the most interesting and endangered mammals in this part of the world.

During the ensuing night, the temperature dropped to 50°F and the dampness made it feel even colder. While a few of our people had already developed persistent coughs, the major ailments were still only blisters and sore muscles. I had given out all my Ace bandages days ago and was now down to my last few sheets of Dr. Scholl's for the blisters. Khaing's feet were badly swollen, because of what he thought was an allergic reaction to leech bites. I gave him all my Benadryl capsules. U Tilawka, who despite his personal stockpile of traditional medicines had been battling a case of constipation for days, reluctantly consumed my Ex-Lax. The most worrisome maladies were also some of the most common up here. The headman appeared to be developing pneumonia, while his wife was plagued with recurrent bouts of malaria.

In addition to everything else, people had to work harder at survival here. The change in agricultural practices after crossing over the Panangdim Pass was immediately obvious. Ever since we had left Putao, rice had been the staple crop, along with maize, yam, tapioca, and sweet potatoes. Starting at Panangdim, rice was replaced by millet. Farther north, wheat, mustard, and beans would also be grown.

But there was another difference that I hadn't expected. After we crossed the Nam Tamai, the wildlife community changed abruptly. The common barking deer, leaf deer, sambar deer, jungle cat, large Indian civet, binturong, Hoolock's gibbon, and other species were left behind on the south side of the river. The pangolin, sun bear, Phayre's leaf monkey, and fishing cat, recorded as common before, made it across the river but were now rare on this side. The takin, musk deer, Himalayan bear, and red goral, known only from the higher, colder mountain habitats, were reportedly common now. Even the bird communities had changed. We had clearly gone beyond the transition zone, helped by the fast-flowing, ice-cold waters of the Nam Tamai, which acted as a dispersal barrier for many species. Now our feet were firmly planted in the Himalayan realm.

The shift in wildlife had no effect on hunting patterns, only on the kinds of species that were now traded for salt and other necessities. In fact, parts from the rare Himalayan wildlife were valued more than were those from the more common species at the lower elevations. And up here, hunters engaged in another collecting activity, one that was more difficult but could bring greater economic rewards than the selling of wildlife parts: the search for a medicinal plant the Myanmar people called *machit,* also known as *pai mu.*

The machit plant, *Fritillaria roylei,* has long been valued by the Chinese. A member of the lily family, this alpine species is a single-stemmed herb that grows about a foot tall and produces only a single flower. Frank Kingdon Ward, while exploring the sources of the Ayeyarwady in 1930, noted that groups of Chinese, Lisu, and Tibetans were coming across from China to search for this plant. At the time, machit was unknown in Putao, but today *machit-u*—the tuber of the machit plant—is a highly prized medicine among the Myanmar people as well.

The dry tuber, powdered and mixed with tea or water, is thought to prolong life if consumed regularly. More commonly, it is used for stomach disorders and pneumonia. Sometimes the tubers are immersed in raw honey; taken twice a day, the medicine supposedly eases the pain of rheumatism. The missionary Eugene Morse, after sending pieces of the tuber to the United States for analysis, was told that the chemicals in the plant provided an effective antidote for tuberculosis bacilli.

Part of the economic value of this alpine lily is due to the difficulty of finding and harvesting it. It grows only in the most inaccessible, snow-covered nooks and crannies above the timberline, at about 12,000 feet. The most valued part of the plant, its bulbous root, is difficult to excavate from the rocky, frozen soil. Hunters say that they typically have to spend several weeks doing dangerous climbing to find this plant, with no guarantee of success.

❦

I spent our last evening in Panangdim showing photographs of different animals from India and Tibet to village hunters with whom I had not yet spoken, still hoping to confirm the presence of some of these species in Myanmar. I let them talk among themselves for a while. Suddenly, one of the hunters got very excited.

"This one here—I know this one!" He pushed the book toward me while Khaing translated. He had continued to leaf through the pictures and was now pointing at a snow leopard.

"My brother-in-law killed two of these, more than five years ago on the edge of the icy mountains, and sold them for 500 yuan in China. I saw the skins he brought back."

He called over another man, who nodded at the picture. The second hunter told me how he had watched a snow leopard nearly twenty years ago while it stalked a takin. This was exciting news. Having confirmed the presence of blue sheep in the mountains near Mount Hkakabo Razi, it was possible that its persistent predator, the snow leopard, was close on its trail, occasionally making its way across the border into Myanmar. But until I saw hard evidence of these animals, I had to treat these reports as hearsay.

I wrote down everything that I'd been told, while they continued to study the pictures and talk among themselves.

"Alan," Khaing said, calling me over to where he was sitting.

"All the hunters insist that this animal is common, especially farther north." He was pointing to a black-and-white picture of an animal known as Fea's muntjac, a dark-skinned barking deer known only from an area along the border with Thailand, far to the south of where we were now. It was one of the pictures I had showed, knowing the animal couldn't be found near here, to test the credibility of the hunters I questioned. But these old hunters seemed sure of what they were talking about.

"Khaing, please tell them that this animal is not around here." I said. "See if they're confusing it with something else."

There was a prolonged exchange among Khaing, a second translator, and the hunters. Then one of the men left and came back minutes later with a knife sheath he'd retrieved from his hut. He walked over and handed it to me. The sheath was made of a skin that still had most of the hair attached. All the hair was black!

"Alan, he says his sheath is made from the skin of that black deer. And that the black deer is the *only* deer that lives on this side of the river." Khaing looked at me, waiting for an explanation.

"Maybe this is the black deer that other hunters told us about," Khaing said. "If it's not Fea's muntjac, maybe it's something we haven't seen before."

I remained silent. But my gut, and the piece of skin I now held, told me that Khaing was probably right.

## CHAPTER 9

# In the Shadow of Hkakabo Razi

The function of man is to live, not to exist. I shall not waste my days trying to prolong them. I shall use my time.

—Jack London

WHEN WE LEFT PANANGDIM we hiked north, staying parallel to the Nam Tamai and climbing steadily in elevation. Daytime temperatures dropped a few degrees, ranging from 46° to 58°F. But it was the continual rains that plagued us. With each passing day, walking up and down the increasingly muddy mountain slopes while rocks spilled down from above became more difficult and dangerous.

Mountains rose straight up all around us, their snowcapped peaks looking so close yet so daunting. The landscape was more pleasing to look at but tougher to hike through. We crossed over Kazong Razi Pass at 6,181 feet. On our right, Htamanghku Razi (10,286 feet) and Paoi Hpawng (10,636 feet) loomed, while on our left were Tanzim Razi (8,730 feet), Mayit Hpawng (8,450 feet), and Hsamra Razi (10,033 feet). Local porters pointed out the moun-

101

tains, their voices becoming quieter and more serious when speaking the names of these towering peaks. It was clear that their conversion to Christianity couldn't completely suppress their animistic
reverence for these natural giants, looming over them with the
power of life and death.

In the days ahead, we would hear a common lament among the
porters. There was not a single village where people didn't die
almost yearly from landslides, falling off cliffs, or being swept down
the river. I said, half-jokingly, that the mountains were angry for
being ignored so long. No one smiled.

"We are Christians," they'd respond. "We don't believe in spirits
anymore." Then, almost surreptitiously, they'd glance to the mountains beyond.

The Rawang villages were spread farther apart now, and sometimes we'd set up camp for the night between villages. With the
increasingly rough terrain, there were fewer flat areas where settlements of any size could exist, and the number of people that did
live in these villages was limited by usable space and the amount of
tillable land nearby. I quickly learned that the concepts of "tillable"
and "near" were relative up here. Some villagers would walk more
than a day to their terraced fields, having located their taungyas on
steep mountainsides that I could barely scale.

I could see why most of these villages weren't on any maps.
Human settlements in this region were dynamic entities, sometimes
shifting locations because of landslides or inability to grow enough
food when the tillable land was played out. Once the steep slopes
around villages had been denuded and stripped of their topsoil, the
frequency of landslides and deaths increased dramatically. An earlier
explorer who trekked through these mountains described the terrain eloquently:

> The miracle of the country was the absence of flat sur-
> faces: steep gradients everywhere, with little visibility.
> Every step was either up or down. . . . Folds and creases,

mountains and valleys—but try to find a level surface! Nature seemed to have stipulated that even if man conquered desert and lowland jungle, this vertical terrain should forever repulse him.

I found it hard to understand why people persisted in living in such an inimical environment until I realized that, in their minds, they had few other options. This was the land of their birth and the way of life that they had always known. Many believed that they were neither physically nor socially suited to live at lower elevations.

✢

Much of our time in camp was spent huddled over fires, trying to dry our clothes for the next day. Five minutes after being back on the trail we'd often be wet again, but it was important psychologically that we put on dry clothes first thing in the morning. It was also important for everyone to have several bowls of hot, steaming rice before setting foot outside. Everyone except me. Despite having dropped two belt sizes by now and feeling hungry all the time, I couldn't hike on a full stomach and I didn't like rice for breakfast. Instead, my breakfast was always a bowl of oatmeal or noodle soup and a cup of heavily sweetened coffee. Lunch was usually a small packet of crackers and hot tea. By midafternoon I would dig into my stash of PowerBars to keep going, allowing myself only half a bar a day so that I could make them last.

As hungry or as tired as I got, I knew that I had never in my life experienced real hunger or total exhaustion. When I imagined I was unbearably hungry, I thought of Captain Robert Falcon Scott's 1910 expedition to the South Pole, when he and his exhausted, starving team ate hallucinatory meals and had continual nightmares about food. They dreamed of shouting at deaf waiters and sitting at food-filled tables with their arms tied behind their backs. In the

end, the entire team perished, collapsing only 11 miles from a supply depot.

I could tell we had climbed into higher elevations and cooler
temperatures even without checking the altimeter and thermometer each evening. The villagers here wore musk deer hats, and we
sat around fires drinking tea on red goral or Himalayan bear skins.
The wildlife was less familiar to me now, and I took more care
when questioning the hunters and examining their kills. I'm glad
I did.

In the village of Ngawa, 15 miles from Panangdim, I spotted a
hunter coming in from the forest with a basket on his back that
looked to have some intriguing contents. Just protruding from a
pile of leaves and plants he'd collected were two small sets of hooves
attached to two black-colored legs. The black hair on the legs was
the same as that I'd seen on the hunter's knife sheath in Panangdim.
He lowered his basket to the ground, and I pushed aside the leaves.
In front of me was the animal I'd been hoping to find—the black
barking deer.

In 1938, Arthur Vernay, supported by the American Museum of
Natural History, mounted an expedition to collect biological specimens and "to solve the mystery of the black barking deer," which
was labeled at the time "the rarest animal of the Burmese hinterland." Sightings of a black deer had been reported from the high
mountains along the northwest border of Myanmar, but many
scientists thought it unlikely that it was the *true* black muntjac,
whose only other known population was more than 1,000 miles
away in southwest China. After collecting more than 1,500 specimens of mammals, they acquired two "smoky-gray barking deer,"
which turned out to be the tufted deer, *Elaphodus cephalophus.* As
a result, H. E. Anthony, then curator of mammals with the American Museum, who accompanied the expedition, concluded the following:

> In newspaper accounts of the proposed field work in
> Burma, before the expedition left the States, some men-

tion was made of a 'black barking deer' never taken in Burma and an exceptional object to be sought. Apparently this statement derived in some way from the fact that there is a true barking deer so called black *Muntiacus crinifrons* of which only three specimens have been recorded (these from Chekiang, China) and that a Chinese name for the tufted deer can be translated as 'black muntjac.' There is no likelihood that the very local *Muntiacus crinifrons* would be encountered in Burma, over 1,000 miles removed from the known records. When I saw the first specimen of the tufted deer I could readily understand how natural a thing it would be for the laymen to call it a 'black barking deer.'

Now, in Ngawa, after carefully examining the entire body of the freshly killed animal in the hunter's basket, as well as another half-dozen "black deer" skins that suddenly appeared when hunters saw my interest in this species, I was certain that Anthony was wrong. What I was looking at was neither the Fea's muntjac nor the tufted deer. Anthony's team had never reached this far north, and from the descriptions in my field books, I was convinced that what I was looking at was the black muntjac, *M. crinifrons,* far removed from its currently known distribution. Final confirmation would come later, after DNA analysis of skin pieces that were brought back to New York. This was another new large mammal record for the country, the third after the blue sheep and the as yet undescribed leaf deer. But the question in my mind now was why this deer was here in the first place. The answer to that piece of the puzzle would come only much later.

For the next week we hiked alongside the Nam Tamai in constant sight and sound of its raging, ice-cold waters. This river, unlike so many others I had slept beside in my life, didn't calm my spirit or lull me to sleep at night. Instead, its incessant roar reminded me of an unbroken mare. It was as if these young towering mountains were spewing forth their life force, challenging any that entered their realm.

I always feel both strengthened and humbled by the almost palpable energy of truly wild places such as this one. It never surprises me that human beings feel a need to worship and appease the power of raging rivers and the indomitable presence of towering mountains. To me it is a manifestation of the intuitive understanding that one has to live with nature, instead of constantly pitting oneself against it, in order to survive. What saddens me, however, is when people learn to suppress such feelings, becoming convinced that humans are apart from nature.

Each day, the countryside seemed more rugged and the people less "civilized" in dress and their reactions to us. Few of these villagers had had much contact with anyone beyond people in the villages immediately around them. The only outsiders regularly coming through were traders from China, usually of Rawang or Tibetan ethnicity.

Each village claimed to have a primary school for their children with at least one or two local teachers who had been trained in Putao. Yet we never saw a class in progress, nor could we usually find the teachers. Class schedules, we were told, depended on when the children were not needed on the plantations and when the teachers were available. A few of the larger villages closest to Putao had a middle school where students from neighboring villages could come and stay during the school term. But the last middle school we'd seen was in Ratbaw, more than 50 miles from where we were now. Most families couldn't afford to have their children go that far away, I was told.

We hiked under waterfalls, through narrow gorges, and up steep mountainsides. Crossing even little feeder streams that flowed into the Nam Tamai was treacherous after more than a week of rain. We assigned a small group of porters to go ahead of us each morning in order to clear and rebuild portions of the trail, or to find the best way to cross over the flooded streams. Sometimes landslides wiped out the main trail, and the porters hacked out what looked like a mountain goat trail into the hillside. I'd edge my way carefully along the edge of sheer rocky drops that plunged 50 or more feet to the raging waters below. When rivers were too dangerous to ford, the porters built bamboo bridges over the rapids that would last until the first heavy rain swept them away.

As we climbed higher and higher, my enthusiasm, my strength, my optimism—all the things I'd been feeling since the start of this trip—began to drain away. With little rest in almost three weeks and the constant stress of getting all the information I could from each village we passed, I felt as if I were running on fumes. Others on the team were similarly tired, but I seemed to be falling into a depression that scared me.

I slept poorly at night. Thoughts and doubts about Salisa were haunting me. Tossing and turning throughout the early morning hours, I'd wake up tired and then push myself even harder during the day in order to avoid thinking. The soldiers were both impressed and intimidated by me, talking among themselves about my strength and my moodiness. None of them liked being assigned to hike with me because of the pace I kept, so they alternated each day. My knee started throbbing painfully during the day, but I was glad to have the pain. It kept my mind from wandering. Still, I wasn't in my 20s anymore, and this terrain was taking its toll. We had a long way to go, and I was inching toward physical limits I'd never tested before.

It all came to a head on one particular day. By early afternoon, a few miles short of the village where we expected to spend the night, I started visualizing scenes, like a television soap opera, playing out in my head. I saw images of Salisa meeting someone she knew, someone who sympathized with her pain, calmed her fears, and didn't turn away from her tears. He was taller than me, better looking in a softer, more cerebral way. She met him three times over a two-week period, once for lunch, twice for dinner. The second dinner was at his apartment, and he cooked. He had good taste in furniture, but the place lacked warmth. He served merlot, her favorite wine, and then talked to her softly and gently, the way I used to talk to her when we first met. He played on her pain with just the right amount of sympathy. She never mentioned my name, and he never asked. Her long black silky hair and beautiful Asian features had long attracted him.

It started raining hard, and I took off my hat to feel the pounding of the water on my head. There was a small side canyon in the distance. I told myself that if I didn't reach that canyon in the next fifteen minutes, it meant that she had kissed him. I look at my watch and sped up. I passed the canyon after twenty minutes. She was feeling guilty now, I thought. The kiss had felt good, but she knew she had gone too far. She knew she should leave, but she didn't feel like going home to an empty apartment and an empty bed. She felt that her life had never been so sad, and she was overwhelmed now by wanting to feel loved.

We topped a hill. Down below, on the other side of the river, I could see the village where we would spend the night. I looked at my watch. If I didn't make it into the village within the next thirty minutes, then Salisa would spend the night with this man, and our marriage was over. There was a little footpath off the main trail, straight down the side of the mountain. It was rocky and steep but would cut perhaps ten minutes off getting to the bridge. My knee was throbbing. I saw the empty bed in our apartment. That son of a bitch hasn't won yet, I thought. I looked over at the soldier who was unfortunate enough to have been assigned to me that day, and smiled. Then I took off, running and sliding down the mountain.

The physical hardships we endured were nothing to the porters. They acted as if they were on holiday, laughing and joking continually, easily handling their loads over the worst of terrain. The line of porters stretched over miles, and the last one wouldn't arrive in camp until long after dark. Yet rarely a night passed when I didn't fall asleep to the sound of their singing. I asked Khaing why they seemed so cheerful—particularly the women, who looked truly exhausted when they staggered into camp at the end of the day.

"Everyone is happy to be making the money we pay them," Khaing responded. "The younger ones are also glad to be seeing new places and meeting new people. And the older women say they are glad to be away from their husbands for a while." He laughed.

With the changing of porters at different villages, the voices and melodies of our nightly serenades also changed. That I never understood the words of the songs never bothered me, until one night I heard a song that was haunting in its intensity.

"It is a song about Mount Hkakabo Razi," Khaing said, after questioning the porters. "They sing of its beauty and the purity of its snow. They also sing of a magic lake high on the mountain, which fills when the snow melts. None of them have ever been there."

The idea of a magic lake on top of Mount Hkakabo Razi seemed pure fancy to Khaing, but I thought there could be something to it. Some of the accounts of early expeditions through this area referred to small, unexplained ponds on the tops of some of the high mountains. The Rawang at that time claimed that these "small lakes" were created by the spirit of that particular mountain; the explorers speculated that they were either human-made or had been gouged out when the glacial ice retreated. Either way, these high mountain pools were believed to be real.

I fell asleep easily that night, my demons calmed. I'd reached the village within my allotted time. As the voices of the porters sang the

praises of Hkakabo Razi, the king of these mountains, even the turbulent roar of the river subsided into the background.

⟨✠⟩

We dispersed salt, clothing, and medicines in almost every village
where we stayed now. The villagers were grateful, and some wanted
to respond in kind. Sometimes they gave me an animal part I was
interested in, such as a serow or red goral head, or they presented
me with the two-inch-long canine of a musk deer on a string to
wear as a necklace. Others gave us live chickens for our larder.

In the village of Gawai, I was given a gift unlike any other we
had received before: two large flower pods. I assumed the pods had
some medicinal value until I saw the excitement on U Saw Lwin's
face. He took them from my hands as if they were Fabergé eggs and
I was unworthy to be holding them. These green pods were rare
wild slipper orchids, locally known as black orchids because of their
dark, purple-green flower.

First discovered for science in 1922 by Frank Kingdon Ward on
a rocky outcrop near the village of Naung Mung, which we'd
passed to the east two days out from Putao, this beautiful dark
orchid, *Paphiopedilum wardii,* flowers only in the winter months and
is restricted to northern Myanmar and the Yunnan Province of
China. Because the plant's nearest relatives were in the Malay
Peninsula and the Philippines, Kingdon Ward considered it an "out-
lier," linking the flora of Malay Peninsula with that of northern
Myanmar. Only now did I realize that U Saw Lwin and our other
botanist on the team had been looking for this plant all along, wondering how far north the black orchid lived and how abundant it
was up here. Although this species is now grown domestically, the
wild variety is one of the world's rarest and is still highly valued by
collectors in places such as Japan and England.

When Khaing had first organized our team, I'd questioned but
not opposed the inclusion of an orchid specialist. It didn't take long

after leaving Putao before U Saw Lwin had me fascinated by the complexity of the largest flowering plant family in the world. While the majority of the 25,000 to 30,000 orchid species were found in the tropics, he explained, the greatest diversity of orchids were at higher elevations.

Pointing out orchids ranging from specimens the size of my thumbnail hidden on the forest floor to spectacularly lush arboreal assemblages high in the forest canopy, U Saw Lwin educated me about the relationship between orchids' floral structure and the animals that pollinate them. Many of the more than 850 orchid species native to Myanmar depended on bees, moths, butterflies, birds, and even bats for pollination. Some orchids could be pollinated only by a single species of insect.

Because so many orchid species are restricted to such small areas, orchids are much more easily threatened by loss of habitat and overcollecting than other kinds of plants. The removal or destruction of even a few orchids from an area could potentially cripple an entire population, reducing fitness and adaptability for the species as a whole. Unfortunately, the popularity of many orchids as ornamental flowers, U Saw Lwin said, had led to rampant overcollecting and an international trade involving substantial sums of money. Japanese traders were already coming to Putao regularly, for example, paying high fees to people there to scour the mountains in search of wild orchids.

We shared our dinner of rice and chicken with the headman, accepting from him some yams, potatoes, and popcorn. A fresh takin carcass, killed the previous day, was offered to me for sale. Takins were common up here, the hunters said, although numbers of these animals were fewer than in the past. I had heard this comment many times already with most of the species I asked about. Yet there was little realization among the hunters that "common but fewer in number" was only a step away from "rare" and then finally "extinct." Some of the older hunters at lower elevations even acknowledged seeing species such as tiger and elephant disappear completely in their lifetime.

The beautiful teddy-bear-like red panda, whose soft fur was used to line the inside of Chinese gloves, was also considered common by these hunters. In reality, its numbers were down to an estimated several thousand individuals spread throughout the high mountainous regions of Nepal, Sikkim, Myanmar, and parts of China. Other increasingly rare animals of these mountains were sharing the same fate. The hunters from this village alone estimated their past year's kills of just three of the most sought-after species at fifty red gorals, ten black barking deer, and a dozen red pandas. The more they killed, they said, the better they could bargain with the Chinese. The idea of self-controlled sustainable hunting didn't seem to be any more intuitive among these people than among people elsewhere.

The takin being shown to me now was a good example of one of the strange and marvelous Himalayan species that was slowly being hunted to extinction. Standing nearly four feet high at the shoulder and weighing up to 600 pounds, this long-snouted, two-horned bovid has a thick yellow-to-brownish coat and lives only near the upper limit of the tree line, at elevations from 6,000 to 12,000 feet. Found sometimes in herds of more than two dozen individuals, takins break into smaller groups when they move to lower elevations during the summer months.

Hunters used snares and spear traps to get the flesh, skin, and horns of this beast. Although no hunters I spoke with had seen herds today that were as large as those they had observed in the past, they still considered the species to be common because they knew where to find the surviving animals. If the hunting of this species wasn't curbed soon, the takin would follow the Sumatran rhino into oblivion.

We reached the village of Tazundam during the third week with the team feeling tired but generally in good health, with a few important exceptions. The rains were more sporadic now but still creating difficult conditions, wearing us down faster and contributing to more illness. Hpa-hti, who stayed up late and woke up early to cater our meals, had developed a chronic cough. My porter, Zawgan, sliced his foot almost to the bone while walking barefoot in the mud after leaving Gawai.

I was also worried about U Tilawka, who had grown feverish and pale and was now having dizzy spells. His thin orange robes and orange wool cap gave little protection against the cold and rain, yet he refused to wear anything over the robes. When we suggested that he rest at a village for a few days and catch up with us later, he refused. It was important to him that he continue to walk with me and lead us personally to his monastery at Tahundan.

The most serious problem was with our zoologist from the university. I had had difficulty working with him from the first day of the trip because of his reluctance to use the standardized questionnaires and protocols I had developed for this trip. A few years my senior, he believed that he knew the best way "to get into people's heads" about hunting and wildlife. He resented my authority and would go into long tirades about how the government prevented academics like him from furthering their careers. Khaing and I agreed to let him do as he wanted, as long as he didn't interfere with our work. Eventually the entire team steered clear of him.

When we noticed the zoologist limping and starting to lag behind, he told us that it was just from a bad blister and that he would care for it himself. By Tazundam, though, he was feverish and leaning heavily on a walking stick. Finally he showed his wound to the major. What may have started out as nothing more than a blister was now a foul-smelling, suppurating wound that was infected and septic. The major cleaned the wound, injected him with antibiotics, and told him how to change the bandages daily. Two of the team were assigned to stay near him at all times. Instead of showing gratitude, he became more morose and uncooperative.

We spent an extra day resting at Tazundam. Here was the junction of the smaller rivers that formed the Nam Tamai—the Seingkhu Wang, coming down from the northwest along the border with India, and the Adung Wang, coming from the northern foothills of Mount Hkakabo Razi and Tibet. Following the Adung Wang Valley three to four days due north would take us to the last village of Tahundan, where we would set up base camp.

The people in Tazundam seemed taller, with more sharply delineated facial features, than the Rawang we'd been seeing until now. When I asked about this, the villagers explained that they were Htalu, a people I'd heard were considered among the most backward and isolated of the Rawang subtribes. The Htalu had been numerous in the past, until earthquakes and landslides during the 1950s caused many deaths and led them to abandon many villages. Interestingly, both Colonel Saw Myint and Frank Kingdon Ward had questioned whether the Htalu were true Rawang at all, believing that they were more similar in physical appearance to the Tibetans.

Until now, U Tilawka had generally been ignored in the Rawang villages we passed. While his presence initially influenced the way villagers viewed our group in these Christian enclaves, we were such an odd mixture of people that any immediate suspicions or discomfort was offset by curiosity. It was difficult to view a group consisting of a monk, an American, Bamar people from Yangon, and soldiers, all asking questions about plants and animals, as having any religious overtones.

After Gawai, however, the reaction toward our party changed. Now we regularly encountered small groups of Tibetans coming down from the farthest northern villages to trade and visit other villages. No matter how narrow the trail or how heavy the load on their backs, when Tibetans encountered U Tilawka, they immediately knelt or bowed their heads in respect. U Tilawka's demeanor also changed. The smiling, boyish face and the playful aspect that emerged when we were alone together were replaced by a contemplative, serious expression. He accepted any show of respect as his due, and in turn bestowed blessings upon the heads of those who understood what his robes signified.

During a break in the rain, I explored the environs of Tazundam and came upon a man working a little plot of land with a simple plow made of wood and bamboo. Nothing would have seemed strange about this scene had it not been for the fact that, instead of livestock pulling the plow, women and children—all grasping a rattan cable thrown over their shoulders—were acting as the beasts of burden. "Beasts of burden" was a misnomer, though: everyone was laughing, singing, slipping in the mud, and enjoying themselves immensely. The man behind the plow was smiling too, as he helped to push the plow while the others pulled.

Because this family had no livestock of their own, this was just another of their necessary chores to produce food. I thought of some of the questions I'd been asking villagers during this trip, trying to pinpoint what made them happy or sad. All the answers had been less than satisfactory, mainly because they had no idea what I was asking. On the surface, these people were like everyone else. They laughed and cried, experienced frustration and pleasure. But the difference, I now realized, was that they didn't dwell on the reasons behind such emotions, nor did they bemoan their lot in life.

The scene in front of me could easily have been construed as slavelike toil by women and children working to overcome hardship and adversity. But that would have been an outsider's perception, not theirs. They were simply a family dependent on each other for survival, playing games while producing food. When they motioned me over, I joined in, helping pull the plow and falling in the mud with them, until they decided it was time for rest. They invited me to their hut for tea and popcorn.

While plowing the mud, I thought of how the heavy rains we'd been experiencing, while simply an inconvenience to us, were of serious concern to the villagers. March and April were the months when old taungya fields or new forests were burned and planted for the coming year. Prolonged rains now meant a shorter growing season and fewer crops. Food would be scarce and people would go hungry. If it went on too long, there would be famine. In a place where survival was a day-to-day affair, any adverse change in the environment could tip the scales from life toward death. When this happened, the very old and the very young suffered the most.

Because the villagers had few pieces of clothing to warm their bodies and seemingly little propensity for cleanliness, the rains also meant that most of them had colds, fever, and diarrhea. Despite an abundance of water, all the children were very dirty, with dried mucus on their unwashed faces, and hands and feet blackened with ground-in dirt and grime. Many believed, in fact, that being overly clean in this cold environment weakened the body and made them susceptible to illness.

Interestingly, a number of villagers were fearful of the rivers, considering them to be living entities that provided life but, if one were not extremely careful, could easily bring death. Incidents of men falling off rock ledges and being swept away by the river were not uncommon. In Putao, there were stories about a giant water snake, the *bu-rin,* 40 to 50 feet long, that attacked swimmers or even small boats. Sounding somewhat like a larger, aquatic version of the Myanmar python, this snake was considered incredibly hostile and dangerous. No one had firsthand knowledge of the creature, yet because of it, children were often discouraged from spending long periods of time in the water.

Few people in this region knew their real age; they had little use for such information. Some of the elders kept track of the passing years by marking on trees the number of plantations that had been cut since a child's birth. For most people, however, it was impossible to assess longevity accurately, and there clearly were not many elderly people around. I also couldn't find any cemeteries. We had seen only two graves during our travels so far, both freshly dug sites along the trail. When the people had been animists, they said, they burned their dead, as the Buddhists did. But as Christians they were obliged to bury the bodies and plant a cross. With so little flat land available, this was a problem. Burial plots had to be randomly placed in available spots that were not immediately needed to grow food.

I was also surprised to have encountered only two crippled people in all the villages we'd visited. Early reports, before the Christian missionaries came, claimed that the Rawang had a "horror of bodily deformities" and killed even goiterous persons. But the Rawang themselves claimed that they would never let crippled babies die, nor did they ostracize crippled adults. There were simply no births of defective children, they insisted.

After our first week on the trail from Putao, we started setting up a health clinic in the headman's house whenever we stayed in a village. When word spread that we were giving out free medicine, the entire village would line up at our door whether they were sick or not. It soon became clear that everyone considered themselves sick, with aches or pains somewhere on their body from which they wanted relief.

Our team doctor, the major, was not particularly sympathetic to the woes of these villagers, nor did he want to spend his time treating them. Unless there was a serious medical issue that required his advice, Khaing, one of the foresters on our team, and I dispensed the medicines. We had to be careful about how we did this, though. No matter how much we emphasized the importance of taking the medicines according to the instructions we gave, everyone believed that more was better. If we gave them fourteen pills to be taken twice a day for a week, they would take them all at once and be back for more the next day. Thus we never gave out more than a single day's dosage of a medicine, nor did we give out anything that could be fatal in larger doses.

Given the modest supplies we had with us, our ability to treat most illnesses was limited, particularly if people wouldn't follow directions on how to take the medicines. So we just tried to make people more comfortable or ease their pain. The bulk of our efforts involved cleaning and treating surface wounds and distributing aspirin, ibuprofen, cough drops, Benadryl, Pepto-Bismol, and throat lozenges. Sometimes, for fatigue or a more serious bronchial cough, I would give a shot of antibiotics or of B-complex.

When we left a village, we'd leave a bag of medicine with the headman or the village schoolteacher, explaining in great detail what the different-colored pills were for and how to administer them. There was no alternative but to hope that they followed our instructions. Later we learned that the villagers would rush to the headman's house soon after we left and request that the drugs be distributed evenly to everyone. The headman usually obliged. People who were not sick would still take the medicine, thinking it would prevent them from getting sick.

Few of these villagers had ever seen or used commercial medicines, and almost none had ever visited a doctor or medical officer. As would be expected in a remote area such as this, any treatment for illness usually involved traditional medicines made from plants or animal parts. Of these treatments, two were employed more frequently than any other for the most common ailments, such as headaches, fever, and body fatigue.

The first was an ancient Chinese technique called cupping (also known as the "horn method" or "fire cup"), mentioned in Chinese writings as early as 281 A.D. The idea was to draw blood to the afflicted area by creating negative pressure on the skin through suction. I had been the recipient of this treatment while surveying wildlife in Taiwan and suffering from the same kind of knee pain as I had now. There I visited a traditional practitioner's office, where he used glass or plastic suction cups attached to either a hand pump or an electrical device that created the suction.

Here in the forest, cupping was still practiced the way it was first described centuries ago. Bamboo cups were placed over a burning piece of paper or leaf, sucking the air from the cup and creating a vacuum that extinguished the flame and held the cup in place. The burning paper was placed on a small piece of green leaf so that the skin was not burned. Both the suction and the heat were meant to be therapeutic. Large red circular blotches, usually on the forehead, were the telltale sign that a villager had recently received this treatment. If an injury was swollen or infected, sometimes it would be pricked with a bamboo needle, and then cupping would be used to draw out the pus, or what was called the "bad blood."

I learned about the second practice when I went out one morning to brush my teeth and saw one of our Forest Department staff squatting on the veranda, shirtless, with extensive red bruises being made on his neck and back. There were beads of sweat on his brow and an agonized expression on his face. A villager was hunched over behind him making the bruises by rubbing his back roughly with a spoon, being careful not to break the skin. This practice, called *meik hkalawng*, is well known in many areas of Myanmar and is meant to stimulate blood flow to the upper body, helping overcome fever and fatigue. I offered some of my private stash of Tylenol to the forester but he politely refused, choosing instead to bear the pain in stoic silence.

The only other "medicine" I saw consumed regularly was the whiskey brewed in certain Tibetan villages from fermented corn. This became the favored medicine of some of our team and soldiers, and I took the "cure" on a few occasions myself. It was a weak concoction and usually in short supply, so I never saw outward signs of drunkenness among the villagers.

I was now wearing two sets of thermal underwear to sleep, along with socks and a hat. My down sleeping bag was rated to 40°F, but with the dampness in the air I was still chilled during the night.

Still, I had better clothes and gear than anyone else on the team, so I didn't complain.

Despite a general malaise, I felt strong and fit. Most of my dark thoughts and invented scenarios of earlier days had dissipated. Aside from chronic athlete's foot and increasingly persistent throbbing in my left knee, I felt in better shape than I had in years. With popcorn and oatmeal for breakfast, biscuits and coffee for lunch, and rice and vegetables for dinner, I was taking in about a notch a week on my belt. Our ornithologist, who had tipped the scales at 220 pounds when we started, looked to be down to a svelte 190.

The realization that Panangdim was a key intersection in this region, linking the country's main Rawang settlements with Putao to the south and China to the east, had been important to my understanding of the social dynamics of this area. Now I viewed this more northern village of Tazundam as another important crossroads. Here, a trail from the western Seingkhu Wang Valley linked Tibetan settlements close to the Indian border with the Adung Wang Valley, where the last settlements of Tibetans and Rawang lived in the far northern hinterland of the country. Hence, Tazundam was a potentially important link in any cross-border activity or trade with India.

After consulting with Khaing and the rest of the team, I decided to change our itinerary. We were only a few days from Tahundan, our primary destination, so barring any disaster, our arrival there was assured. We decided to put off the final push to Tahundan for a few days and travel northwest up the Seingkhu Wang Valley to visit the Tibetan villages of Guba and Madaing. The trail was less frequented and more rugged than what we had been traveling on, so only a few of us would go, leaving the rest of the team to recuperate in Tazundam. We also asked U Tilawka to take several porters and go ahead of us to Tahundan. He was too ill to make this side trip with us and would be better cared for at his own village. To our surprise, he readily agreed, saying he would prepare the monastery for our arrival. Then he took my hand, squeezed it, and looked at me sadly, as if he were somehow letting me down. I felt as if I were parting with a lover instead of a monk.

## CHAPTER 10

# Lost Tribes of Tibet

Seize the mountain spirits, make them divulge their secrets. Only with strength is there discovery.

—Deng Ming-Dao

THE EIGHT-MILE WALK to Guba was more diffi-
cult and treacherous than anything we had encountered before. The
Tibetans, who were relative latecomers to this region and preferred
to live at higher elevations, occupied the more narrow, less traveled
river valleys nestled among the snowcapped mountains. Trails and
small bridges between these villages were maintained poorly, if at
all, and the strategy for cutting trails seemed based on line of sight,
regardless of slope or terrain. Trudging up and down rocky wet
slopes, hugging rock ledges, and rock-hopping across icy streams all
took its toll on our already depleted energy reserves. My left knee
was aching continually now, and I had to use a walking stick. And
it was raining again.

The first day we came to a place where a landslide had wiped
out the trail the year before, sweeping two women carrying firewood off the mountain to their deaths. Our only alternative to

123

backtracking and climbing over the top of the mountain was to use a narrow animal path, perhaps a foot wide, that snaked along the edge of a sheer drop to the Seingkhu Wang River about 100 feet below.

Inching sideways with my face toward the rock wall, I wondered how long Salisa would mourn if I were to meet my death in this desolate place. Unbeknownst to me, one of the porters decided I was moving too slowly and went to pass above me, using smaller, even more treacherous foot- and handholds than I. Suddenly, a shower of stones started rolling down onto my head, and then a rock the size of a baseball swept by my cheek. Distracted by other thoughts, I panicked. Earthquake! I thought. The walking stick I was carrying slid from my hand and went sailing toward the river below as I flattened myself against the wall, frantically searching for handholds.

I grabbed onto the jagged edge of a rock protruding from the slope, slicing the palm of my right hand in the process. Pain shot up my arm. I closed my eyes against the fear and the pain, and found myself back in my sixth-grade classroom. The teacher was calling on me to read a short story I had handed in the week before. It was a made-up story about a boy who talked to animals because no one else would listen to him. Only it wasn't made up, and it was never meant to be read aloud. Students were looking at me, especially Sarah, a girl I liked but had never had the nerve to talk to. Now I'd have to get up and stutter, and the whole class would see the spitting, the head jerks, and everything else that made me look like a fool. Some kids would laugh, and others would look away because they pitied me. That was what I hated most—the pity.

I dropped my pencil to the floor, making it look like an accident, and then bent below the desk to pick it up. Without stopping to think, I stabbed the point of the pencil into the palm of my hand, hard. The pain was immediate, shooting up into my arm the way the ache from the jagged rock was doing now. I was rushed immediately to the nurse, just as I had hoped. I never had to read the story.

I felt someone grab my arm and opened my eyes to see one of the foresters on our team, who had caught up with me on the ledge. He hollered what sounded like a reprimand at the unseen porter above us. I was embarrassed, but his eyes showed only concern as I pulled my hand away from the rock and he saw the blood. I shook my head, indicating that it was nothing, and then started moving again. Pain was bearable; humiliation was not.

Part of what had triggered my reaction on the slope was the thought that we were moving through an active earthquake zone. This part of Asia was known for its seismic activity, recorded diligently by the India Meteorological Department since 1898. And the particular area through which we were traveling was part of the Great Boundary Fault—where Tibet, Assam, and Myanmar meet. This was the eastern edge of the youthful, unstable, and still growing Himalayas, where any subterranean movement could have massive repercussions on the surface, as Kingdon Ward had come to learn too well decades earlier:

> Suddenly a most extraordinary rumbling noise broke out, and the earth began to shudder violently. Shattering the dead silence of the night in that remote, mountain retreat, the ominous rumble swelled to a deafening roar. It was as though the keystone had fallen out of the universe and the arch of the sky were collapsing. . . . All four of us held hands and lay flat, waiting for the end.

The quake of 1950, whose epicenter was in Assam, less than 50 miles as the crow flies from where we stood now, lasted only four minutes, and Kingdon Ward was in a sheltered valley. But in the days ahead he witnessed the extent of one of the worst earthquakes the world had experienced in historical times. A land area of more than one million square miles was affected. Whole villages were buried, rivers dammed, mountain ripped apart, and drainage patterns permanently altered.

Along one tributary of the Bramaputra River alone, a flash flood took 500 lives. Forests were transformed into "deserts of stone." Of the hills in the northern border region, an estimated 75 percent were mutilated by landslides, while 50 percent of the wild animals in the area might have been killed. The face of the region was changed forever, and survivors suffered greatly from the after-effects of the quake for years to come. Nothing of that magnitude has happened since, but lesser tremors were still common—certainly ones large enough to cause an avalanche along our path.

We descended the mountain only a short way before reaching Guba, nestled in a valley more than 6,000 feet high. A second village, Madaing, was less than three miles farther on. Guba was a small village of only six houses, while Madaing had fifteen houses. The way of life of the Tibetans here was clearly different from that of the Rawang we had visited earlier. Most of the Tibetan houses were built of sturdy logs, raised eight to ten feet off the ground, with wood shingle roofs. The logs held heat better than wooden planks or thatch, but the Tibetans usually left large gaps between them, providing ventilation but making the houses cold and drafty.

If the Rawang had generally been friendly and hospitable to us throughout the trip, the Tibetans welcomed us like long-lost relatives. The smiles that readily spread across their faces were almost beatific, and their apparently immediate trust of us was heartwarming. It helped to dispel the fatigue we were all feeling.

No one knows exactly when the first Tibetans settled in Myanmar, but they'd been coming down to Rawang villages to trade medicinal herbs for salt for as long as anyone could remember. At some point, a few daring individuals were captivated by these unspoiled remote wild valleys and decided to settle here.

Borders meant little to the people of this region. The Tibetans knew that they resided in a country called Myanmar, but they never lost touch with their homeland. U Tilawka made occasional visits to these villages and was respected for the Theravada Buddhist teachings that he represented. But these villagers remained loyal Tibetan Buddhists, worshiping the Dalai Lama, inviting Tibetan monks to visit, and making annual pilgrimages to Tibet. China was about a seven-day walk from Madaing, while the border of India was nearly twice that distance.

The high mountain valleys of the Tibetan villages were extraordinarily lush. The Tibetans were the archetypal agriculturists, growing different varieties of crops and rotating them in a way that we never saw among the Rawang. Life was by no means easy up here, but resigning themselves to just subsistence-level survival was obviously not part of the Tibetan mind-set. They were an industrious people, keeping livestock to help plow the fields, and using dung and fallen leaves to refertilize fallow plots. They even learned to plant fast-growing trees along slopes susceptible to landslides, and kept these areas off-limits to cutting for firewood. It was clear that Khaing and other members of the team felt much more comfortable among these Tibetans than they had among the Rawang.

The Tibetans hunted like everyone else, but they seemed less enthusiastic about it than the Rawang or Lisu. This was partly because of their Buddhist beliefs and partly because the Rawang had been here much longer and already controlled the best hunting territories. Still, the Tibetans too needed the trade goods from China, so they hunted wherever they could. When I asked about tigers, they claimed that tigers had roamed the mountains in their grandfathers' time, but now their livestock was never bothered, so it seemed that all the cats had disappeared.

Maize was one of the main crops in this northern region, and in every house we visited we were offered either popcorn or a plate of dry, yellow powder, both of which were used to fill the stomach after coming back from working on the plantation. When making popcorn, the women mixed the corn kernels with sand in a large wok placed over the fire. The sand distributed the heat evenly and prevented the corn from being burned, but it made the popcorn taste gritty. The yellow powder, Khaing explained, was a mixture of fried corn, wheat, and millet, ground together on hand-hewn stone grinders. It tasted like a mashed-up version of my PowerBar.

Sometimes we were given a large chunk of flat bread made from ground millet or wheat. The obligatory tea was no longer the simple black tea used by the Rawang, but Tibetan tea, a mixture of tea, milk, salt, and butter with the viscosity of fuel oil. I would drink a little of the mixture while it was still hot, just to be polite. But I couldn't stand even a sip once the tea had cooled off and the butter had coagulated on the surface.

As I sat around the fire writing notes in my journal, a young girl entered the house with a large bamboo container filled with water from the stream. Her mother stood in the corner making butter in a bamboo churn with a specially fitted plunger that was forced up and down repeatedly with great effort. The man of the house poured tea into bamboo cups for Khaing and me, and then went back to cutting dried bamboo leaves to fletch newly spliced bamboo arrows for his crossbow.

This wasn't the first time I'd marveled at the incredible versatility of bamboo. Many a night I lay in my sleeping bag listening to bamboo leaves flutter in the wind, or hearing the hollow stems knocking upon one another, almost drumlike, as the plants swayed to and fro. Everything about bamboo evoked images of beauty and vitality, even its name. Malay in origin, the term *bamboo* is thought to be onomatopoetic for the explosions that occur during a fire, when the air in the sealed bases of the hollow bamboo trunks expands and blows the stalks apart.

Throughout my years of work in southeast Asia, I had continually been reminded of how essential bamboo was to the lives of the people of the region. On this trip I'd seen bamboo used for medicinal cures; for cooking and eating utensils; to build bridges, houses, dams, plows, and livestock pens; for hunting and fishing; and to make baskets and water pipes. And I was certain this list barely scratched the surface. A thorough investigation of bamboo by an early-twentieth-century author listed at least 1,546 uses of the plant in Japan alone.

Because there are more than 1,000 species of bamboo worldwide (60 percent from Asia), it has been suggested that archaeologists would be justified in defining a Bamboo Age comparable with the Stone or Bronze Age. Given that bamboo has played a role in virtually every aspect of life in Asia, some believe that it has influenced human cultural evolution more than any other plant in the world. Until the mid-twentieth century, ancient Asia was categorized in the West as a region of "cultural retardation" because of the paucity there of stone tools, believed to be prime indicators of more advanced learning and cultures. Now it is recognized that sophisticated Asian cultures relied heavily on tools from bamboo, which, unlike stone tools, were not preserved in the fossil record.

As I sat by the fire interviewing hunters and examining the myriad musk deer, red panda, and red goral skins that were ready for trade, one particular skin caught my eye. It was a red serow—a different race than the black serow, which was relatively common south of here, in forested mountains more than 3,000 feet in elevation. This was the fourth red serow skin I'd seen in Guba and Madaing. Strangely, hunters claimed that only the red serow could be found in these mountains, although black was the predominant color of the serow near all the villages we'd visited earlier. I suspected that hunting and habitat fragmentation had localized many serow populations, causing genetic isolation and racial variation.

I wondered if the situation was similar for other species in this terrain. Takin, red panda, and red goral all ranged at elevations starting at about 6,000 feet. During the winter months the animals moved down the mountains near the villages, the hunters said, while in summer they headed back above the tree line. Only the musk deer stayed year-round at the highest elevations, 9,000 feet and above. But the rugged terrain of this region encouraged more creatures than just the serow to live in restricted pockets of habitat instead of moving freely over wide areas. Animals in these disjunct pockets of habitat were more likely to develop lasting genetic differences that set them apart from animals of the same species elsewhere.

Another hunter I spoke with identified the picture of a wolf in my photo album, a species long suspected of being in Myanmar but never confirmed. He'd seen this animal twice within the last three years, he said, not far from the Indian border. This was the second report I'd had of a hunter having seen a wolf in the northern mountains, but I still had no definitive evidence of this species from Myanmar.

I was so absorbed in listening to Khaing translate the hunter's words that it was almost too late when I smelled the burning rubber. Suddenly, I realized that my sneakers were on fire, and they were still on my feet! I jumped up and rushed around till the flames were extinguished, much to the delight of the people in the house. Fortunately, only the thick rear rubber section was damaged. But it was a big event for the household, and no more information was forthcoming from the hunters. All they wanted to do now was drink tea and talk about my shoes catching on fire.

That night we feasted on mithan, a rare treat since it was a valued animal of the Tibetans. This mithan had broken its leg and had to be killed, much to the dismay of the owner. The mithan, also called gayal, occupies only a limited region of south-central Asia centered in Assam, Arunachal Pradesh, and northern Myanmar. Averaging five and a half feet tall at the withers and weighing up to 1,300 pounds, it is considered its own species, *Bos frontalis*, although its origins remain in dispute. Some believe it is a domesticated form of the gaur, a wild cattle species, while others think it is a hybrid of gaur and domestic cattle.

Known for the high butterfat content of their milk and their unusually quiet and gentle disposition, mithan are kept in a partially domesticated state by both the Rawang and the Tibetans. As well as providing milk and butter, mithan are highly valued for barter and bride purchases. Only when absolutely necessary are mithan used for manual labor, and only on rare occasions, such as severe illness of a family member, will they be sacrificed. The villagers allow mithan to graze and wander at will, knowing that the animals will return in the evening for their salt rations. Such a relationship supports the view that the local people originally domesticated cattle by inducing them to develop a dependence on regular gifts of salt.

Although it hadn't surprised me to see mithan in some Rawang villages, I expected to see yak as well in the Tibetan villages. Yak had been in northern Myanmar when Kingdon Ward came through the region in the 1930s and again when Colonel Saw Myint did his northern frontier reconnaissance in 1954. Another large grazing bovine that has been domesticated for at least 3,000 years, the yak is common in the high elevations of Tibet, where it provides the people of the region with a source of milk, butter, meat, hides, and dung for fuel wood. But yaks much prefer elevations above 6,500 feet; they do poorly at lower altitudes, where their heavy coat makes it difficult for them to dissipate heat and where they become easily exhausted and susceptible to infections. The Tibetans in Myanmar, all living below 6,500 feet, said that they had stopped keeping yaks years ago because of the need to move them to colder, higher elevations during the summer months. Instead, they adopted the Rawang use of the mithan, which they found better adapted for this area.

The Tibetans were cleaner than the Rawang, with less of an aversion toward bathing. On the other hand, they seemed to care less about toilet facilities. If we wanted an outhouse in a Tibetan village, we had to make our own. Otherwise it was just a matter of finding a spot that was not in the direct line of sight of anyone passing by at the time. Avoiding the livestock, however, was another matter entirely. If the pigs weren't trying to get your feces, the mithan were eagerly waiting to lap up your urine for its salt content.

While pigs could be bullied, nothing seemed to deter the gentle but overzealous mithan, always wanting to drink the urine right from its source. This might have been humorous if not for their horns, more than a foot long, lingering dangerously close to your genitals. One night a particularly presumptuous mithan came up quietly behind me and jammed his head between my legs while my pants were down. As soon as I determined that his blunt horns had caused no major damage, I closed my legs and locked his head between them. Then I gave him what he wanted. I urinated on his head.

Our stay in Guba and Madaing was far too short and we were reluctant to leave the Tibetans, having felt more welcome and comfortable while among them than at any other time during our trip. But we had to rejoin the rest of the team and continue onward so that we didn't fall far behind our schedule. As we left Guba, laden with gifts of chickens, Tibetan bread, and Tibetan tea, it saddened me that, despite how hard and long these Tibetans worked the land, they were seen as latecomers and outsiders by the neighboring Rawang. The Rawang even claimed much of the land around Tibetan settlements as their own traditional hunting territories. If the Tibetans wanted to hunt certain species, such as musk deer, they had to travel far distances into the icy mountains or ask permission from the Rawang to hunt their territory.

These Myanmar Tibetans were caught between two worlds. They were viewed as "primitive" by their own people across the border in Tibet as well, they said, because they had adopted some Rawang practices (such as the use of mithan) and had combined traditional Tibetan Buddhist practices with animistic beliefs that involved paying respect to the natural forces around them. As long as they remained in these remote valleys, they would always be "lost" from Tibet, one hunter said wistfully. This was the price of crossing new frontiers and carving a better life out of the harshest of environments. But I had no doubt that, while the fortunes of others might wane, these people would always have food in their homes and smiles on their faces.

## CHAPTER 11

# Pygmies of the Adung Wang Valley

It is only with the heart that one can see rightly; what is
essential is invisible to the eye.

—Antoine de Saint-Exupéry

ALTHOUGH IT WOULD HAVE SEEMED impossi-
ble to me a few days earlier, I returned to Tazundam more tired
than when I had left. The members of the team who had stayed
behind were well rested and eager to be off again, but we needed
to rest an extra day. Not only were both knees bothering me continuously now, but my left knee was also swollen with fluid. Zawgan had fashioned a new walking stick for me, and I used it constantly. Hobbling along, sporting a monthlong gray beard on my
face, I felt very old.

I tried to maintain the illusion that if I just ignored the pain, it
would go away. It had worked when I was younger. In my more
lucid moments, however, I realized that my age and the abuse I had
inflicted upon my body over the years were catching up with me.
Injury, illness, and even the possibility of an untimely death were
realities that I'd learned to deal with during my years in the field.

But aging, manifested by the irreversible breakdown of my body parts, was something I couldn't yet accept.

The next village on the trail from Tazundam, Tazhutu, was only six miles or a three-hour hike away, but we ended up spending the night there. The monk had been through several days earlier, looking weak and feverish, but we heard that he was back safely at his monastery now. Zawgan, who had been teasing me about walking like an old man, sprained his ankle. It gave me some satisfaction that we'd both be limping to our final destination. That evening, the team had an infusion of animal protein, feasting on a freshly killed Assamese macaque brought in by a hunter. I ate some of the meat but passed on the offer of a special dish of cooked brain.

We were nearly four weeks into the expedition. Despite the fluid in my knee, I still walked faster than anyone else on our team. Fortunately, the soldiers no longer felt the need to keep someone assigned to me, so my solitary walks were more pleasant. I was alone when I rounded a bend in the trail and saw the large swinging bridge spanning the Adung Wang River. On the far side, I could hear children's voices and dogs barking among the nearly thirty huts that dotted the narrow piece of land between the river and the mountains. The sights and sounds were like those of all the other Rawang villages we had visited so far, but my heart beat faster as I approached the bridge. This was not just any village. I had been anticipating this moment since the morning I had burst into Khaing's room over the railroad station in Myitkyina. Soon a mystery would be solved. This was the home of the Taron.

In 1954, the Myanmar military officer Colonel Saw Myint, while leading a reconnaissance expedition to the northern borders of the country, came upon a group of fifty-eight people (twenty-six males, thirty-two females) living in three settlements in the Adung Wang Valley; most were in the village of Arundam, which I was looking at now. In his report to the government, Colonel Saw Myint called them Taron, describing them as a separate pygmoid racial group originating in the upper reaches of the Tarong River in China, with distinctive behavior, language, and cultural beliefs.

The Taron first migrated into Burma in the 1800s, the elders told him, when they were trying to escape tribal warfare with the Tibetans who dominated the Tarong River basin at that time.

Earlier explorers who had also met these people described them as "a pygmy forest tribe of unknown origin" and "queer, stunted simian beings . . . with scarcely any clothes, an unsavory smell, and great mops of curly black hair." But they had mistakenly grouped them together with another Rawang tribe, the Daru, which also lived in the area. Eight years after Colonel Saw Myint's expedition, a team from the Burma Medical Research Society journeyed to collect physical and physiological data on the Taron. Their report, published in the book I had shown Khaing and in the international journal *Nature,* stated that the sixty-nine pygmies they examined were of Mongoloid racial stock. Due to inbreeding, the Taron had a disturbingly high rate of infant mortality, insanity, cretinism, and mental retardation. Such defects, combined with the natural hardships and dangers of living in this rugged region, took a heavy toll, as illustrated by the family tree Colonel Saw Myint recorded of a 70-year-old Taron male who had taken two wives:

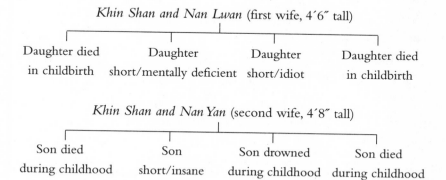

*Khin Shan and Nan Lwan* (first wife, 4´6˝ tall)

| Daughter died in childbirth | Daughter short/mentally deficient | Daughter short/idiot | Daughter died in childbirth |

*Khin Shan and Nan Yan* (second wife, 4´8˝ tall)

| Son died during childhood | Son short/insane | Son drowned during childhood | Son died during childhood |

In the decades that followed, the outside world had lost touch with the Taron, and I didn't know what I would find. We were about to learn the status of perhaps the only pygmies of Asian ancestry in the world.

To most people, the capitalized term *Pygmies* refers to the several hundred thousand racially distinct people of equatorial Africa who have been around for at least 4,000 years. Of these, the Mbuti Pygmies of the Ituri Forest in Congo (formerly Zaire) are the smallest, with the men averaging less than five feet tall and 106 pounds, and the women averaging less than four and a half feet tall and 92 pounds. But the lowercase term *pygmy* can refer to any short person with a stunted or dwarfish condition. It is a diminutive of a Greek word meaning "fist," originally used to refer to a measure of length from the elbow to the fist. The earliest use of the word is most often ascribed to Homer, who used it when describing a battle between Greek and Trojan forces in the *Iliad*.

The Myanmar Medical Society Expedition of 1962 found the average height of the Taron to be four and a half feet for both men and women, with the men averaging 91 pounds and the women 84 pounds. Professor Mya-Tu, who led the expedition, noted the similarities in stature between the Taron and both the African pygmies and the Oceanic Negrito pygmies, but the Taron had typical Mongoloid, not Negrito, features, he commented, and differed in other ways as well. One of the generally accepted theories among nineteenth-century anthropologists was that all people of small stature, typically those living in humid tropical areas of Asia, Oceania, and Africa, belonged to the same racial group. It was not until the 1960s that this theory was disproved, when studies using blood groups as genetic markers showed that pygmies of various geographic regions are more similar to their non-pygmy neighbors than to each other.

As I crossed the bridge and entered the village, now renamed Karaung, all movement and sound around me ceased. The houses here were rougher, more poorly built than those in other Rawang villages. My first impression was that the village, rather than being filled with short-statured Taron, was populated by people who were merely less attractive, aberrant forms of the Rawang. I stopped to take a picture of a woman who looked terrified of me and had frozen in place as I approached her. Focusing the camera, I felt, and then saw out of the corner of my eye, a child brushing up against my leg. Turning with the camera still to my face, I was surprised to watch the viewfinder fill not with the body of a child but with the misshapen, dwarfish form of an old man with sad, rheumy eyes. Before I could snap the picture, the viewfinder was empty. I looked up in time to see him hobbling off before disappearing into a nearby house. I had just seen my first Taron.

That night we bought a chicken and some eggs from the village headman and asked him to join us for dinner. During the meal I learned why the people of this village, apart from the Taron, looked different from other Rawang. Of the twenty-eight families comprising 170 people in the village, most were Htalu, with nearly a third of them claiming Taron blood from mixed marriages. I suspected that the proportion of mixed-blood families might in fact be even higher, because few of these people had the characteristic taller stature and sharply delineated facial features that we had seen among the Htalu in Tazundam.

Over tea, I asked the headman why I saw so few of the Taron, and how the Htalu had come to live with them in the first place. He seemed reluctant to answer and changed the subject. A little later I instructed Khaing to give the headman a bag of medicine that we had planned to leave for the village. He was grateful for such an important gift, as I knew he would be. Then I asked my questions again.

"The Taron have a hard life," the headman finally answered. "Many people have hurt them. We help them build houses and cut their taungyas now. But soon there will be only Htalu. That is better."

I asked what he meant by that last statement, but he wouldn't explain. Would he help me talk with the remaining Taron in the village? He looked toward his elder daughter, who had been standing unnoticed in the shadows. She nodded. Then she moved into the firelight as her father stood and left the room.

I spent that evening and the next day visiting the few huts where the Taron lived. In contrast to the friendliness and hospitality of other tribal groups, the Taron seemed fearful, listless, and sad. Colonel Saw Myint had reported that the Taron were extremely shy in the presence of outsiders, harboring feelings of inferiority built up through a history of persecution and enslavement by neighboring Tibetans and Chinese. At one point, he said, the Taron had built their huts in trees in order to escape continual slave raids. Even during Colonel Saw Myint's trip, Tibetans in the village of Tahundan still owned Taron slaves.

Using the headman's daughter as a translator, I was shocked to learn that while there were sixty-eight people from sixteen families who claimed mixed Rawang-Taron heritage, there were only twelve pure-blood Taron left, down from more than a hundred just forty years earlier. I thought again of Colonel Saw Myint's report, which stated that after the Taron crossed the mountains into Myanmar, they lost contact with their original tribal settlements in China when earthquakes closed the passes and isolated their settlements. No longer able to obtain matrimonial partners from other Taron groups, the Taron here started condoning marriage between brothers and sisters in an effort to maintain ethnic purity. The result was a high rate of infant mortality and a sizable proportion of mentally defective children. Yet that still didn't seem to fully explain how quickly and dramatically the Taron's situation had deteriorated.

Questioning the Taron was a laborious and sometimes frustrating process. I would pose a question to Khaing, and he would translate from English to Burmese for our local Rawang forester, U Myat Soe. U Myat Soe talked to the headman's daughter, translating from Burmese to Rawang. The headman's daughter questioned the Taron in the local Htalu dialect, which the Taron could speak and understand even though it wasn't their first language.

The Taron were reluctant to talk about their past, and it turned out that much of their oral history was forgotten. I was also uncertain as to the accuracy of the translations I was getting. Answers to questions about animals and hunting were much easier to confirm than responses to personal questions. Sometimes I asked the same question three or four different ways to make sure I understood the answer. But there was always some doubt in my mind as to the original wording of the answer from the mouths of the Taron.

The Taron houses were more decrepit than those of other Rawang groups, as were the Taron themselves. Although they had a lighter facial complexion than the Rawang, my first impression was that the few Taron left looked much like the typical portrayals of Stone Age people. They were disheveled and dirty, their simple cotton clothing almost in tatters, as if they cared nothing about their appearance. Even in Colonel Saw Myint's time, the simple coarse cloth dress of the Taron, barely covering much of their bodies, was described as "inferior" and as little better than what one would expect from "jungle-dwelling savages."

The remaining Taron were mostly elderly. Two individuals I interviewed were retarded, and a third had advanced goiter. Colonel Saw Myint described watching Taron male children wrestling and playing with crossbows while Taron girls wove cloth alongside their mothers. There was none of that now. Instead, I was struck by the look of resignation on the villagers' faces. It was a look I had seen only once before in my life, in an AIDS ward in a New York City hospital.

The results of the Taron-Htalu marriages in the village didn't seem advantageous to the Htalu, whose children were shorter and far less physically attractive than the Htalu we'd seen in Tazundam. The diet of the village was mostly wheat, corn, beans, millet, and taro from local village plantations. The Taron, unlike the Htalu and other Rawang, had no livestock and rarely included meat or fish in their diet anymore, although they were considered skillful hunters in the past, with the ability to bring in any species they desired.

Colonel Saw Myint speculated that the appearance of the Taron was due to dietary deficiencies in nutrients such as iodine, but the medical team that came later found the Taron to be no more nutritionally deficient than any other human group in the area.

The Taron men became excited for the first time when I showed them pictures of animals, as memories of their past suddenly surfaced. Before their conversion to Christianity, I was told, a special ceremony overseen by a shaman was held after the birth of a Taron male child, involving small models of animals that they valued, such as serow, bear, and musk deer. These models were placed around a foot-high sculpted mountain made of corn flour, and the corn mountain was burned to invoke the protection of the Spirit of the Mountain. Afterward the animal figures were taken into the forest to ensure the hunting success of the child when he reached adulthood.

One old Taron started jabbing his gnarled hand at one of the pictures in my book. I had seen this behavior often by now, usually when the hunter was familiar with the species. This time the picture was of a yellow-throated marten, a four- to five-pound weasel-like animal that was common over a wide area in forests between 600 and 9,000 feet in elevation.

The Taron reached behind him and pulled a small rolled-up skin from under a bundle of clothes, then handed it to me. I didn't really want to see the skin of another yellow-throated marten, but I felt I had to examine it to be polite. As I unrolled the skin, I was already framing the false words of admiration I'd use. But the words died in my throat.

"Ask him where exactly he killed this animal, and if there are many others like it around here," I said to the headman's daughter through Khaing.

"He says there are some, but not many," Khaing eventually replied. "He is giving you the skin as a present."

It was a present I wanted. The skin I held was not from a yellow-throated marten but from a stone marten, a related species that was known mostly from central China and the Himalayas above 4,500 feet in elevation. Although it was not uncommon at higher elevations, its fur was valued by traders and it had never before been documented in Myanmar. This was the fourth new mammal species I had identified in the country.

Khaing was unusually quiet that first night when we returned to our hut. I thought he was exhausted after hours of helping me with tedious translation. As we prepared our bedrolls, we agreed to give the Taron all the extra salt and clothing we had left. They seemed the neediest of all the groups we'd met so far. I asked Khaing what he thought about the Taron.

"They are a pitiful people," he said. "When I was translating for you, I felt bad for the Taron, and I had to be careful that I didn't put my own feelings into what they said. Sometimes the meaning of what I was told they said was difficult to understand."

"You did the best you could," I said. "We learned a lot." I crawled into my sleeping bag.

"I told you they don't like themselves," he said, suddenly stopping what he was doing and looking up at me through the light of the candle on the floor between us. "I think that was right, although it might have been said with different words. But I didn't tell you something I should have. U Myat Soe said that the Taron said of themselves that they are ugly. *I* thought they were ugly too. So I wasn't sure if we were just putting our own feelings into words that were supposed to have come from them. How could they know what 'ugly' is? I felt bad about what I was thinking, so I didn't tell you this."

I sat up, leaning on one elbow and facing Khaing. He had my full attention now.

"If we're to understand anything about these people, I need to know exactly what they say, or at least what you think they say. You know that, Khaing." He nodded sheepishly. "Besides, I was thinking and feeling the same things you were as we talked with them. I didn't even want to sit close to them."

"But maybe they're not ugly to each other," Khaing said. "Maybe we're putting words in their mouth."

"That's possible. In such a short time, it's hard to really know what's going on here," I replied. "But I think you were right about what they said. I think they see in each other some of what we see from the outside, though maybe they wouldn't describe it as we do."

I wrote in my field notes what Khaing had just revealed to me and then lay back in my sleeping bag, letting the candle burn itself out. In the darkness, I again faced toward where Khaing was lying.

"You still awake?" I asked, hearing snoring from another part of the hut.

"Yes," he said, in a way that suggested he was still thinking about our conversation.

I tried to explain to Khaing why I had said what I did. The beliefs that "beauty is in the eye of the beholder" and that physical attraction is completely culturally determined were not borne out by scientific studies, I said. While the criteria for beauty were often influenced by our cultural backgrounds, there actually seemed to be a universal perception of attractiveness, one that was governed by natural selection and was programmed in the circuitry of the human brain. In other words, features that were considered universally beautiful in women might be external cues to men indicating that a woman is herself healthy and fertile and thus capable of bearing healthy children. Features considered attractive in men were often those indicating strength and dominance in a group. That's why it would be no surprise to me, I said, if some of the Taron and even the mixed Taron-Htalu appeared unattractive not only to us but also to themselves.

⚬✕⚬

As soon as I entered the hut, the man sitting by the fire turned away from me. He had known I was coming. Two Taron women, his older and younger sisters, stood beside him. As Khaing worked with the translator to ask the women questions, I sat down beside the man, sipping tea and looking into the fire. Out of the corner of my eye, I saw him cast furtive glances toward me. I waited.

I reached for the teapot sitting in the fire, forgetting that my hands were not as work-hardened as those of the villagers whom I'd watched do this many times.

"Yow!" I hollered, dropping the pot, spilling the tea, and spraying myself with hot ashes. "Damn," I said, pounding out the smoking embers that were burning holes in my clothes. Suddenly, I heard the strangest sound and turned. The Taron man was now facing me, rocking back and forth, cackling with high-pitched laughter. Unwittingly, I had broken the ice between us.

His name was Dawi and, at 39, this stocky, impish-looking man was the youngest of the surviving Taron in Myanmar. He and his two sisters were the only pure Taron family left. The other eight Taron were part of Htalu families. As he poured the tea for me, I took out my last remaining PowerBar, which I'd been saving for an emergency, and gave it to him.

He sat facing me now. He was wearing a coarse, dirty blanket thrown over his shoulder, light cloth pants tied at the knees, and cloth leggings that ended at black, hardened feet that had never seen shoes. He was one of the few who still wore remnants of the Taron traditional dress. I asked him several questions that went unanswered. He nibbled around the edges of the PowerBar, smiling and speaking to his sisters in the Taron dialect; suddenly, the whole bar was gone in a gulp.

After many cups of tea and a long hard look at me, Dawi began to speak, straining to put into words thoughts he'd perhaps never voiced before. He'd remembered everything I had asked him, and the intensity of his gaze hinted at an intelligence that had probably been long suppressed.

"For many years the Taron only marry each other," Dawi started, almost in a whisper. "But when we have babies, the babies have small brains and small bodies. It was no good." He turned his eyes away for a moment and then looked back at me.

"We don't want Taron babies anymore," Dawi continued. "Long ago, the Taron decided not to have babies with each other. Only with Htalu. Some Htalu marry Taron, many do not want to. If Htalu won't marry Taron, then we die alone."

His voice became almost defiant. "There are few Taron left. Many die alone."

Dawi shifted his body away from me again and faced the fire. It must have taken a lot for him to tell me what he did, to face images of a past that was gone and a future that would never be. Kingdon Ward called the Taron "one of nature's unsuccessful experiments." I think Dawi might have agreed. I didn't need to ask him what he thought of his own future. He was among the last. And he was dying alone.

## ❧ CHAPTER 12 ❧

# The Last Village

When we know how to read our own hearts, we acquire wisdom of the hearts of others.

—Denis Diderot

AN EASY TWO-HOUR WALK from Karaung brought us to Tahundan, the last village in northern Myanmar, nestled in a valley at 6,300 feet. It was an absolutely beautiful day— clear blue sky, cool breeze sweeping down off the mountains, shimmering snowcapped peaks hovering above dark evergreen forest in the distance. After nearly four weeks of hiking, we had reached our destination, and we were finally getting the beautiful weather that we felt we deserved. April was just around the corner. This was a dry month, the villagers said, when they cut, burned, and planted their taungyas for the coming year.

I couldn't get the Taron out of my mind. Dawi's face, as he looked into the fire, haunted me. If the translation and my understanding of his words were correct, his people had become active participants in their own extinction. Unless there were others elsewhere, an entire ethnic group of which the world was largely ignorant would soon be gone. It would be as if they had never existed. I had to see them again.

I spotted U Tilawka in the distance long before he saw me. He was standing on a little rise above the river where the trail crossed, anxiously awaiting our arrival. His face broke into a huge smile, ear to ear. Despite the reservations I'd had about him during our travels, the sight of his smiling face, a WCS hat on his shaved head and his health obviously improved, cheered me instantly. All thoughts of the Taron were pushed to the back of my mind. We embraced, and his eyes glistened. Then he took my hand and led me into the village.

U Tilawka's "monastery" was a simple structure situated on a little hilltop above the rest of the village, with a sweeping vista in every direction. It was a one-room cabin raised off the ground, 25 feet long by 15 feet wide, built with boards instead of logs and with a zinc roof overhead, the first I'd seen since Tazundam. There was a small detached cooking area off to one side. Against one wall of the main room was a raised platform on which U Tilawka slept, with a silk scroll bearing a Buddha image hanging above his bedroll. Nearby were several shelves holding Buddha images, incense burners, and candles. On a little knoll behind the cabin sat a 20-foot-tall white Buddhist chedi, built in 1994 by order of the head monk of the Theravada Buddhist Mission of the Kachin State, based in Myitkyina. The cost was approximately $15,000, and local soldiers had to be used to transport the concrete needed to build the structure because the Rawang refused to carry anything intended to promote Buddhism in the region.

At U Tilawka's insistence, Khaing, U Saw Lwin, and I stayed with him in the monastery. It was the cleanest house we had been in since the start of our trip. It was a pleasure to be able to spread out our belongings without having to sweep the floor of old bones and decaying animal skins, continually chase out chickens and dogs, or spray our sleeping area for fleas and bedbugs. The rest of the team was invited to stay at the house of U Namar Jon Sein, a 25-year-old

Tibetan who had gained notoriety for himself and the village when he accompanied the Japanese climber Ozaki on his successful second attempt to reach the peak of Mount Hkakabo Razi a year earlier.

That first night I woke at 3 A.M. shivering, colder than I'd been at any other time during the trip. The thermometer I had put near my head read 39°F. Tahundan was at 6,300 feet, similar to the elevations of Guba and Madaing. I tried snuggling deeper into the sleeping bag but finally, unable to sleep and needing to urinate anyway, I put on my warmest clothes and wandered outside.

My initial enthusiasm about staying in the monastery was gone. It was the cleanest house in the village, but it was also the coldest. U Tilawka's desire to have what he considered "civilized" living conditions was not the best strategy in this environment. The wood planks and zinc roof didn't retain the heat from the sun the way logs and thatching did. Also, the roof had a large, triangular "window" at one end that provided lots of light and a magnificent view of the snowcapped peaks but was a conduit for the nightly winds sweeping down the valley. Worst of all, there was no central hearth in the main room, only a small one in the detached kitchen. U Tilawka was compulsive about cleanliness, and he disliked the smoke and carbon residue that were generated from these fires. He also disliked dirt and malodorous bodies, which, I assumed, was why I rarely saw him out among the villagers. After several days in the monastery, I yearned for the warmth of the dark, dirty, smoke-filled local huts. Instead, I simply lived in my thermal underwear.

Over the next few days we settled in, wandered about the village, and discussed our next moves. After experiencing life in the Tibetan villages of Guba and Madaing, I wasn't surprised at how comfortable we felt here. Tensions that had built up between some of the team members dissipated quickly.

My mornings would start with the arrival of several women at the monastery, ostensibly coming to see the monk and bring him Tibetan tea and plates of millet and popcorn. But instead of returning home, they huddled in a corner of the monastery and watched me, sometimes for hours. They watched me read, they watched me write, they watched me brush my teeth, and I'd even wake up some mornings to see them watching me sleep. Every movement, every sniffle, was of interest. If I did something particularly fascinating, such as sharpen my pencil or inflate my sleeping pad, they would whisper among themselves for several minutes and then watch for my next strange action.

When I made eye contact, wide smiles would break across their faces, smiles unlike any I'd ever seen before. Their smiles were guileless, with nothing behind them other than the desire to convey the pleasure of being there. It was a wonderful way to start a day, and I came to look forward to waking up to the sight of them. It reminded me of how little people needed speech to convey the most important feelings. I wished I had been more aware of that in my youth, especially the times I crawled into the corner of my closet and pushed my fists into my cheeks until I couldn't stand the pain, physically trying to reshape my mouth so that I wouldn't stutter anymore.

The major and U Saw Lwin were keen to continue hiking beyond the village so that they could report to the Myanmar Mountaineering Club that we had pushed farther north than any other Myanmar expedition. The villagers warned us, however, that we risked encountering avalanches and soft snow at the higher elevations at this time of year. Another consideration was the condition of our team and the anticipated four-week return trip. The zoologist's foot was still not fully healed, and he was weak and emaciated. Hpa-hti's chronic cough sounded worse than ever, and we were treating it with a regular regime of antibiotics. He was also laid up with dysentery, so one of the village women was cooking for us. Khaing and I both had persistent knee problems that necessitated the use of walking sticks. He was treating himself with a traditional Myanmar liniment called the Great Wall Miraculous Pain Relief Medicine, while I was taking my own traditional mixture of anti-inflammatory and codeine pills. The rest of the team members had the normal assortment of aches and pains but were doing fine.

Another consideration was food. Our supplies were holding out well, although we had given away more food at villages along the way than we had planned to. We had also had to help feed our porters, even though they were supposed to have brought their own food with them. But on the upside, we had been able to purchase chickens, eggs, and vegetables from many villages without causing any undue stress on local food supplies.

The real food issue was rice. If we ever ran out of rice, I was sure that some of our team members would mutiny, while others might just lay down and die. Every time I heard that rice was a factor in planning our activities, I had to suppress my feelings of frustration that the success of our expedition depended on the supply of a particular food group. I constantly reminded myself of the importance of this simple grain, which not only is the main food of half the earth's population but is at the heart of many Asian cultural traditions.

To Asian peoples, rice is not simply food but the manifestation of the earth mother herself. In many cultures in Asia, rice is viewed as the embodiment of a tender, beautiful, timid woman who dislikes being handled by men. Men can prepare the land for rice, but women have to plant, weed, winnow, and cook it. Harvest time is when the earth mother is pregnant. The final white, soft grains that are produced and eaten are treated gently, like a shy young girl. Rice is not to be thrown on the floor or wasted. Rice is the model of acceptable public behavior—unassuming, gentle, and sensitive. At its most basic level, the consumption of rice is not simply the eating of a meal but a bonding with the earth.

If we were to spend a week exploring beyond Tahundan, we would have just enough rice for the return walk. Since the beginning of the trip, Hpa-hti had been conservative with our supplies, preparing simple but tasty meals—usually rice with fish paste, fermented tofu, and soup from local vegetables. I had enjoyed such

simple meals but, since reaching Tahundan, I had developed a crav-
ing for something sweet and flavorful. Besides raw sugar and honey,
we had run out of snacks and candies long ago, mostly due to my
inclination to freely dispense what we had among village children.
·I'd even given my last PowerBar to Dawi. My problem was solved
one evening as I was putting on my Vaseline lip conditioner. The
cherry flavoring was so satisfying that I bit off a little piece and ate
it. Having felt no ill effects by morning, I developed a ritual of nib-
bling at the lip balm each evening as an after-dinner treat.

I sat in the main room of the headman's house, looking across the
fire into the face of his elder son. The decor was similar to that of
every other hut we had been in on this trip, little beyond the bare
essentials. The headman's son was sitting on a Himalayan black bear
skin, weaving a basket with bamboo strips. The headman's grand-
child was playing with the horn of a goral, next to a pile of red goral
skins in the corner. A fresh takin skin was stretched and drying outside. The headman's 22-year-old daughter came out from a back
room and placed a bowl of millet mixed with honey in front of me.
Her knee touched mine and she smiled.

"U Ga Nar," I said, turning to the headman and using his given
name for the first time. "This is a beautiful place, with many beautiful animals. I know that sometimes you kill for food, but most animals die for the Chinese traders. It makes me sad." Khaing translated, and the headman nodded.

"You can see that life is hard in these mountains," the headman
responded. "Much of the time, there is enough to eat. The land is
good to us. But we need salt. If there is no salt, food is not good and
we get weak. Also, the livestock die. We need things that come from
the traders." He paused, choosing his next words carefully.

"When you come, you bring us salt, medicine, and some
clothes, and I thank you for that. But you will probably never come

again. When we have these things, we can spend more time taking care of the land and growing more food. But if we do not have them, we must hunt."

"If I could bring you what you need, would you stop hunting more than just for meat?" I asked. "Would you let animals live if you didn't have to kill them?"

"Some people like hunting," the headman responded. "Sometimes it is for more than food. But alive is better than dead. If we do not have to hunt, it is good. People can grow more food."

"But if I gave you what you get from the traders, how would I know if people were still hunting or not?" I asked.

"I am the headman," he said, looking a bit chagrined. "I can tell you who hunts and who does not hunt. I can show you the fresh sign of animals that are alive."

He stiffened his back as if waiting for me to challenge him further. But my mind was elsewhere. The seed of an idea was just starting to take root.

Despite the peace and calm I felt in the village, I was getting restless. We had pushed hard to get here, and I was afraid that if we got too comfortable, it would be tougher to make the trip back. I had gotten over my neurotic visions of my wife with another man, but other images of Salisa and home were intruding more and more frequently into my daily thoughts, making me homesick.

That evening, the team met to discuss what we should do next. As usual, all discourse was in Burmese. I waited patiently for Khaing to translate or summarize what had been said.

When you can't understand what is being said around you day to day, your mind becomes more focused and your awareness more acute. All other senses are heightened, trying to interpret facial movements and body language, listening to tones and pauses. I continually strained to pick up the gist of what was going on around me. It became a game, seeing how right or wrong I was when Khaing finally translated people's words. Sometimes I was way off, but usually I wasn't. Eventually, I came to rely more on my gut feelings than on what the translation was telling me. People's words didn't always convey the core of what they felt, thus explaining why those who put too much faith in what people say are often shocked when subsequent actions don't coincide with the words they heard.

At 2 A.M. I awoke abruptly, fragments of dreams dissipating into the night air. There was an unsettled feeling in my gut, so I got up and went outside. A nearly full moon lit up the snowcapped peaks in the distance, and I decided to visit the chedi. Despite the cold, I removed my shoes before stepping over the small rock wall onto the ground around this religious structure, considered sacred.

I circled the chedi three times, as I had done with Khaing at the Shwedagon Pagoda in Yangon. It seemed a lifetime ago. Near the river's edge in the valley below, I could make out Tibetan prayer flags in honor of the dead fluttering in the wind. The flags had originally been placed up near the chedi until U Tilawka voiced his disapproval: the practice of flying flags for the dead clashed with his own beliefs.

I stopped before the gold Buddha that occupied a special niche built into the wall of the chedi. Leaning deep into the niche to shelter my lighter from the wind, I lit three sticks of incense and placed them in the cup in front of the Buddha. Then I kneeled in respect. The fragrant smoke of the incense wrapped around the Buddha, obscuring his face for a moment.

A strange interplay between the smoke and the moonlight created an impression that can occur only in the early morning hours, when the psyche is susceptible to shifts in perception. I saw the Buddha's face transform, becoming haggard and tired. A strong feeling of desperation overwhelmed me. I felt scared. I saw Dawi sitting alone in his hut. Then I saw myself, much older in years, sitting beside him.

The next morning I discussed an idea with Khaing before talking with the rest of the team. The previous evening, everyone else had been unanimous in their feeling that we should continue on as far north as we could. They felt it was an opportunity that might not come again. The weaker members of the team had agreed to remain in Tahundan, while the others would push forward. But in my own mind, it was not as simple as that. The outcome of this trip would determine how much more WCS could do for this area and other places like it in Myanmar. If something went wrong now, it could end all my plans. The final decision was mine to make.

Our itinerary called for us to walk out by the same route we had come in, which would take at least three weeks if we started now. It was the end of March, and the rains we'd experienced coming up here were nothing compared to what could fall from the sky by mid- to late April, when the rainy season started in earnest. Given the same rough terrain on the walk out, there was no doubt we'd be pushing the physical limits of many of our team members. If we delayed our walk out for one to two weeks by going farther north, the situation could be worse. Our food supplies would be just that much more depleted, and meals would be sparser than they had been, just when we needed the energy the most. I was already worried by the hacking coughs I heard coming from the sleeping bags of our team members each night. On the other hand, passing up an opportunity to explore farther when we might never come this way again was almost unthinkable.

Before our trip, General Chit Swe had said that if we made it to Tahundan, he might come in by helicopter to meet us. I hadn't given much thought to the remark because I felt it was said offhandedly. But I now realized it left open an option that I hadn't even considered earlier. I asked our radio signalman to try to make contact with the minister in Yangon. We would relate the success of our trip and request a helicopter to take us out. Our chances were slim, but a precedent had been set with Ozaki the previous year when he climbed Mount Hkakabo Razi. We had nothing to lose and much to gain.

In the meantime, I compromised and agreed that some of us would remain here while the rest would split into three teams to explore the terrain a bit more. The major and some of the soldiers would proceed as far north as they could safely go and still be back within a week's time. U Saw Lwin would lead a botanical group accompanying the major, then split off to look for orchids and survey the forest types. Khaing, two Forest Department staff, and I would travel north in a different direction, following hunting trails to the snow line in search of animal signs. We would also collect more information here in Tahundan and from the smaller village of Talahtu, which we'd passed but not yet visited. Khaing was disappointed, wanting to go with the major's team to see more of the high mountain habitats. But I needed him for translation, and I wanted him to save his energy for the walk out.

That afternoon two young hunters arrived in Tahundan looking for me. They carried a rattan basket bulging with what looked like a pile of dark skins, but as they approached, I saw the skins move.

In the basket was a young female serow. One of the men had captured it in a snare around his plantation and kept it alive for four days before making the 10-mile trip to try selling it to me. The poor beast, no more than six months old and less than three feet tall, was terrified and had developed a bloody sore on its head from rubbing against the small, cramped basket. I instructed Khaing to pay them what they would have gotten for selling the skin and meat to traders. Then I sent for U Tilawka and asked the two hunters, along with other hunters from Tahundan, to accompany me across the river and into the forest.

A short way from the village, I asked the hunters to set down the basket with the serow beneath a large spruce tree. Then I did something I rarely do—I lectured the local people, asking Khaing to translate my words exactly. I had reached the limit of my ability to turn a blind eye to all the killing of wildlife on this trip. It was easier when the animals were long dead and cut up into pieces. But the imminent death of a young female, whose womb contained the potential for several generations of her kind, was too much for me to take.

"I know you have to hunt," I started. "I also know that because you have hunted and traded for many years, you think there will always be animals here. But every hunter knows that you now have to walk farther and work harder to get the animals you want. You know why this is."

A few hunters nodded, but most faces were expressionless. The whole scene seemed bizarre, even to me.

"There is no reason for any of you to kill young animals or pregnant females. You get little from the traders for young animals. I know traders pay a lot for the unborn fetus of pregnant females, but it is foolish for you to kill pregnant females because of this. You lose more than you get. These animals are your future, for the time when food is scarce or when your children need to hunt. If you keep on killing the young ones and the females, you will have nothing. Hunting is harder now. It will be even harder next year and the year after. Soon it will be impossible for you to find many of the animals that you depend on. There will come a day when you are hungry and wonder where all the animals have gone."

I was worked up, but I wasn't angry. It was impossible for me to be angry toward people just struggling to survive. The last thing they needed was proselytizing, I knew, but I had to do something. Khaing, I could tell, thought I was wasting my time. But the thousands of skins and body parts I'd already seen being sold for handfuls of salt or a few cooking pots all seemed to be summed up in the life of this one little serow. There had to be a better way to help both the people and the animals.

After extracting a promise from everyone there that this serow wouldn't be killed after we set it free, I signaled for the hunters to open the basket and lift out the serow. U Tilawka, at my request, blessed the animal. When he was finished, I motioned for everyone to step back. Fifteen seconds passed before the serow struggled to her feet and stood wobbling. Finally, realizing there was nothing holding her back, she dashed into the woods, fell once, then regained her footing, and went up the mountain.

That day was U Tilawka's forty-first birthday. He mentioned it to us that evening when we presented him with the robes, incense, candles, and two Buddhas that had been brought for his monastery. He, in turn, gave Khaing a bottle of wild honey with a large ginseng root inside for strength, and he gave U Saw Lwin a bottle of highly prized machit powder. Then, from behind a Buddha on one of the shelves near his sleeping platform, he pulled out two items: an old brass half-pound measuring weight molded into the figure of a duck, and a five-inch-tall brass Buddha figure. He walked over and laid them before me. Then he turned to Khaing and spoke at some length.

"The monk says you gave him a very special birthday present today when you set free the serow and had him bless it," Khaing explained to me. "It was a true act of Buddhism, and you made him feel very good. He wants to give you something special in return."

U Tilawka reached out and closed his hands around mine while Khaing continued translating.

"This weight is old," Khaing said. "It will guide you in understanding your past. Carry it for a time and then put it aside. The Buddha is from Tibet and is also very old. But the Buddha's teachings are timeless. Hold it when you need to, but never put it aside for long. It will help you in the future."

Khaing seemed to approve of what the monk was saying, but something else was obviously bothering him. I asked why he seemed annoyed.

"Those are special things the monk gave to you," Khaing said. "They have come over long distances. The weight is the shell duck we call Hintha Lay, from the city of Bago. According to our history, the migration of the shell duck along the Ayeyarwady showed the Myanmar people where to build ports for trade. They are considered very special animals. These pieces are yours now, and you should respect them, as the monk says. But they were not his to give away. They were given to him by others, to be buried under the chedi. He favors you too much, while he ignores the needs of others, especially the people of this village. He is a good man, but he still has much to learn."

I knew Khaing was right. Even if he had not said it, I felt that the precious gifts I held, representing the hopes and dreams of others, were not meant to be sitting on a shelf in New York City. In a strange way, I felt I was a bad influence on U Tilawka. From that day on, I resolved to put a little more distance between myself and the monk.

✑✖✎

Khaing and I saw the other two teams off. We stayed behind in the village for a few more days to wait for word about the helicopter. Women and children continued to come by the monastery every day to sit and watch me. I learned to ignore them, but they didn't care. One night I made the mistake of recording them with my video camera and then playing it back to them. They laughed and hid their heads behind each other, amazed and embarrassed to be seeing their own faces looking and talking back at them.

The next day nearly the entire village crowded into the monastery to see themselves on the little video screen. Few had ever seen television before, and many had never even looked upon their own faces as closely as they were doing now. Putao was the farthest south that even the oldest of the villagers had ventured. Unfortunately, they wanted repeated showings, which I had to refuse after the first few. There was no way to recharge my batteries up here.

When I had free time I wandered the village, which included only eleven houses with an average of seven people per house. I watched the woman of one house go out every morning and offer food and popcorn at an altar, a raised platform of bamboo surrounded by Tibetan prayer flags. Along with the food, leaves and scented pine kindling were burned, generating large plumes of smoke that carried hopes for good health and good harvest to the spirit world. During the ceremony, she blew on a conch shell so that the spirits would heed her prayers. It was an example of the convergence of Buddhism and spirit worship up here that, as the headman in Madaing said, set these Tibetans apart from others of their kind.

I followed villagers as they collected wood for their fires. I helped the men build bamboo drying racks to stretch the skins of recent kills. I watched the children taking care of each other while they helped with whatever chores had to be done around the house or in the gardens. The hardships of life here, and the lack of formal schooling, forced children to take on adult responsibilities and to mature more quickly than their counterparts elsewhere. But every now and then, when the children slipped in the mud, splashed water on each other, or fell and rolled down a hill, their laughter showed them to be like any other children anyplace in the world.

I also finally got a closer look at what appeared to be sections of tree trunks atop large rocks placed close to plantations. On several occasions the Tibetans had given us bowls of the most delicious honey I had ever tasted, and U Tilawka told me that honey was in abundance here. Now I learned that these disconnected three- to four-foot-high tree pieces, plugged up on both ends with wooden slabs and held down on top by a large stone, were the village bee-hives.

Tree cavities are the typical nesting sites for honeybees in temperate climates, containing colonies that store a much larger amount of honey for surviving the winter than do colonies farther south. Since bee swarms generally move no farther than 1,000 to 2,000 feet away from old nests, the local villagers had learned where to search for new supplies of wild honey.

Although the Rawang didn't typically cultivate honey, I saw the

Htalu in Karaung maintaining an active honeybee nest in a live tree at the village. They had opened up the cavity and then sealed it again with boards, so that the nest could still be used by the bees but the villagers could get to the honey when they wanted. The Tibetans, not surprisingly, were much more industrious. They cut down the trees, sealed the ends, and created natural honeybee nest boxes. Honey was an essential part of the diet of the Tibetans and, given its fuel value of about 1,500 calories per pound, it was probably one of the reasons that they were more vigorous than other tribal groups.

❧

Once I felt comfortable enough in the village, I started just showing up at the doors of people's huts, walking inside, and ensconcing myself next to their fire, as they did with each other. At first, the entire household stopped what they were doing and focused their attention on me. Eventually, they just acknowledged my presence with a smile, served me tea and popcorn, and then went about their business, ignoring me as easily as I had the onlookers at the monastery.

My favorite house was the home of Daw Sri Daraemer, matriarch of her family and of the village, with an estimated age somewhere between 75 and 80. She was the last woman in the village who could use a loom, which in this place was made of wood and bamboo. Though her eyesight was failing and her fingers were arthritic, she had recently acquired a pair of spectacles from a Chinese trader and she still made clothes for her six grandchildren. My first visit to her house was made at her request, because one of her grandchildren was sick.

As soon as I saw the little girl, my heart sank. No more than four years old, little Ma Phae Darae looked as though she had acute conjunctivitis, an inflammation of the mucous membrane lining the inner surface of the eyelid and part of the eyeball, commonly known as pinkeye. It had advanced to the point of almost disfiguring the right side of her face and she was in considerable pain, crying constantly and unable to sleep at night. The entire household was worried. While pinkeye is easily treated in the United States with sulfa drugs and antibiotic ointment, I had neither. There was little I could do other than administer some Benadryl to help the child sleep at night.

It was during one of my visits to check on the girl, as I sat writing notes in my journal, that I felt a body lean against my back, then saw a head appear at my left shoulder. I looked up into the piercing eyes of Kaw Yan Htawgyi, a 14-year-old boy whom I'd seen occasionally following me at a distance during my wanderings around the village.

I turned back to my writing. When I didn't react to his presence, Htawgyi pushed closer. He was watching my hand make scrawling movements across the page. I looked into his face again, and he smiled. There was an intensity about this young man that reminded me of Dawi; he seemed different from the other young people in the village. Daw Sri Daraemer, who was sitting by the wall mending her daughter's clothes, said something to Htawgyi that caused him to back away a bit. I shifted my own body just enough to reestablish the contact and let him know it was okay. I was surprised at how good it felt to me.

Later, after asking Khaing to inquire for me, I learned that Htawgyi was an orphan. His father had died when he was a child, and his mother went off to Tibet, remarried, and never returned. Daw Sri Daraemer looked after him. After that day at his house, I started picking him out among the youngsters and watching him more intently. He would always do things that the others with him wouldn't do—look under logs, climb steep rocks, watch fish in the river. Sometimes I'd see him staring off into the distance toward the icy mountains.

I knew what was special about this boy. His mind was alive and curious, and he was trying to reach out beyond the boundaries of his world. When I looked at his face, or when he met my stare with his own, I was looking into a mirror thirty years in my past.

CHAPTER 13

# Touching the Snow

The shadow past is shaped by everything that never happened. Invisible, it melts the present like rain through karst. A biography of longing. It steers us like magnetism, a spirit torque.

—Anne Michaels

$W$HEN THERE WAS NO WORD from General Chit Swe on our helicopter request, or even an acknowledgment of our message, Khaing and I decided to accompany some hunters on a day trip north of the village. We planned to follow the Gwelang Wang, the branch of the Adung Wang River that flowed through Tahundan, to its source in Gwelang Razi, the mountain whose snowcapped peak at 14,360 feet could be seen from the village. This river was one of the many branches that eventually came together to form the Ayeyarwady, and the idea of reaching the origin of at least one of this famous river's sources appealed to me. More importantly, the distant mountains marked the end of the Adung Wang Valley and the beginning of a higher, colder Himalayan habitat that stretched into Tibet. There were no trails where we were going, so we followed the river.

Soon after leaving the village, we ascended to 7,000 feet into moist, temperate forest containing a mixture of deciduous and ever-green broadleaf trees and conifers, dominated by blue pine, spruce, hemlock, walnut, and oak. On sites of recent landslides, stands of alder had taken root. About an hour out, as the river narrowed and turned toward the mountains, we found ourselves in a clearing in which stood a lone thatched hut that seemed as out of place as any human habitation we had yet encountered. A small bamboo basket lay on its side by the door, and some ragged pieces of material, which might have once looked like clothing, hung from a vine clothesline in back.

I approached the door to look inside, wondering why someone had chosen to live in such an isolated, lonely spot. Thinking it was abandoned, I pushed open the front door and heard a small cry from the darkness within. There was no fire burning in the hearth, but from the slivers of light coming through the bamboo wall I could make out the figure of an old woman clutching a little bun-dle to her chest. The bundle was a little baby. There was another cry that trailed off into a whimper, but whether it came from the woman or the baby I couldn't tell. Something about that sound, fear mixed with desperation, disturbed me so greatly that I stepped back outside.

"Three women and a baby live here," Khaing said after speak-ing with one of the hunters from Tahundan. "They are not Tibetan. They are Rawang from Karaung. It is a very sad story."

The father and the son-in-law had both died in landslides, Khaing translated. Now the women had to fend for themselves, and they settled on this little piece of unused land where they were try-ing to do the backbreaking work of making a plantation. It was too much for them. Sometimes they'd come to Tahundan to beg for food, and the Tibetans tried to help them when they could. Last year the daughter gave birth to a new baby. No one knew who the father was.

I only half listened to what Khaing was telling me. That cry from the darkness still bothered me. It triggered memories of a little boy looking for dark hiding places, wanting to squeeze into corners where no one could find him. That same sound had once come from my own lips when my parents found me huddled in the closet.

"We have to help them," I said.

"The hunter says to leave them alone," Khaing said. "We need to move on if we're to get back before dark. This is what their life is."

I walked away from the house after leaving them the food that we'd brought with us for lunch. As I turned back for a last look, a single eye peered at me from an opening in the wall. I thought of Dawi looking at me across the fire. I thought of Htawgyi pressing his face close to mine. I thought of the little boy in the closet, squeezing his eyes shut and hoping that when he opened them again, the world would be different.

We moved away from the river and bushwhacked up a little canyon that would save us time climbing the mountain. Almost immediately, the hunters spotted fresh goral tracks. Their entire demeanor changed; instead of guides, they were predators. There was no conversing now as they continually scanned the cliffs or checked the banks near stream crossings for tracks. Suddenly, one of the hunters pointed to the top of a cliff overshadowing the canyon. The second hunter looked up and nodded in affirmation. I saw nothing. They pulled out two poison-tipped arrows and placed one behind each ear, then started climbing the cliff face. I trained my binoculars on the spot where they had pointed. On a small rock outcrop far above us, a lone red goral balanced precariously.

"Call the hunters back," I hollered to Khaing, breaking the silence. "I'll pay them for the animal. There will be no killing on this trip." I trained the binoculars back on the animal.

The red goral is a magnificent beast, one of the rarest animals in this part of the world. First collected from Myanmar in 1931 but only identified as a red goral in 1961, this combination goat-ante-lope of primitive ancestry is the premier mountaineer of the Himalayan ungulates. The goral saw us now and froze. It was alone, as goral often are, particularly females getting ready to give birth. Then it moved again, realizing that as long as we stayed far below, we were of no threat. I marveled at its surefootedness as it moved along ledges I couldn't even see.

Every now and then the goral's head dipped as it grabbed or nibbled at something sticking out from the rocks. Once a hoof slipped, ever so slightly, and a few stones tumbled downward. The animal looked down at us, almost as if we were to blame for its near fall, and then headed for the mountaintop. There, for a moment, it paused, the goral's beautiful red coat silhouetted against the blue sky. Then it was gone.

Few people in the world have ever seen this animal in the wild. Yet, ironically, along with the black barking deer, which I didn't even know existed here before this trip, goral were the most hunted species in this part of the country. Their skins, piled in almost every hunter's house, were greatly valued by traders for coats and other leather products. The blue sheep was also well known to these hunters, although they had seen it only rarely. They confirmed what we'd been told by other hunters earlier, that it was found only in small numbers, mostly near the base of Mount Hkakabo Razi.

By the time we crossed out of the canyon and were partway up Gwelang Razi, it was early afternoon and the river had narrowed to a small stream. Soon afterward it became a trickle and then disappeared completely into a rocky moraine that continued up the side of the mountain. We followed the moraine, hopping and climbing over jumbles of rocks and dirt left by retreating glaciers. One member of our team suddenly shouted with delight. He had reached the snow.

Most of our group had never seen snow before. I showed them how to make snowballs, and they played among themselves while I walked on alone farther up the mountain, thinking about how this long tongue of whiteness connected to a glacial cap in the

Himalayas. We were at the edge of what was called a valley glacier, formed by melted ice moving down the valley. The almost straight line of sight up the mountain was the result of glaciers modifying preexisting stream-cut valleys through a process called valley straightening. Because the bulk and weight of the highly viscous glacial ice couldn't easily turn sharp corners, it carved out a U-shaped profile whose steep sides and relatively flat floor were in contrast to the normal V-shaped profile of stream-eroded mountain canyons. On the upper walls of the small valley I spotted striated boulders whose grooved and scratched surfaces were a result of being dragged along by the glacial ice.

I flattened a little area in the snow and sat down, out of sight of the rest of the team but still able to hear their laughter. I listened to the wind sweep down the mountain and felt engulfed by the deep blue sky. Not much lived here compared to the forested pockets lower down. But it made sense that anything that did survive in this terrain would be different in appearance and behavior from their forest neighbors. It was the edge of another world, a world where only the hardiest of living organisms could survive and flourish. A world where one could believe in mountain spirits.

I remembered the stories I had heard in Putao from the few hunters who had been to this region, in the heart of what they called the icy mountains. To a man, they all spoke of the strange, inexplicable feelings that came over them after spending weeks and even months living and hunting in these mountains. They described feelings of "love" that tormented them when they were away from the area. One hunter said he asked his wife not to wash his clothes for at least a week after he returned, so that he would still be able to smell the mountains. She was convinced that he had fallen in love with another woman. Another hunter told me of seeing "snow people" covered in white hair. The snow women were beautiful, he said, but their legs were ugly. He too quarreled with his wife, who was convinced that he had made love to these women.

We returned to the village late in the afternoon and were met by some of the military members of our team, who were hiking out to meet us. The Ministry of Forestry had finally replied to our radio message. General Chit Swe was considering our request for a helicopter, but he had to confer with the Ministry of Defense first. In the meantime, the government wanted to know the names of the sick and injured, and had asked if I was one of them.

When Khaing related the last part of the message to me, I was confused. He hadn't told me that, in sending our request for a helicopter pickup, he had taken it upon himself to tell the minister that some of our team members were injured and others were so weakened that the walk out could be dangerous for them. While what he said was true, I wasn't sure I would have played that card with the minister.

No one on the team wanted us to report individual names to the government, for fear that it might somehow be used against those people later. Also, Khaing was bothered that General Chit Swe was asking about me specifically. He believed that our chances of getting helicopter support would be much less if the government learned that my health was not in jeopardy.

I wasn't about to lie to the government or do anything to hurt our future efforts in this country. But I also wanted the helicopter. In the end, we agreed to simply ignore the question. The signalman was instructed to send back a message thanking the minister for considering our request and suggesting that a helicopter pickup would ensure the complete success of the expedition and the well-being of everyone involved.

After we returned from the glacial valley, Khaing seemed particularly distracted. I thought it was about the helicopter, but when I asked, his response came as a complete surprise.

"Do you remember the hut on our walk to the mountain?"

I nodded, remembering it only too well. It was Khaing who had seemed disinterested.

"The villagers think the baby will die. The women have little food to eat, and the mother can't take care of the baby while she works in the plantation."

"We can send food up to her, whatever we can spare," I said, thinking this was where Khaing's thoughts were going. "We can also give up some of our extra clothes."

"I am thinking of something else," Khaing said. "I am thinking that my wife might like another child, and that my daughters might like a baby sister."

I was speechless, completely thrown by what Khaing was implying.

"Khaing, you need to ask your wife about this first, and that's impossible up here. This is not a decision you should make by yourself."

But Khaing wasn't listening. He had already acted on his feelings.

"I've told the headman of Tahundan to send someone out to the mother to ask if she will talk to me," he said. "I will take the baby back to Yangon and raise it as my own, if she is willing to give it up. I hope this is the right thing. What do you think?"

I looked at Khaing, unsure of what he really needed or wanted from me just then. Although he had already made up his mind, he was asking for my support. I felt I was the last person who knew what the "right thing" was in this situation.

"A monk I once knew in the forests of Thailand told me that if you act from the heart, it is always the right thing," I said, suddenly thinking of my friend Supanyo and remembering how different that monk was from U Tilawka.

Khaing looked up at me and smiled. Then he nodded in agreement.

As we waited for a response to our last radio message, Khaing and I discussed the idea of proposing that this area of northern Myanmar be made a national park. Given the importance of both the watersheds and the wildlife here, there was no doubt that this area needed strict protection and management. These rugged mountains were the primary source of the Ayeyarwady River. But also, this remote corner of the Himalayas, I was convinced, was a living laboratory of evolution, and its ecological and cultural diversity was of global importance. There was even potential to encourage visits from certain kinds of tourists—those who would pay to venture through a wild, remote landscape where the way of life had remained static for generations. Such activities would certainly change things here, but some changes were needed if wildife was to be saved and the people's lives improved.

We discussed the need for permanent Forest Department staff to manage the area, working from a headquarters in Putao. Then we talked of proposing at least two forest guard stations at the major crossroads: Panangdim and Tazundam, where cross-border trade and hunting would be monitored and, if possible, regulated. We also considered the potential of a small research and forest guard station at Tahundan, where scientists could study a relatively undisturbed Himalayan ecosystem.

The next day, U Saw Lwin's botanical team returned from the field, thrilled to have added several new orchid species to their collection on their trip 26 miles to the north. And that afternoon we received our next radio message. The good news was that the military had agreed to send a single helicopter from an army base in Myitkyina to pick us up. The bad news was that the price would be the same as what they had charged Ozaki on his first attempt to climb Mount Hkakabo Razi: U.S.$6,000 per hour, to be paid in U.S. dollars, starting from Myitkyina. The helicopter would overnight in Putao, for which we'd have to pay extra, and then attempt to get us out as soon as the sky was clear. With only a single helicopter, we'd need two trips from Putao. The short of it was that we could be out of here relatively soon for the paltry sum of U.S.$40,000–$50,000. The government awaited our confirmation and again inquired about my health.

I didn't need to ponder this message for long. The fee was higher than anything I could or would authorize. Beyond that, it was an unreasonable request since the expedition was for the country's benefit, and it had been sponsored by the Myanmar Forest Department. This was not a tourist outing. I told Khaing to hold off on answering until the next morning so that we could discuss how best to phrase our reply. We wanted to keep our options open.

The message we eventually sent contained what all of us considered a reasonable compromise. We understood the need to defray all costs and to pay extra for the army's time and effort. Since this was a Myanmar expedition sponsored by the Myanmar Forest Department, however, we would agree to pay what the government was asking, but we'd pay it in Myanmar kyats instead of U.S. dollars. At the government's own official exchange rate of $1 = 6 kyats, the U.S.$50,000 was equivalent to 300,000 kyats. This was the sum we would pay. Anything more was impossible. Of course, it was left unsaid that at the current street exchange rate of 200 kyats to a dollar, the pickup would cost me less than U.S.$1,500, a price I could afford to pay if it saved us a month of walking out. In response to the question about my health, we again remained silent.

The major's survey team returned a day later, and we all sat around discussing what they had found. Everyone on his team was rosy-cheeked and bright-eyed, as if the days spent in the womb of the icy mountains had healed their bodies and rejuvenated their spirits. They had reached Rasadan Camp, 31 miles north of Tahundan, and explored four miles along the Tali Wang tributary to the northeast. Along the way, two red gorals were spotted on high mountain cliffs. Although he had wanted to push farther north, the major reluctantly turned around at the camp where the Ozaki team had diverted to the west to climb Hkakabo Razi. The snow was too soft and unstable beyond this point.

Several days passed with no reply to our last radio message. Meanwhile, the rains had started coming down again with a vengeance. Our dry hiatus seemed to be over, and the villagers worried whether enough land had been burned for the coming harvest.

I asked Khaing to send the radio message again and to ask for an immediate answer. He told me to be patient awhile longer. Making demands on the government was not a wise strategy.

In two or three days we would start using food supplies that were needed for the walk back. Meanwhile, more team members were getting sick. Zawgan and one of our survey men were down with a fever and diarrhea; Hpa-hti's cough was worse than ever; the zoologist seemed almost catatonic at times, spending long periods sitting by the river, not moving or responding to anyone who approached him.

Htawgyi started visiting me regularly at the monastery, but he kept his distance. He knew when I wanted to be left alone, and he never made body contact with me again. When I encouraged him by showing him pictures of animals or just talking to him, he'd inch closer. I liked talking to Htawgyi. I could always speak to him without stuttering, just as when I spoke with animals, since neither could understand my words nor judge me. He liked hearing me talk, watching my face and seeming to understand my feelings if not my words. He looked at me and listened with no expectations, just an open heart, as I hoped that a child of my own would do someday.

It was probably watching me interact with Htawgyi that made U Tilawka determined to try harder than ever to share his feelings with me. Until now, we had had to either mime or speak through Khaing, who increasingly disapproved of how U Tilawka kept himself apart from the people here. But I was not comfortable just sitting with the monk in silence, as I was with Htawgyi. I felt bad that I could not help this gentle man who carried his own burden of unresolved issues. Although his Buddhist name, U Tilawka, meant "master of three worlds," he was still trying to come to grips with the one in which he lived right now.

U Tilawka had become a monk when he was 17 years old, at the wishes of his mother who, according to Buddhist beliefs, gained merit for his sacrifice. Consequently, he had never really experienced adolescence nor come to terms with his own sexuality. Although he had spent more than twenty years as a monk, those issues still simmered below the surface, and I think I represented to him another path his life might have followed. What I didn't understand was why, given such inner turmoil, he had chosen to forgo even a normal monk's life to live alone up here. His sacrifice was not for himself but for his mother, he said when I asked him. When his mother was gone, he'd be free of the obligation. Then maybe he would take off his robes.

I spent more and more time sitting along the river, or wandering up the mountains into the forest, so that I could watch the village from a distance. There was no false facade here in this remote Tibetan enclave filled with gentle people and beautiful smiles. But it was also clear that life here was as much a struggle as in every other village we'd been through. The little girl with pinkeye was getting worse and cried continuously throughout the night. Daw Sri Daraemer's face would contort with pain as she mended clothes with her arthritic hands. The headman's hacking cough had worsened, and he was now spitting up blood and pieces of what looked like his lung. An older widow, living alone, was slowly wasting away in her hut from what looked like a stroke.

I told Khaing that if we didn't get a radio message within two days, we should start walking back. He urged me again to be patient.

"They will come for us. I am sure now," he said emphatically. "Last night I dreamed that an eagle landed at Tahundan."

I wasn't appeased a bit. "Now I feel much better," I said sarcastically. "If we don't leave soon, that eagle is going to change into a vulture that feeds on our carcasses."

❦

I wandered back down to the river, a little away from the village, to a place that had become my favorite hideaway. Two larger rocks were configured in just such a way that I could lay my head back and look up at the mountains merging into the sky while listening to the river, freshly born from melting ice, on its quest to the ocean. I thought of home, and I thought of Salisa, and I thought about how our marriage might not last another year.

In the midst of my musings, I saw Htawgyi out of the corner of my eye. He had known where to find me but, as usual, didn't approach beyond a certain point. He had his own rock that he settled himself onto when we were both here together. Usually we just sat in silence. Today I needed to talk.

"When I was younger, I dreamed of traveling, of seeing and experiencing as much of life as I could," I said, looking up into the sky and not acknowledging Htawgyi's presence.

"Nature was my reality. I hated New York, where I grew up. Everyone was caught up in their petty worries and living by the clock. People were afraid of me because I was different. Or they pitied me. For many years I wanted to fight them all, pound into them the truth of who I was. Then I realized I didn't need them. People were a burden. I could rely only on myself. When I finally escaped New York, I found comfort in the forest. For the first time, I felt alive and in control of myself. I loved it. I still love it."

I looked over at Htawgyi now. He was listening intently, but he wasn't smiling as he usually did. I turned my eyes back to the sky.

"Now I realize that some of what I so easily walked away from when I was young—love, family, the daily struggles of building a life—are maybe the most important realities of all. But now maybe it's too late." I closed my eyes.

"You know what? I'm scared. I'm scared that it really is too late. I'm scared that I will lose a woman who has loved me unconditionally. I'm scared that I will never have a child to whom I can give what's in my head and in my heart. And the thought of going back to the emptiness inside that I felt when I was young is too much to bear."

I closed my eyes, pressing the lids down tight. In the darkness of my mind I listened to the river. As I drifted off, I pleaded with the mountain spirits to soothe my aching heart.

✠

Salisa turned her back to me and was crying again. I reached out for her and then pulled back. It was better to be alone, I thought. I still had so much work to do. I got up out of bed to urinate and walked outside into the darkness. An owl hooted in the woods nearby. There was a cry of pain from the house. I ran back inside and saw Salisa reaching out, blood on her arms. I climbed into bed and held her tightly.

"Don't die, please don't die," I said as a warmth spread between my legs. "I'm sorry, I think I pissed myself." I felt embarrassed. Salisa was smiling.

I pulled back the cover and a little head appeared. A baby's head. I reached out and stroked it.

✠

A chill woke me. The sun had dropped behind the mountains and the sound of the river seemed softer, as if it had slowed down for the night. I felt a weight on my legs and looked down to see Htaw-gyi fast asleep, his head resting in my lap. My hand was stroking his head.

## CHAPTER 14

# Child of Beyond

What makes a place special is the way it buries itself inside the heart, not whether it's flat or rugged, rich or austere, wet or arid, gentle or harsh, warm or cold, wild or tame.

—Richard Nelson

"COMING, COMING!" hollered the young signalman in English as he ran toward me on the trail. At first I thought something horrible had happened, until I saw the smile on his face. Then I got excited. I followed him to the monastery, where Khaing was talking with the monk. After listening to the soldier carefully, Khaing looked at me and nodded. Word had come. Our terms were accepted and a helicopter was coming to get us. Khaing went off to discuss the details of our departure with the soldiers.

"My dream was right," Khaing said to me proudly when he returned. "A helicopter has already been sent from Myitkyina to Putao. We have to clear a landing area for it immediately and pile up brush for signal fires. They will come for us as soon as there is a break in the weather."

The workings of this government amazed me. We'd spent days

179

waiting for our request to work its way through the system with no clear indication of whether we'd be walking out or not. But once our request got to the single person who could make a decision, no time was wasted in carrying out orders. "Wait, wait, hurry, hurry, then wait again some more"—that seemed to be the mantra for working in this country.

That night we made plans to leave, knowing that with the current weather patterns, our departure could be tomorrow or a week from now. Only one helicopter was being sent, a Polish model of Russian design called a Sokal, similar to the Russian MI-6. It would be flown by the squadron commander who, with eighteen years of flying under his belt, was considered one of Myanmar's best helicopter pilots.

From Putao the pilot could make a beeline to Naung Mung. After that, it would become more tricky. With several 6,000- to 8,000-foot mountains ahead and no other landmarks, the pilot would follow a compass bearing between the Mali Hka and Nmai Hka drainages until reaching Panangdim Pass at 6,000 feet. With no navigation equipment aboard, the pilot would need line of sight to get through the pass.

At this time of year, even if the weather was good in Putao and Tahundan, the pass might be clouded over. And if the way was clear, the window of opportunity for getting through it and back out again was only a few hours. Clouds usually obscured the pass early in the morning and late in the afternoon. Once the helicopter did make it through, the pilot had to stay in the canyons, following the Nam Tamai from Panangdim to Tazundam, then heading north up the Tazung Wang River to Tahundan. It was the same route we had walked but, from the air, differentiating villages and waterways could be confusing. If two trips were to be made, there could be no loitering on the ground once the helicopter touched down.

The helicopter could carry a maximum load of 1,850 pounds besides the two pilots and the mechanic who would already be aboard. Two trips would be able to take out all fifteen primary team members and most of our luggage. The six baskets of animal and plant parts I had collected on our journey were coming on the helicopter, no matter what else had to be left behind. The rest of our permanent party, including some local Forest Department staff and the porters we'd brought from Putao, would have to walk back, carrying the rest of our baggage. All the food that wasn't needed by the group on foot would be given out at Tahundan, with some sent to the villagers at Karaung.

U Tilawka wanted to return to Putao with us, but Khaing and I rejected the idea. Space was limited on the helicopter, and we both felt that he should spend more time with the people in Tahundan, whether he wanted to or not. His presence alone was important to the villagers here, even if he did little else.

By the following day, a landing site had been cleared by the soldiers and villagers, with brush accumulated around the perimeter for signal fires. The fires wouldn't be lit until we heard from the radio signalman that the helicopter had made it through the pass. We were all packed and ready to go, most of us having already left the area psychologically, thinking now about home and family. It was hard not to get excited about being back in Putao within a few days when the alternative was nearly a month of walking.

Late that first afternoon, hours after we received word that the helicopter was coming, a young woman appeared at the door to the monastery. Half hidden behind her was an older woman. Neither of them was Tibetan. I was sitting on my backpack in a corner of the room writing some notes when U Tilawka, upon seeing them, went over and spoke quietly to Khaing. Khaing looked up from his writing, his expression pensive.

Suddenly, a sound from a shawl wrapped around the old woman caught my attention. It was the same sound that had come from the darkness of the hut I'd stepped into not many days before, only this time a cherubic little face was attached to it. I walked outside to get a closer look at the baby, while the younger woman entered the monastery and approached Khaing.

The old woman wouldn't meet my eyes as I opened the shawl and let the baby grab my finger. A tear dripped from the woman's face onto my hand. For the first time I noticed another child, about eight years old, standing off to the side. This was the family from the hut in the clearing north of the village. Khaing was suddenly behind me, looking down at the baby, who turned and buried her head in her grandmother's chest.

"She wants to give me her baby," Khaing said softly. "It is a little girl named Chanrin Nina. She loves the baby, but their lives are too hard. She worries that if they have another bad year, the baby might die. It will have a better life with me."

"So why is she coming to you now," I asked, "when we are just about to leave?"

"She was putting off her decision until the last minute, and then she heard that the helicopter was coming for us." Khaing was quiet for a moment.

"I am going to take the baby home with me," he continued. "She wants me to promise that someday I will bring her back. I promised. But the truth is, I can only promise that her daughter will know who her mother is, and that she will understand why her mother had to give her up. After that, the choice will be hers to make."

We fed the family at the monastery while U Tilawka made arrangements for them to stay in a house in the village until the helicopter arrived. That first night, it snowed on the mountaintops and rained in the village. By morning we were socked in by fog, with no chance of getting out that day.

Throughout the day, each family in the village came to the monastery to say their good-byes to us in their own way. Usually this meant just sitting and spending time with us. Htawgyi came early and stayed close to me throughout the day. The soft, beautiful smiles were still on every Tibetan face, but there was a heaviness in the air. That evening, I gave Htawgyi a little bundle that I had put together for him—a pocketknife, a whistle, a bar of soap, and a shirt of mine that he liked, although it would take him ten years to grow into it.

Two days of beautiful weather followed that first day of fog, but there was still no helicopter. Each morning we went to the landing site with our gear to sit and wait. Everyone from Tahundan stayed home from their plantations to see the helicopter come in. By late afternoon, we knew there was no chance of the copter coming that day, but not until 5 P.M. did Putao send a radio message confirming the obvious. No explanation ever followed.

Would the helicopter really come for us after all? Maybe the government had reconsidered the bargain we had struck. I started to prepare myself for walking out. Khaing wasn't talking about seeing eagles in his dreams anymore, yet everyone seemed to accept the situation with complete aplomb. I seemed to be the only one becoming increasingly frustrated. Of course, my periodic ranting was looked upon with complete incredulity by the Tibetans.

"You must learn to accept what you can't change," Khaing would say to me repeatedly. But such a fatalistic attitude was foreign to me.

"Khaing, I agree that there are things in life that you can't change. But there are also things in life that you can try to change even when told to accept them. And I reserve the right to rage against even those things I can't change." I smiled. "It reminds me that I'm still alive."

❧

On the fourth day of waiting, with a clear blue sky again over Tahundan, word came that the helicopter had lifted off from Putao.

"The eagle has flown," Khaing said to me.

We sat at the helipad, eagerly awaiting the "eagle." It took two more days, though. On the first attempt, the pilot couldn't get through a bank of clouds obscuring the pass. On the second day, he made it over the pass, followed the river to Tazundam, and then took a wrong turn—he had been given incorrect directions, we later learned, and then became concerned about his diminishing fuel level. He hadn't realized that he was only 17 miles away when he turned back to Putao.

That evening we received a radio message telling us that there was enough aviation fuel left for only one more attempt and no more was expected in Putao anytime soon. The pilot assured us that he would try the next day even if the weather wasn't ideal, as long as he could safely get through the pass. If the attempt failed, we would have to walk out.

Tensions ran high that night. I wouldn't speak to anyone. I felt like packing my bags and just leaving Tahundan on foot in the middle of the night. Khaing knew better than to try to calm me at this point, and he was clearly worried himself. We had dug heavily into our remaining rations, even feasting over the last two days, assured of the helicopter's arrival. Field gear and rations that the group walking out wouldn't need had already been given away to the villagers. If we all had to walk back to Putao now, we would have to live on the food of the villagers we met on the way. U Saw Lwin, who had given away his extra blankets to one of the village families, had asked for them back twice now. That night, as the temperature dropped and the wind rattled our zinc roof, more than one pair of eyes remained open, looking into the darkness and wondering what the next day would—or would not—bring.

It wasn't raining the next day, but scattered clouds almost guaranteed that the pass wouldn't be completely clear. Then we got some good news: the pilot had made it through the pass anyway and was making a beeline for us. He wanted us to be ready to climb in the helicopter with our gear as soon as he touched down. He wasn't even going to shut off the engines. There would have to be three more trips through the pass if he was to get the whole team out.

We were warned that he might not be able to return for the second group.

Although I wanted to leave as soon as possible, I offered to switch to the second group. Khaing wouldn't hear of it. We'd stick to our original plan, he said. The government would be furious if I ended up stuck here while others got out. Khaing, U Saw Lwin, U Khin Maung Zaw, Hpa-hti, the zoologist, the two other university lecturers, and I would be on the first trip. The major and the rest of the Forest Department staff would be in the second group. The soldiers lit the brush, and plumes of smoke rose out of our hidden valley.

It was one of the soldiers who first heard the helicopter coming down the canyon. I looked behind me at the villagers huddled close together, both frightened and excited by such a momentous event. The first time any of them had seen a helicopter was when Ozaki was airlifted out from here two years earlier.

I turned to find Htawgyi. He was at his grandmother's side, already wearing the shirt I'd given him. They both waved and smiled when they saw me looking at them. U Tilawka wasn't far away. He was wearing his WCS baseball cap and trying not to look downcast. I was sorry I had not been able to give him what he wanted or needed. Perhaps our relationship would have been different under other circumstances.

Off to one side of the crowd of villagers stood a separate group—the old woman, her daughter, and her granddaughter. As all eyes turned to the sky to watch the helicopter round the bend and enter the valley, I looked over at the young mother. Into her eyes, already red and puffy from crying, came a look of sheer terror as the realization swept over her. She had only moments more with her baby.

Suddenly, someone was tugging at my arm. The helicopter had landed. They were loading our gear, and we had to get in and strap down. I covered my face against the downdraft from the blades and climbed through the open doorway, choosing a seat where I could look out at the villagers. Khaing was the last to board and, once inside, gave a prearranged signal for one of the foresters to bring the daughter and baby under the swirling blades.

"Get everyone inside and close the door," the pilot turned and hollered. "We've got to move!" He had no idea what was transpiring in the moments before takeoff.

The daughter stood by the door and clutched her baby tightly. Khaing reached out. She motioned to hand the baby over and then pulled back. I thought she was going to change her mind. Finally, she turned back the blanket covering her child's face and placed her face close, tears spilling onto the baby. Her lips moved, explaining and apologizing all at once, I guessed. Then she closed her eyes tightly and delivered the baby into Khaing's arms.

# CHAPTER 15

# Back into the World

Our experience is composed rather of illusions lost than
wisdom acquired.

—Joseph Roux

A MONTH OF WALKING was transformed into a
forty-five-minute trip out by helicopter. My initial feeling that we
had somehow diminished the accomplishments of our expedition
by flying back was quickly dispelled. The immensity of the area—
the deeply bisected river valleys of the former Irrawaddy Plateau,
the glacial caps, and the miles upon miles of unsettled wilderness—
was laid out visually before me in a way that I could never have
comprehended from the ground. Now I had a better understanding of the natural topographic features that could be used to delin-
eate the southern boundary of the national park I was planning to
propose.

Once we crossed the Nam Tamai, we saw the pass ahead. There
were scattered clouds, but the pilot had line of sight through the gap
in the mountains. Apart from a few tense moments immersed in the
clouds, and the continuous crying of Khaing's new baby, the trip

went smoothly. We landed at the Putao airport as a light rain began to fall. The pilot never hesitated, dropping us off and immediately taking off again for the return trip. The second team arrived an hour later after a much rougher flight than we had had.

Usually when I end a successful field trip, there is a feeling of release, as if a great burden has been lifted from my shoulders. I don't have to dwell on the specter of potential failure anymore, and I am no longer responsible for anyone or anything besides myself. The ending of this trip in particular should have felt great. It was the most physically exhausting journey of my life, but one of the most successful biological surveys I had ever undertaken. The wildlife discoveries, the survey data, and the information on hunting and trade would fill at least half a dozen scientific papers and popular articles. But instead I felt disoriented, restless, as if I had left something unfinished.

For the first two nights in Putao, I couldn't sleep. Having remained healthy for most of the trip, apart from my knees, that first morning I felt congested and ill. Perhaps if I shaved my beard I would feel better, I thought. When I mimed for hot water to shave with, I was brought hot tea.

I used a cuticle scissors to trim the long hairs, and a towel soaked in the tea to soften my face. Then, with my last two razor blades, already dulled from use, I used the miniature mirror from my compass case to hack away at the monthlong growth. When I was finished I did feel better, although my face felt as though I had shaved with a rock.

When I went outside, I realized immediately that the way I looked at Putao had now changed. What had just a short time ago seemed like a fascinating remote frontier town, far removed from the civilized world, now felt like just another emotionally impoverished city going through the motions. The smiles on people's faces were not as quick or genuine as they had been in Tahundan. The greetings were not as heartfelt. I was back in the "real world," and I didn't like it.

When I walked into town on the second of the five days we

spent there, Khaing told me that the DLORC chairman of Putao had surprised him with the news that he was organizing a party to celebrate our success. Of course, we would have to pay for it. I thought of all the villagers who had brought us food and given us their chickens, neither wanting anything in return nor even considering whether they had enough food for their own sustenance in the coming months. I agreed to pay for the party if the DLORC chairman helped to get us seats and baggage space on one of the biweekly flights to Yangon.

Putao was originally called Fort Hertz, after the fort built here in 1918 by the British to establish their control over the region. As we walked past the remnants of the fort, I chuckled. When Khaing asked what was funny, I told him that the fort reminded me of something I'd read before our trip. The British, when trying to staff the Indian army with Myanmar soldiers, had claimed that they got their best recruits in the most remote areas, such as here. The British believed that the farther one moved from civilization, the greater the discipline and trustworthiness of the local people.

At some point in my childhood, maybe the first time I tried to speak and the only sound out of my mouth was an unintelligible stutter, I lost the ability to laugh, even to smile, without conscious thought or effort. I was judged by my words or, rather, by my inability to produce them in the way that others did. From then on, I learned to trust no one and to speak only when absolutely necessary. As far as I was concerned, trusting led to betrayal and pain, and speaking was an unbearable horror. Words were my enemy.

Until I could physically escape my circumstances, I learned to fight my way through my shame, but I found solace only when I was alone. Years later, when I had the opportunity to travel, it was only in the most remote areas overseas that I felt at peace. The lack of a common language was like being alone, and it was a ready excuse for not having to speak. I hid so deeply within myself that when the time came to open my heart to someone I really cared about, I didn't know how to do it. All I had to give were fragments. The whole had broken apart long ago.

Now, in a little valley nestled in the Himalayas, I had started to smile without knowing why, and I had started to dream of the tomorrows that could still be. Borne on the unburdened laughter of a group of remote Tibetans, the gentle friendship of a confused monk, the unrequited love of a fatherless boy, the purposeful acceptance of a lonely death by the last Taron, and the selfless pain endured by a mother giving up her baby, my heart was lifted up through the darkness and given back to me. For the very first time in my life, I felt almost whole.

I realized now what the hunters meant when they talked of the "love" they felt after having touched the trees and walked in the snows of the icy mountains. I knew why they tried to hold on to those feelings, and why they kept the smell in their clothes as long as they could. I did the same. I put aside one particular shirt and a pair of pants that were saturated with the smoke of scores of village fires and stained by the mud of the hills, and that had been on my body while I watched a lone red goral disappear into the recesses of the snowcapped peaks. Some memories of the trip, I realized, were already beginning to slip away. I needed to hold on to them as long as I could. The world I had stepped back into paled in comparison.

Attending a party, only days after leaving Tahundan, seemed strange to all of us. I was still on field time—going to bed at 7 P.M., getting up once in the night, and then rising at 5 A.M. Still, I played my role as guest of honor among a crowd of officials, and I let myself be plied with too much cheap whiskey. After dinner, a group of young boys and girls from Putao put on a cultural show for us as the chairman beamed with pride and looked at me for approval.

As the young dancers ran on and off the stage, changing costumes and recreating the songs and dances of the peoples in the areas we had just visited, the whole scene struck me as Kafkaesque. Their clothes, which to them were costumes, were clean and colorful. They acted out tilling the fields and hauling wood in baskets while singing the songs of the forest in front of fake trees.

But they weren't stooped low enough, and their brows weren't furrowed in concentrated effort. Their feet, hands, and faces were clean, not blackened with dirt and soot, and they didn't have the look of having had to mature long before their time. There was not an earthy, unwashed smell to their bodies, and their eyes did not glisten with that faraway look of the mountains as they sang. Most important, the smiles and laughter were forced. It was a show, in which words and dress were meant to convey reality. But the reality I knew, and had always known, had nothing to do with words or dress.

The next day, I accompanied Khaing on a pilgrimage to the village of Kaung Mulon, nearly 10 miles south of Putao. This was one of the last settlements of the Shan people, one that had existed since the time when they dominated this region, before the incursion of the Kachin and other Tibeto-Burman groups. In anticipation of a visit that week by Senior General Than Shwe, one of the most powerful men in the government, a new dirt road had just been opened to the village using "voluntary labor."

This was an important trip for Khaing. The pagoda there, built about 2,000 years ago by King Asoka, was one of the three oldest and most sacred Buddhist sites in the country, along with the Shwedagon Pagoda in Yangon and the Shwezigon Pagoda in Bagan, and it was considered good fortune to have visited all three sites in one's lifetime. Also, Khaing said, we needed to give thanks for our safe return.

I sat on the rock wall surrounding the pagoda, not wanting to remove my shoes to approach the decaying, unimpressive structure. It was a peaceful place, located atop a hill overlooking the Mali Hka River. But my night in the moonlight at U Tilawka's little pagoda on the hill had been much more of a spiritual experience for me. There would be no visions here.

In the days before leaving Putao, I wrote feverishly in my journal—trying, as much as words would allow, to keep the sights, sounds, and smells of the expedition alive. "A man writes to throw off the poison which he has accumulated," Henry Miller once said, but while trying to recapture his innocence, all he does "is to inoculate the world with the virus of disillusionment." Was that what I was doing, I wondered.

Soon I would be on an airplane to Myitkyina, then Yangon, then Bangkok, then New York: bigger and bigger places with more and more people trying to figure out what to do next with their lives. Soon I would again be husband, son, scientist, homeowner, and neighbor, with all the expectations that accompanied these roles. But would I ever again be smiled at, touched, or listened to as I had been in Tahundan, with no qualifications whatsoever? How long, I wondered, before I started breaking apart again?

I stood over the table at our office in Yangon, staring at the maps of northern Myanmar and drawing boundary lines with a black felt-tip marker. The maps were more than half a century old, published for the government of Burma by the surveyor general of India. But the terrain remained essentially unchanged. I had given the team members a week to put together their reports for me, so that Khaing and I could prepare our final document for the Forest Department and General Chit Swe.

When I finally surveyed all the results of our trip, I was surprised at how much we had accomplished as a team. The botanists had

The monk U Thilawka traveling with us on the 1997 trip to his monastery in Tahundan. (Alan Rabinowitz)

Rawang headman in traditional dress shopping in Putao market for salt and other basic necessities for his family. (Courtesy of Steve Winter)

Author crossing a bamboo and rattan bridge built by local villagers and spanning one of the many ice-cold whitewater streams we encountered during the trips. (U Saw Tun Khaing)

Author with porters hiking in a rocky riverbed through the Adung Wang Valley during dry season. (Courtesy of Steve Winter)

The author standing with Dawi, the youngest living male Taron, in front of his log home. (Courtesy of Steve Winter)

Dawi (far right) standing with his family, the only remaining pure Taron family left. Dawi's mother (center) died from illness not long after this photo was taken. (Alan Rabinowitz)

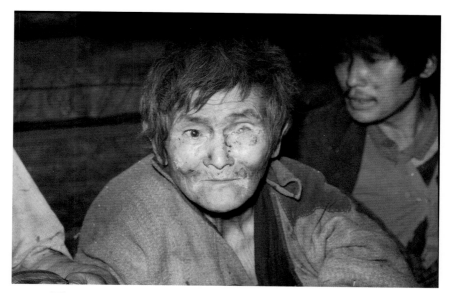

The headman of the remaining Taron. He fell to his death off a cliff before I returned in January 2000. (Alan Rabinowitz)

Tibetan women from Tahundan coming to visit at the monastery. (Alan Rabinowitz)

Tibetan hunter returning to Tahundan with his crossbow, dogs, and a red goral carcass over his shoulders. (Alan Rabinowitz)

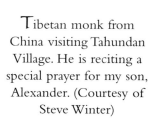

Tibetan monk from China visiting Tahundan Village. He is reciting a special prayer for my son, Alexander. (Courtesy of Steve Winter)

Tahundan villager (on right) accepting salt from Chinese trader in exchange for red panda, red goral, and black barking deer skins. (Courtesy of Steve Winter)

One of the high mountains that we had to cross once beyond the last village. (Alan Rabinowitz)

The author in January 2000 training the newly appointed Hkakabo Razi National Park staff about data collection on wildlife kills in Tahundan. (Courtesy of Steve Winter)

The author and team caught in a snowstorm in Karaung Village while waiting for a helicopter pick-up during the January 2000 trip. From left to right, U Min Thein, Hpa-hti, U Saw Lwin, the author, U Saw Tun Khaing, U Than Myint, and U Thein Aung. (Courtesy of Steve Winter)

brought back more than 500 plant specimens. I had collected nearly 200 animal parts. At least 150 bird species had been positively identified by our ornithologist. The Forest Department surveyors had sketched maps of the route and surrounding areas, showing known and reported village settlements. Our social ecology team had compiled extensive information on ethnic and religious affiliations of villages, agricultural and hunting practices, and trade routes.

There were years of work to be done in this area. Our job had been to blaze the trail and lay the groundwork. We had gathered excellent data and made important new discoveries, but we had just scratched the surface. I hadn't even looked at the communities of small mammals, reptiles, fishes, and insects. I envied the scientists who would come after me and the discoveries that they would make. I wanted to be one of them. But right now I had more pressing work to do. Everything else would be meaningless if this region wasn't protected as soon as possible.

There are scores of books and scientific papers expounding theories of protected area designation, design, and management. Statisticians have developed formulas to calculate how many individuals must be in an area to maintain viable populations of a species. Wildlife biologists argue over the ideal size and shape of areas needed to protect key wildlife populations. Some experts speak of the need to consider future global climatic shifts when choosing and designing protected areas. Many anthropologists and social scientists claim that indigenous people and local communities must have rights in, or control over, protected areas that impinge upon their lives.

The extensive body of literature on these subjects has been written by some of the best minds in their respective fields, and it offers some important guidelines. I'd considered the words and ideas of these contributors carefully over the last two decades, especially when I had the opportunity to help set up some special protected areas: the Cockscomb Basin Jaguar Preserve in Belize, the Tawu Mountain Nature Reserve in Taiwan, and the Lampi Island

Marine National Park in Myanmar. But I had learned in the field during that time that conservation is never clear-cut, people's actions are often unpredictable, and one is rarely given a free hand to choose the best course of action. I came to realize that the most important rule about setting up new protected areas, amid the various political, social, and economic concerns of a country, can be expressed in one sentence: Take whatever you can get, under whatever conditions are mandated, and do whatever you have to do to make it work.

People must be part of the equation for saving wildlife. But many of the theories popular today, which claim to have a blueprint for how wildlife conservation should be carried out—concepts such as sustainable use, community empowerment over protected areas, and integration of conservation and development—have proven largely unsuccessful in accomplishing their mission. Why? Because they often place people first, even in the last refuges set aside for vanishing species of wildlife.

Only by first understanding and then providing for the needs of wildlife in the areas where we wish these animals to survive can we implement strategies to make local people part of the process. There is no set formula for doing this, because circumstances and laws often dictate the parameters within which we can work. The strategies may take the form of employing local people as forest guards, or giving local communities exclusive rights over tourism or service concessions. They may mean substituting something better in people's lives to replace what they perceive themselves as having lost because of restrictions on activities in the designated areas.

But the protection of wildlife must be the first priority in saving wildlife. Whatever actions need to be carried out toward that end, from restricting people's activities to providing for their relocation to a new living space, must be taken in areas where we wish to save wildlife. Whenever possible, the burden on local people should be minimized. Any costs that are incurred, be they social or economic, should be mitigated or paid for by local or national governments and the international conservation community. For, in the end, if people are left feeling disfranchised by conservation actions, with nothing to compensate them for or replace what they feel they have lost, wildlife will continue to suffer, no matter how strict the regulations or enforcement designed to protect it.

⁕

"What do you think of this boundary?" I asked Khaing, turning the map around so that it faced him. "This is what we talked about on the trip."

I had drawn a big black line from the border with India to the west, following first the Seingkhu Wang and then the Nam Tamai River southeast to where it joined the Nmai Hka, then continuing east along the Tarong River to the border with the Yunnan Province of China. It was a natural boundary, using the country's borders and a prominent river system to encompass the whole northern tip of Myanmar. This would be the biggest protected area in the country. Khaing was nonplussed.

"That's just the Hkakabo Razi region," he said. "That's good. We need to protect that area for sure. But what about where we found the new leaf deer? What about what you called the transition zone area between Putao and the Nam Tamai?"

"You're right, Khaing. That's what bothers me," I said. "But here's what I was thinking. The government has said that local people can't be moved out of new protected areas if they are already settled there. They have to be incorporated into the management of the area forever. In this far northern region I circled, there are fewer than 2,000 people living in nearly 1,500 square miles of wilderness. Even with the hunting and trade we've seen, I think that's manageable."

I moved my marker down to the area where we first discovered the leaf deer.

"The transition zone is more problematic," I said, staring again at the map and hoping some novel idea would jump out at me.

"Part of the problem is, we don't know very much about this area. It's more heavily settled, has better agricultural land, and includes the town of Naung Mung, with nearly 7,000 people and a military base. We could try to exclude Naung Mung, but there are no natural boundaries to use. It would make the whole protected area less definitive and much more difficult to protect. And I don't know how much land we can realistically ask the government for."

"I don't know either," Khaing said. "General Chit Swe is on our side, and the government wants new protected areas. They don't know themselves where to draw boundary lines. So we should try to get as much as we can."

In the end, Khaing and I agreed to keep the Nam Tamai River as the southern boundary. We went after the largest chunk of land that made the most sense to us for wildlife and that we thought could be most easily justified to the government. Once I had read all the reports from the team, I drafted a proposal to the Myanmar Forest Department clearly delineating and attempting to justify the park boundaries we had in mind. I also recommended, as a separate issue, that the forests connected to the proposed park, particularly the lower-elevation habitats of the transition zone, be designated under the general category the Forest Department called "protected forest," which would prohibit clear-cutting of the forests but allow for other activities.

The biological and cultural diversity that I detailed in the proposal spoke for itself. However, I knew that some of the strongest arguments for protection were that this region contained no large stands of commercial timber and that continued degradation of the watershed would threaten the viability of the Ayeyarwady River, the country's most important waterway. National park status, while allowing the indigenous settlements to remain, could also allow for recreational use of the area, particularly adventure tourism, bringing in much-needed dollars and potentially assisting local communities in positive ways. Before I tried to convince the government to protect and manage this area as a national park, however, I had to be sure that a realistic plan could be developed to curtail the killing of wildlife without having a negative impact on the lives of people in the region. Right now, killing animals for cross-border trade was necessary to their survival.

By the time we met with General Chit Swe and the director-general of the Forest Department, Khaing and I had talked several more times and developed a detailed plan of action based on some of my earlier conversations with U Ga Nar, the headman at Tahundan. Bartering for salt was a major reason that indigenous people of the region killed so much wildlife. In our plan, salt would be used as the incentive to protect wildlife.

I proposed that once the area was formally declared a park, several key villages should begin to receive regular shipments of good-quality salt and other necessities, for sale locally at very minimal cost. We'd already learned that salt got marked up in price nearly eightfold just when moving from Myitkyina, where it sold for 6 kyats a pound, to Putao, where it sold for 44 kyats a pound. By the time salt reached Tahundan, its price was 170 kyats per pound, nearly thirty times its cost in Myitkyina. Since the park staff needed to monitor and patrol the area on a regular basis anyway, we could absorb the transport costs and bring the price way down.

I also proposed that certain hunters be hired to work with the park guards as part of a monitoring system that followed population trends of species such as red goral and black barking deer. Park staff would learn from the hunters, while the hunters would benefit financially from studying the wildlife instead of killing it. I offered to help train the park staff and to set up the monitoring system myself. Village headmen would be enlisted to oversee these activities and to monitor hunting and trade within their own village areas. The rewards for cooperation and success would include additional subsidies for salt and other goods. This would make the wildlife more valuable to the headmen alive than dead.

I was under no illusions about the potential problems involved in setting up and enforcing a system like this. That's why I wanted every village headman, and many of the hunters, to understand and agree with what we hoped to do in their area. There would be no punishment for lack of cooperation. Cheaper salt would still be sold to all those living within the park, and essentials such as medicine would be sold or distributed according to need, so that the creation of the park would benefit everyone. But those villages that did also work with us would be the first to be rewarded with subsidies and community programs that improved their way of life. In the meantime, park staff could take steps to curtail the illegal trade in wildlife in Putao and at border crossings to reduce both the demand for and the supply of wildlife parts.

Once the proposal was submitted, Khaing and I spent our time discussing exactly how we might develop programs in the proposed park that would help the villagers become more efficient in their use of forest resources and in their food productivity. Khaing mentioned the potential of introducing certain fast-growing tree species that could be used for fuel wood. I thought about different species of corn, and other crops, that would provide more nutrients or that could be grown at different times of year. We both wondered whether there were better systems of crop rotation that could work in this region. Clearly, we needed to consult with agronomists and farmers in order to understand the possible risks as well as the benefits of various changes. But there were good prospects here for programs that could improve the lives of these remote villages while steering them away from some of their hunting and trading activities.

If the park was established, I told the Forest Department, WCS would commit funds to assist in implementing everything we were proposing. I had the authority to make such a promise, although I knew it would mean more time in New York helping to raise funds.

It would be the government's responsibility to assign park staff and provide some funds for that staff, but I knew that the park budget would be a few thousand dollars at most and would barely cover staff living and housing expenses.

On behalf of WCS, I was willing to commit at least an additional $10,000 to $20,000 per year for the park, at least for the first five years. What seemed like a relatively small sum of money in the West would go a long way up here and would pay for nearly everything we wanted to do, as well as improve the livelihood of the park staff themselves. After five years, we would reevaluate what was needed for the park. I had learned from experience that large sums of money were not always necessary for good research and conservation efforts in wild areas; in fact, they often encouraged financial corruption and abuse.

The Fasten Seat Belt sign came on as the pilot announced that we were cleared for final approach into New York's Kennedy Airport. It was April 25, and I'd been away from home a little more than two months. Strange, I thought to myself. Not that long ago, "home" was in the field. Now I had a wife, a house, and mortgage payments.

I'd been three weeks out of Tahundan, first in Putao and then in Yangon, working with Khaing and the Forest Department on our proposal for what we were now calling Hkakabo Razi National Park. We had heard nothing from General Chit Swe during that time, which seemed unusual. Meanwhile, I hadn't had a single decent night's sleep nor an entire day with complete peace of mind since leaving Tahundan. I had called New York and spoken with Salisa several times, but our conversations seemed forced. I still had the feeling of being disconnected, out of sync, of having left northern Myanmar and the people there too soon. Something had been left unfinished, but I still didn't know what it was.

Music leaked from the headphones of the middle-aged man sit-

ting next to me. I smiled to myself, recognizing the words of an old
Eagles song telling me not to let the sound of my own wheels drive
me crazy, that I should lighten up while I still could. As the plane
banked, I could see the bright lights and big city below. Salisa was
waiting. Was she as nervous as I was?

I suddenly thought of Htawgyi, and how he would sit and smile
and want just to be close to me. The flow of feelings between us
had seemed so natural. It had been that way with Salisa too at first.
That was one of the reasons I knew I loved her. But I remembered
the day I started stuttering around her, and the look of pain that
appeared on her face. Neither of us spoke of it, but we both knew
that something was lost between us that day. Another piece broken.

I went through the motions at the airport as I had dozens of
times in my life, loading my duffel bags and backpack onto the baggage cart and then wheeling it in front of the customs official. I
always wondered what they thought when they saw me. My passport showed multiple trips of several months each to countries like
Burma, Thailand, and Laos. Did I fit their profile of a drug courier?
There was always a longer look and a few extra questions after
examining my passport. Then I would tell them I worked for the
Bronx Zoo, and their demeanor would change immediately. I'd get
animal questions as they recalled childhood memories. I'd smile, just
waiting for the final nod that would allow me to pass through the
automatic doors and get the hell out of the airport.

I wheeled the baggage cart into the mob crowded around the
exit. All around me were expectant faces, cries of joy, tears and hugs.
Suddenly, I saw her, standing by a pillar away from the crowds. I
could tell that she'd seen me already and had been watching my
face, looking for indications that would determine her next move.
Her beautiful long black hair was now cut stylishly short. It made
her look older, less dependent, but even more beautiful.

I walked over and squeezed her tightly to my breast, then buried
my face in her hair. Her smell brought back our first nights of love

and a thousand little intimacies that we'd shared beneath the sheets of darkened rooms. I trembled with a deep burning desire.

"What are you thinking?" she whispered in my ear, her voice breaking a little.

I felt the warmth of a little boy sleeping on my lap. I heard a child whimper in the darkness of a hut. I saw Dawi drying his hardened black feet by the fire. I watched a mother take one last look at her baby before giving it away forever. My eyes were wet.

"It's good to be home," I said.

## CHAPTER 16

# Genetic Fingerprints

These incidents of intense perception with their disturbing leaven of the spirit are fresh in my own memory, but they were not turning points so much as mile-
stones on a long journey.

—F. Fraser Darling

AFTER WE HAD RETURNED to Yangon from
Tahundan, I had immediately started reexamining all the wildlife
samples I'd brought back, particularly the eight skulls and three
skins of the strange little animal called the leaf deer. Only then did
I have the time to take a closer look at the tiny spiked antlers on
the males, the prominent bony "bump" on the frontal part of the
small skull, and the long canine teeth on both sexes. None of these
were familiar characteristics of any known muntjac species. The
implications of a completely new deer species found in this part of
the world were exciting.

With permission from the Forest Department, I brought some
of the specimens back to New York and left them with George
Amato, director of the genetics program at the Bronx Zoo. He was

familiar with my practice of returning from remote areas of the world and dumping strange-looking pieces of animals on his desk. Since much of his time was spent looking at the genetic profiles of our familiar zoo animals, my saying "I don't know what this is, George" would get him as excited as if I'd placed a living dinosaur in front of him. This time, inadvertently, that's almost what I had done.

Four years earlier, while still director of Asia programs for WCS, I had taken advantage of an opportunity to get into Lao P.D.R., then a socialist country that was just opening its doors to the Western world for the first time since the end of the Vietnam War. After more than a year negotiating with the government in Vientiane, I was given permission to organize the first biological survey in one of their largest and wildest regions, the Annamite Mountains on the border with Vietnam. A year earlier, a joint team of American and Vietnamese biologists had discovered the body parts of what looked to be a new bovid species in these mountains, one that scientists had not previously seen in the wild. It was called saola by local hunters because of its nearly two-foot-long, spindlelike horns.

During several expeditions over the next few years, WCS scientists whom I'd brought in to help with the surveys not only uncovered the main population of extant saola in Laos but also discovered five species of large mammals in the Annamites that were new to science or thought long extinct. I was one of the first Westerners to look upon the approximately 200-pound adult saola, captured alive by the indigenous Hmong who lived and hunted in the area. The discoveries, along with Amato's subsequent genetic analysis confirming the identification and lineages of these Annamite species, led to the realization that the old-growth evergreen forest of these mountains was a unique Pleistocene refuge. Surrounded by drier mixed deciduous forest at lower elevations, this moist forest relic preserved exceptional numbers of native species restricted only to this habitat, and might have been a center of speciation for a spectrum of species—particularly muntjacs, or barking deer.

The remote Annamite Mountains, situated in the midst of decades of conflict and warfare, thus turned out to be a remarkable biological treasure. As the implications of our discoveries became better known, the Annamite region was labeled an area of exceptional biodiversity—an "ecological hotspot"—by the international conservation community. As fascinating as the Annamites were, however, I was convinced that they were not unique in the secrets that they had kept hidden for so long.

I had pored over maps of the region and saw that these mountains were just one arm of a complex web of sharply defined mountain ranges originating in southeast Tibet and northern Myanmar. Both the topographic features and the current forest types had been greatly affected by the Pleistocene Epoch's glacial and interglacial periods, when the polar ice cap expanded and retreated during alternating periods of cooler and warmer temperatures, respectively. There was every reason to suspect that the biological changes which accompanied such dramatic physical transformations of the landscape were equally profound. But any living evidence of such effects would be found today only in the most remote, undisturbed areas. There were not many such areas left. One of them had been the Annamites. Another was northern Myanmar.

I pestered Amato continuously, urging him to confirm definitively what I already suspected was true, that the leaf deer was a species new to science. Having examined eight head parts, two skins, and one entire body of this animal, I knew that there were significant morphological differences in size and skull structure between this and examples of other barking deer species I had seen. But I had too few specimens and too little data to validate this observation. The most important question now was how this leaf deer's genetic blueprint, as manifested by its DNA, compared with that of other deer species.

It would be a high point of my career to discover a large mammal new to science, but I wanted this discovery for another reason. As Khaing had first pointed out, the proposed new national park in the far north did not include the area where we'd found this deer. In fact, the proposed boundary of the park, the Nam Tamai, seemed to be a barrier to its dispersal farther north. But if this distinct transition area between Putao and the Nam Tamai contained a deer species known nowhere else in the world, that fact would help me later plead for a new wildlife sanctuary contiguous to the area we were proposing.

Amato, as Khaing had done so often, told me to be patient. Just to obtain all the proper samples required much more effort than I'd imagined. Two of the muntjac specimens had to be acquired from a collection in China. Most of the others had to be obtained from museums in the United States, which were not always amenable to providing such samples. Amato also had to make sure that all the samples he used came from specimens that were properly vouchered and unambiguously identified as the correct species.

Once we had the samples, it was not simply a question of extracting DNA and immediately determining the "genetic fingerprint" of the animal. Amato first had to decide what pieces of DNA to isolate, and then carefully and methodically compare those pieces to the same pieces of DNA from a number of representative specimens of other known species of muntjac. Such an analysis and comparison of the DNA of all the world's barking deer species had never been done before.

Had I been expecting a phone call or note saying "Eureka!" or even "Congratulations," I would have been sorely disappointed. Instead, Salisa, who worked with Amato, came home one evening carrying a two-page note that she forgot to give me until after dinner. If I hadn't been so excited about what I was sure the note would tell me, I might have fallen asleep trying to wade through the jargon:

> We compared a 498 base-pair fragment of 16 S mito-chondrial ribosomal DNA, a 380 base-pair fragment of 12 S mt rDNA, a 1183 base-pair fragment of cytochrome b mtDNA gene, and a 381 bp fragment of control region (Dloop) from known species of muntjac with samples from this unknown taxon. A preliminary phylogenetic analysis was conducted by searching for minimum-length cladograms. . . .

Having been briefed on some of the techniques beforehand, I understood most of what Amato was saying. He had carefully chosen particular segments of mitochondrial DNA that would be analyzed and compared among the species. Mitochondrial DNA was used because, in vertebrates, it evolves rapidly and provides a higher resolution for distinguishing between closely related organisms. Mitochondria are inherited only through the maternal line, so the potential for changes during cell division, which exists with nuclear DNA and which can create differences between individuals of the same species, does not exist with mitochondrial DNA. In addition, one of the ways Amato was analyzing the results was by arranging the data to form a cladogram, or a phylogenetic tree, showing the relatedness of the various species to one another, based on differences in their observed DNA characteristics.

I finally reached the end of the note:

> Fourteen DNA characters (12 S(1), 16 S(2), cyt b(7), and Dloop(4)) unambiguously diagnose this taxon from all other species of muntjac.

"Goddamn it, George," I said out loud. "Just say it. It's a new damn species!"

I turned to Salisa. "Did you read this?"

"Yeah, George told me all about. Great, isn't it? You've got a new species. Now you've got to name it." She turned back to washing the dishes. I went over and hugged her, whispering in her ear.

"Are all you geneticists this exciting?" I asked.

I named the deer *Muntiacus putaoensis,* after the town of Putao, the closest recognizable locality for the species. Its common name, already given it by the local hunters, was apt—leaf deer, or phet gyi. Although Amato and other molecular biologists were comfortable defining a species based on diagnostic DNA data alone, Amato was, in fact, breaking new ground. Using molecular genetics in biological surveys and conservation efforts was a relatively new approach. Some were still skeptical about it, despite the enormous promise it held for situations where wildlife could not be easily seen or sampled. The Annamites and northern Myanmar were perfect examples of areas where it might have taken years to validate the existence of relatively large, forest-dwelling mammal species if we had not had the toolbox of molecular genetics.

Still, the confirmation of a new species was only the beginning. Now I needed to know the hows, whys, and wheres of the animal. Without detailed data on the animal's distribution and its morphological, anatomical, and behavioral characteristics, I had no real foundation on which to look at possible ecological, evolutionary, and conservation questions.

While waiting for word from the government about our national park proposal, I told the Myanmar Forest Department about the confirmation of the leaf deer as a species new to science and mentioned the name I had given it. Some officials were peeved that I had not let the government name the new species, but everyone still felt that naming it after the town of Putao was appropriate.

I applied for permission to return to the area between Putao and the Nam Tamai watershed. As much as I wanted to go farther north, back to the Adung Wang Valley, that trip would have to wait. I would have to think carefully about making that walk myself again, and I would do it only if the government approved the new national park. In the meantime, we needed to gather data on our new leaf deer, about which we knew almost nothing except that it was being killed frequently.

In November 1997 I received some unexpected and very disturbing news from Khaing. The military oligarchy, SLORC, had changed its name to the State Peace and Development Council, or SPDC. More importantly, they had issued a proclamation in the local newspaper, *The New Light of Myanmar,* declaring a "reconstitution" of the government in which General Chit Swe was no longer listed as minister of forestry. A second proclamation in the same newpaper stated that the general and thirteen other ministers had been placed on a special "advisory group" for the newly reconstituted government.

Within a week, the advisory group had been disbanded and four of the former top ministers had been placed under house arrest on corruption charges. No one in the Forest Department knew what was happening or why, Khaing said. No one had been able to contact General Chit Swe, and we didn't know if he was one of the four under house arrest. I started to imagine the worst.

I had last seen the minister when he had hosted a small party for the expedition team upon our return to Yangon. He was frustrated by the lack of much government action on conservation and ecotourism. Still, he had high hopes for the future. If he even remotely suspected that there were people working to bring him down, I saw no hint of it.

I worried for the man whom I had started to think of as a friend. And I worried for the future of our conservation work in the country. General Chit Swe had been one of our staunchest supporters, and much of what we had accomplished already was due to his assistance or intervention. I was heartened a bit when informed that General Chit Swe's deputy minister had been appointed to replace him. Though I'd heard he was far less enthusiastic about conservation than was the general, Khaing said he was a fair and decent person and already knew about WCS and our work in Myanmar. I fervently hoped that this change would not derail our plans for Hkakabo Razi.

Since I had returned home, my relationship with Salisa had grown stronger, in large part due to changes in me. I no longer had doubts about our marriage or about the bond that had started forming the very first time I'd laid eyes on her. But the biggest change was that I was no longer equivocal about having a child. The fear of commitment, of permanency, of irrevocably linking my life to that of another—all that had begun to fade.

Salisa got pregnant two months after I returned from Myanmar. My joy was indescribable. We spent more time together, touching and talking the way we had when we first met. I analyzed and wrote up the data from the trip during the day, and I read Conrad's *Heart of Darkness* to her belly at night. I sent word to Khaing asking him to delay our departure date for the trip to study the leaf deer so that I could be with Salisa for at least a month after she gave birth.

The higher you soar in your happiness, the farther you fall in your despair. At the end of the first trimester, days after we had seen a tiny fledgling fetus on the ultrasound machine, severe cramps during the night followed by bloody sheets led to the unthinkable—miscarriage. Salisa's emotions were in a shambles, particularly after she was scraped and suctioned in order to get out all the pieces of what could have been our child. At first I felt an irrational anger at not being given a chance to fight whatever it was that had done this to her and my baby. Then I became numb, wishing we had never seen the ultrasound. I yearned to get back into the field, to run away.

We dealt with the miscarriage in the worst way possible. We never talked about it and instead acted like polite strangers in our own house. When Khaing learned what had happened, he took it upon himself to approach the government and request special permission for Salisa to join our leaf deer team on the next trip to northern Myanmar. He wanted to surprise me with the news when he was sure it had been approved.

In the two years since we had started working together, my relationship with Khaing had evolved into a close friendship. While we both recognized the sometimes considerable differences in our opinions and personalities, we were bound by a common passion— saving wildlife. Although trained as a forester, Khaing had quickly become knowledgeable about wildlife and conservation by watching and listening carefully during our trips.

I came to respect Khaing immensely for his compassion toward people and for sticking to his principles with a government that sometimes severely punished those who did not tow the party line. I knew that he, in turn, respected me for my knowledge and for my desire to keep alive some of the wildness in the world. Despite the frustrations and disagreements that arose between us, we trusted each other to do the right thing. He knew of my turbulent childhood, and recently he had become quite worried about my troubled marriage. He staunchly believed that the bond between husband and wife was sacred, no matter what problems arose.

Salisa didn't even glance up from the book she was reading when I sat down beside her and told her that permission had come through for my leaf deer expedition to northern Myanmar. But when I also told her that Khaing had gotten permission for her to come along with us, her head jerked up and she stared hard at me to gauge the truth of my words. Then she smiled and lay her head on my shoulder. She had been thinking that I wanted to get away from her, and she worried, as I did, that our relationship couldn't survive another separation. This trip would help her heal and bring us close again, I hoped. She became our team's geneticist, responsible for collecting tissue samples of the leaf deer to bring back for additional genetic analysis.

In the weeks before our trip, Salisa was excited, almost cheerful. She would see her family in Thailand again after almost two years away, and we would be together in the field. Everything seemed almost normal again. It was only when she thought I wasn't watching that a look of intense sadness would sweep over her face.

## CHAPTER 17

# The Mysterious Leaf Deer

I believe that all naturalists at some time in their lives
have had one great adventure, and that the shock,
ecstasy, beauty, wonder, tragedy, or intellectual illumina-
tion of that moment, hour, or day, they carry with them
the rest of their lives.

—John K. Terres

I MET WITH GENERAL CHIT SWE in Yangon in
April 1998, almost six months after his "retirement." He had not
been under house arrest, it turned out; nevertheless, he was persona
non grata with the government now. My continued association
with him might hurt WCS activities, I was told, and friends in the
Forest Department advised me to avoid him. After weighing the
possible consequences carefully, I decided that I couldn't turn my
back on a friend, no matter what the cost. He had helped me when
I needed him, and his concern for conservation in Myanmar had
been genuine. I had to at least thank him for his friendship.

General Chit Swe seemed relaxed and more at peace with himself than at any other time I had seen him. He was playing golf,
meditating, and spending more time with his wife and grandchil-

dren. He could come and go as he pleased as long as he did not venture near government offices. He made no mention of what had happened to him or why. He sounded only hopeful about possible future involvement in conservation activities, and I said I would look forward to working with him again in the future—recognizing, though, that it was not likely. Before parting we shook hands, and I looked into those eyes that had scared me so much when we'd first met. His gaze seemed less intense now, and his smile sagged at the corners.

"We've done some really good things in this country with your help," I said to him. "And anything we do in the future will be because of how you helped us in the beginning. I want to thank you for everything. I value your friendship."

He nodded in silent affirmation and then turned away. It was the last time I saw him.

⌒✕⌒

Salisa and I arrived in Putao on April 25, 1998, a year to the day since I had landed at Kennedy Airport wondering what I was coming home to. I showed Salisa around as if I were an old resident here, and I delighted in seeing the look of wonder on her face. At the open-air market, the prices of wildlife parts had gone up—probably a result of the further devaluation of the Myanmar kyat since our last trip. I counted five sets of takin horns, more than on any previous trip, and one merchant said he'd already sold eight sets over the last two months to traders from Myitkyina for 5,000 kyats each. I caught sight of a beautiful set of gaur horns, the tips nearly two feet apart. This large wild cattle species had been all but extirpated from the area, I knew. This set came from another remote region called the Hukaung Valley, the merchant said, southwest of Putao.

The government had issued a new directive for Putao, requiring all foreigners to stay in the military compound for U.S.$20 a night. Although few foreigners ever came here, the government wanted any foreign currency they could get their hands on. They just didn't want to have to do anything in return. I took no issue with paying the fee, but I wasn't happy about the unwashed bedsheets and the bedbugs. Khaing and the rest of the team stayed for free at a cleaner house in town belonging to the Forest Department.

This trip was scheduled to take a month and had been set up to be much more efficient than the last. We knew exactly where we were going, and we knew how to get there. I asked Khaing to keep the team small and not to invite people we didn't know well. Hpahti was back as our cook, and U Saw Lwin returned with another orchid specialist, U Kyaw Nyunt. U Thein Aung, a senior forest officer and ornithologist who had been with me in Htamanthi Wildlife Sanctuary three years previously, also joined us. A new WCS staff member was with us too, U Than Myint, who would take over the training program for foresters and wildlife officers. Finally, we invited U Than Zaw, a young master's student in zoology at the University of Yangon, who would assist me and use the leaf deer data for his thesis.

Once word of our arrival in Putao was out, Zawgan appeared and asked to be my porter again. I was flattered. I was also pleased to learn that U Tilawka was currently residing at the monastery in Putao, although for the sake of the Tahundan villagers I would have preferred to hear he was still in the north. Just before leaving Putao, I brought Salisa to meet him.

Though a bit reserved in front of Salisa, U Tilawka seemed truly pleased to see me. He served us coffee and biscuits, and we talked about the people at Tahundan. Khaing related stories about Chanrin Nina, the baby he had brought back; she was adjusting to the heat of Yangon and was being pampered by everyone in his family. Then he asked about the baby's mother. After the helicopter left, she returned with her family to the hut in the woods, and U Tilawka had not seen her since.

A second, aged monk came in from a back room, and U Tilawka nodded to him deferentially. This was U Einda Sara, the chief monk, who had first established this monastery in Putao thirty-five years previously. He sat quietly, seemingly absorbed in his own thoughts, until I asked Khaing to tell him of our problems with the Christian preachers who were acting as wildlife traders. The old monk perked up and related a story of his own.

"A Christian preacher once came to the monastery and asked if he could preach to me," U Einda Sara said. "He was young and very full of himself, and he thought he could earn great merit by converting me." The old monk smiled at the recollection.

"I told the preacher I would give him one hour, and I would stay completely silent during that time. The only thing I asked in return was that, afterward, he give me one hour to talk about the Lord Buddha. Well, the preacher was dismayed at such a bargain and had to think about it for a while. Then he said: 'I am sorry, but I can't do this. I am a preacher, and I have been told that I must preach. I have not been told that I can listen.'"

Khaing laughed as he translated the ending for me, and agreed that most tribal preachers didn't seem to understand the true meaning of Christian teachings. I was thinking that the same could be said for some Buddhist monks. As the old monk was telling his story, I noticed that he was rubbing a little metal ball in his left hand. When he was done speaking, I asked about it.

"This was made by pouring acid over brass and silver, creating an ash," he said, holding up the ball. "Water was added to neutralize the acid, and then mercury was mixed with the ash to make it pliable. Finally, citrus juice was used to remove the ash. When all that was done, the mixture was rolled continuously until it became a ball. Someday, the ball may become gold."

I suddenly realized that this revered monk was discussing alchemy, a practice that I thought had died out long ago and that I never would have associated with Buddhism. The monk saw the look on my face and hastily added that he was not actually trying to create gold but rather was embracing a spiritually powerful "tool" that could aid in meditation and even be used to heal.

Although people in the West often associate alchemy only with medieval Europe, historically India was the first real center of alchemy, from which it spread to Europe and other parts of the world, finding its way into Myanmar in the fifth century. In early Myanmar, alchemy was known as *aggiya,* meaning "the work with fire," and it developed a powerful following, becoming almost a religious cult until the eleventh century, when Buddhism was introduced and became the predominant way of life of the people.

The practice of alchemy, although frowned upon by Buddhism, never completely died out, however. Instead, refuge was taken in the alchemical belief that the ultimate goal was not simply to transmute base metals into silver or gold but to create the equivalent of what some called "the Philosopher's Stone," which would give the alchemist youthful, disease-free life for thousands of years and almost superhuman powers to help others and chase away evil spirits.

Sadly, alchemy never evolved into modern chemistry in Myanmar as it did in Europe. Instead, chemistry was brought from the West with the British conquest, while alchemy lived on as a superstitous practice among a small group of monks within Myanmar. It was claimed that of all the religious cults that existed in Burma before Buddhism, alchemy was the noblest, for it aimed at conquering nature and preserving the human body in its vigor and beauty. That pursuit was still alive, at least in one monastary in the town of Putao.

We left U Tilawka waving good-bye, happily ensconced among the other monks at the monastery. He was clearly more at peace here in Putao than among the Tibetans. Everyone has to find their own way, I thought. Even the old alchemist.

The nearly 160-mile expedition we had planned this time was very different from the previous one. Half the walk was through new territory, to the west of where we'd been on the last expedition. The terrain was relatively easy, and the way of life here was familiar to me now. I knew I wouldn't find out what I wanted to know about the leaf deer if we continually moved between villages, as we had on the last trip. Instead, I planned to set up a base camp for two weeks in Naung Mung, the largest settlement north of Putao. I wanted hunters to know exactly where and how to find me.

We left Putao by a different route, heading north for the mountains and crossing a pass at 6,469 feet over Langa Bum. In two days we reached Naung Mung and were given a little cabin that had been specially built for VIPs visiting the area. The cabin was clean and comfortable, situated between the village and the army outpost. We even had the luxury of a private outhouse.

Evidence from our first trip pointed to Naung Mung as the heart of leaf deer country. It didn't take long for me to realize that the animal parts we saw for sale in the Putao market were mostly overflow. The majority of deer skins that came down from the north ended up in Naung Mung and were sent directly from there to Mandalay. Other items of value, such as horns, antlers, musk sacs, and gall bladders, all left Naung Mung on a direct route to China, just as in the Hkakabo Razi region.

The leaf deer was well known to hunters in the area. Traders valued a skin based on the number of open hands they could lay across its width. Although the small skin and tiny antlers of the leaf deer were not as valuable as parts from other species, the leaf deer was considered abundant and easy to kill.

With a little less than 7,000 people in 1,000 households, Naung Mung (which means "outside the city") was a small town compared to Putao, which had nearly nine times the population. Originally set up by the Shan people as an outpost to stem the advance of other tribal groups coming over from Tibet, Naung Mung eventually was settled by the Kachin, who themselves came to dominate the region. Now Naung Mung was a thriving settlement, and just a three-day walk north of here was the southern boundary of our proposed Hkakabo Razi National Park.

Despite its size, there were still no real roads in Naung Mung, and the only shops were a few wooden stalls with a small selection of sundries brought in from Putao or China. One stall was selling coagulated lumps of sambar deer blood in little vials for 100 kyats, meant to be put in alcohol and drunk for increased vitality. A villager standing nearby had a baby gibbon on a rope. Her husband had killed the mother and they had eaten the meat. She would get 7,000 kyats for the baby, she said.

Several villages were situated within a day's walk of Naung Mung, so we sent runners to all the outlying settlements to spread word that I would pay hunters to examine the whole bodies of any deer they killed on their hunts, particularly leaf deer. Typically, hunters ate the meat and sold the skin of the leaf deer for 200 kyats, discarding everything else. I offered 500 kyats if the hunters brought me the entire animal to weigh and measure, and then helped me to skin it. They could keep the meat. I wanted the skin, the skull, the stomach, and a little piece of tissue for genetic analysis.

While waiting to see what turned up, Salisa and I visited homes around Naung Mung in order to examine and measure the leaf deer heads found on trophy boards there. One hunter finally showed me the leaf that the deer was named after. It came from a plant, called *taungzin phet* in Burmese and *Phrynum capitatum* in Latin nomenclature, containing only a single leaf that was about 32 inches long and a little more than 15 inches wide. He admitted that it often took several leaves, not one, to wrap an entire leaf deer's body for transport.

Most of the hunters in this area used snares and jaw traps from China, with their crossbow as a secondary weapon. The snares were easier to use and enabled them to catch everything from pangolins to bears. It was a bonus if an animal was pregnant, because the Chinese considered a fetus to be powerful medicine and paid up to 20,000 kyat (about U.S.$70) for some species. Since the town of Putao was only two days away, it did not surprise me that these villagers were much more knowledgable and active in the commercial trade in animal parts than those we'd seen elsewhere, especially when I learned that the trade in Naung Mung was organized and controlled by the village preacher and his son.

Every surrounding mountainside and valley was someone's territory for trap lines. Larger mountains had more extensive trap lines, which might be maintained by three or four hunters. Usually, a barrier made from bamboo, brush, and trees would be constructed from the ridgetop to the valley. Most animals would follow the wall, even if they could easily scale it. About every 100 feet would be an opening through which an animal might think it could pass. But in these openings were snares or other kinds of traps. I had seen similar barriers built by indigenous tribal groups in Laos; I called them "walls of death" because they wiped out an entire valley of wildlife within a few seasons.

Hunters here ran their trap lines only in the winter season, from November to April. The rest of the year they spent in their plantations, or taungyas. Because there was more flat land at this lower elevation, these plantations were larger and more productive than those in the rugged sloped terrain beyond the Nam Tamai. Both wet and shifting cultivation could be practiced here, allowing the villagers to grow rice as well as maize, yams, mustard, sweet potatoes, sugarcane, and tapioca. Still, nearly every adult male also trapped wildlife. It had not always been like this, I was told, but in the last three or four years the high prices being offered by traders for animal parts encouraged everyone to hunt.

When traps were open, they were checked every three to ten days. Only a few species, such as wild pigs and wild dogs, were of no value to traders; with these, hunters would eat the meat and discard the rest. For the most valued animals, special trap situations were created. The walls of death might have an opening placed about three feet off the ground for bears to climb through. A string in the opening triggered a poisoned arrow or wooden spike that penetrated the bear's chest. Right now, bear gall bladder was worth 10,000 kyat to traders in Putao and Naung Mung. Another kind of trap triggered a log to fall and crush smaller animals walking on the ground. This was often set for pangolins, now fetching about 8,000 kyat per animal from traders.

While running trap lines was the predominant hunting method, crossbows and poison arrows were never far from reach for the occasional deer, monkey, or even serow that crossed a hunter's path. Since the killing of wildlife was much more methodical and efficient in this region, there was actually less time spent hunting than what I'd seen farther north. Perhaps as a result, there was also less respect for the animals killed. Animals caught in trap lines were considered just another crop. If traps couldn't be checked when they were supposed to be, no one worried much about it. Many of the parts from a rotting carcass were just as valuable as those from a fresh kill.

"These animals were put on earth to serve man," the preacher pronounced when I talked to him about hunting. Almost in the same breath, he told me that he needed to spend more time "civilizing" his more primitive neighbors to the north.

By the end of my two weeks in Naung Mung, hunters from near and far had brought me a strange menagerie of animals, hoping I might buy them. I saw more than twenty species of wildlife, including everything from the fetus of a pangolin to live fruit bats, a live baby wild pig, and the bones of a marbled cat. I treated the hunters respectfully, questioning them and serving tea, but I paid only for the dozen freshly killed leaf deer bodies that were brought in. Of six male leaf deer, three were less than a year old; the rest were adults. Of six female leaf deer, one was a juvenile, one adult was pregnant, and a third was lactating. By now, I had also accumulated data from more than a hundred leaf deer head parts found in village huts.

Several things struck me immediately. Except for the males' diminutive, unbranched antlers, which averaged a little more than an inch long, adult male and female leaf deer were identical in size and appearance. They both weighed about 25 pounds, and they both had prominent canines almost an inch long. In addition, while all the other deer species I knew about were born with spots and retained them for the first two to six months of life, there was no spotting on the coats of either the newborn or the two juvenile leaf deer that I examined.

The stomach contents of the dead deer revealed a diet heavy in fruit species, which, the hunters said, were found only in the distant hills. Finally, all the adult males and nearly half of the adult females had old wounds on their ears, a characteristic sign of aggressive behavior. All of these data, on top of the repeated assertions by hunters that leaf deer were almost always found alone, added up to some exciting possibilities that could never have been suggested by genetic analysis alone.

Having never previously taken much of an interest in the deer family, Cervidae, I had to catch up on a lot of information before this trip. I was glad I did, or I might not have understood the implications of what I was seeing. Based on the weight and size of the adults I'd seen, the leaf deer was clearly one of the smallest living true deer in the world, matched only by the pudu of South America and possibly by the Truongson muntjac, newly discovered in 1997 in the Annamite Mountains. I had suspected this to be true ever since first examining the leaf deer kill of the Lisu hunter the year before. What excited me even more, however, was that all the other data indicated a solitary, fruit-eating species with no obvious morphological differences between the sexes, and a social system in which females actively competed with males for limited food resources in the temperate mountain forests of the north. And all of this pointed to one thing—a very primitive species!

Science has shown that the evolution of deer species has been characterized by certain changes: an increase in body size, loss of canines, greater complexity of antler development, and a tendency toward more gregarious social behavior. This means that deer evolved from being small, solitary, selective browsers of dense forest areas to being large-bodied bulk grazers, forming herds in open woodlands, grasslands, or swamps. The particular group of deer called muntjacs, or barking deer, with their relatively short antlers, solitary habits, and prominent tusklike canines in males, bear a striking resemblance to early fossil deer and have all the physical and ecological attributes of a more ancient deer group.

But the tiny antlers on the male leaf deer, the lack of spotting on the coats of juveniles, their frugivorous feeding behavior, and the equally long canines in both males and females all pointed to the leaf deer as perhaps the *most* primitive of the already primitive muntjac group. This was further supported by secondary characteristics also considered "primitive" by deer biologists: broad, rounded ears and large preorbital fossa, or openings, in the skull, which were indicative of large facial glands.

My mind was filled with questions. Was the leaf deer part of an old, ancestral line that had become isolated after the Pleistocene glacial ice last receded about 10,000 years ago? The geologic events and climatic changes at that time would have left fragmented forests and dispersed food resources. Since muntjacs, as a group, are known to be less capable of exploiting new habitats than are other deer species, the smallest muntjacs might have originated from a more wide-ranging ancestor and then become more restricted in their distribution.

Or could it be that the leaf deer was the product of a more recent evolutionary event, becoming ecologically and genetically isolated in the hills of the transition zone between jungles and snowcapped mountains, exploiting particular food resources, such as fruit, that were not favored by other deer species? I couldn't answer these questions now. But as Khaing had pointed out to me during the previous year's expedition, the questions themselves were the important first step. We had opened an evolutionary window into a world that might have disappeared before we even knew it existed. Now I had to keep that window open.

⚶

The time in the field was like a new beginning for Salisa. Evidence of the past year's stress and disappointments vanished from her face as both the physical exhilaration of the hike and the opportunity to use her skills and knowledge blotted out everything else. She laughed and smiled easily now. As we made quiet, hurried love on the floors of village huts, I could almost pretend we were newlyweds again.

Examining leaf deer that had been alive only hours or days earlier was not a pleasant task for either of us. Sometimes the bodies were still warm. I kept saying to Salisa that this work was necessary because until we understood the present, we couldn't change the future. Then the first adult female was brought to us.

She had been dead only hours and still had warm milk in her lactating breasts. Salisa stood by quietly, the sadness showing clearly on her face. We both knew what this meant. There was a baby leaf deer in the forest right now, waiting for its mother to return. Salisa remained quiet all that evening. And then it got worse.

A hunter brought in another adult female the next day, and I moaned when I saw the swollen nipples again. Fortunately, Salisa was in the house resting, and I tried to cut open the deer and do what had to be done before she saw it. But as I opened her up, my heart sank. I put my gloved hand into the blood pooling in the body cavity and pulled out an enlarged, fluid-filled sac. It contained a 10-inch-long, half-pound leaf deer fetus. It looked almost full term, with little bumps where the pedicels would grow and tiny little hooves. I turned to tell Khaing that we had to hide this fetus for now, but Salisa was standing behind me. Tears were just forming in the corners of her eyes, and her face showed a hurt that gave me an empty, lonely feeling in the pit of my stomach. She looked at the fetus as if it were her own, then looked up at me as if I had been responsible for its death. She turned and went back in the house, not saying a word to anyone for the next two days.

We were getting close to our planned departure from Naung Mung, so I sent out word that we didn't need any more leaf deer. We had enough data. I was repacking our tissue samples when U Than Myint burst through the door. I'd never seen him this excited.

"Alan, you won't believe this. I don't know if you want this or not, but a hunter just brought another leaf deer in a basket."

"Good. More data before we leave. Lay it out on the cutting table. I'll be right out," I said, continuing to pack.

"No, you don't understand. This deer is alive!"

It was a tiny little thing, only 11 pounds, squeezed into a bamboo basket like the serow they had brought to me in Tahundan. The hunter said it was a young female. He'd captured its mother in a snare near his plantation and killed her, but the juvenile was standing nearby and refused to leave, even as he ran up and grabbed her. Only after he had gotten back to his village did someone tell him that a foreigner in Naung Mung was buying these deer.

I didn't know what to do. We were scheduled to leave in two days. The deer looked less than two months old. If I bought the animal and released it, it would certainly die. If I paid the hunter for his trouble but told him to keep the deer, the same fate would befall it. Killing it myself was out of the question. I turned to Khaing and asked what he thought.

"We can bring it with us to Putao," he said. Then he shrugged, as if to say he had no idea what to do with it after that. I looked at him as if he were crazy.

"We have 100 miles to walk and about a dozen villages to overnight in," I said. "We don't know what this deer eats, we have no medicine for it if it gets sick, we don't know where it will sleep—and what do we do with it once we reach Putao?"

Khaing motioned for me to turn around and look at the deer. The end of her nose was sticking out of the basket, and Salisa was caressing it. The deer's big green eyes were looking directly at my wife, who was smiling for the first time in days. I turned back to Khaing.

"Tell the men to collect twigs and leaves and convert the extra room in our cabin into a bedroom for the deer. Board up the windows and put a latch on the door. Then send U Than Zaw to question the hunters about where we can collect some of the types of fruit we've been finding in the stomachs of these deer. Get whomever is left to start building a bamboo cage where the animal can lie comfortably while two men carry it. We have a new team member."

We put off our departure from Naung Mung so that we could give this little deer at least three days to acclimate to us. Both Salisa and I spent much of our free time with her. I tried out different foods and cleaned up her droppings while Salisa talked quietly to her, stroking her flanks. Salisa called her simply Phet Gyi, the Burmese word for leaf deer. I had decided she could represent her species at the Yangon Zoo and perhaps help us to protect the others still out here.

Phet Gyi loved watercress and some of the wild fruits from the forest. But since these foods might be increasingly hard to get as we headed south, we tried testing her on rice gruel and other easily digestible foods. I had no idea whether the Yangon Zoo would even want this deer, but that didn't concern me now. We still had 100 miles to walk.

The day before we were to leave Naung Mung, another live leaf deer was brought to me. It was a young male, slightly larger than Phet Gyi, that had been caught in a snare. Its left front leg was badly swollen, and it couldn't even stand. The men worked late into the evening building a second cage, while I injected the deer with an anti-inflammatory drug and antibiotics. Salisa and I alternated staying up with him through the night, but the trauma of capture and his injuries were too much for this young life to bear. At 3 A.M. his breathing became labored and his heartbeat weak. Letting out a final yelp like a wounded, scared child, he died. Phet Gyi lay awake in the corner, watching.

After breakfast, Salisa went to calm Phet Gyi before we put her into the new bamboo cage that had been built to carry her. A special team of six porters was assigned to take turns being with the deer at all times, making sure that she didn't overheat and that she had plenty of food and water. I was more determined than ever that this animal would survive, no matter what. I'd seen enough death. A long pole through the top of the cage allowed two porters to carry her easily. Just before we brought the cage inside the house to load her in, Salisa called to me.

"Alan, you won't believe this." My stomach started to knot. Usually when I heard that on these trips, something bad had happened. As I approached Salisa, I saw that she was holding the leaf deer's head gently between her two hands. Only she could do this with Phet Gyi, I thought, as I got on my hands and knees to crawl over to them without scaring the deer.

"Look where my index fingers are on the top of its head," she whispered.

I looked and smiled. Phet Gyi had had us all fooled. Under the hair atop its head were two little bumps just coming through to form the first set of antlers. Our beautiful little she-deer was a he-deer.

It took only ten days to get to Putao. At each village where we spent the night, we brought in leaves and twigs to fix up a special room in the hut where the leaf deer could get to his feet and walk around. Now Phet Gyi was the center of attention instead of me. I was surprised that no one thought it strange that we were carrying a live deer and sleeping with it in our huts. Even the owners of the huts didn't complain. Then again, the deer was cleaner than the dogs, chickens, and most of the people who also slept inside.

I always slept against the wall of the room adjoining the room where Phet Gyi was kept. I was a light sleeper, so I knew I would wake early if there were anything wrong with him or if he made any noise out of the ordinary. One morning, about a week out from Naung Mung, I dreamed that Salisa was caressing my face. I woke to feel the warm, damp nose of the leaf deer pushing against my face through a space in the rattan dividing wall. This was the closest he had ever gotten to me, and I could feel his body pressed against the wall on the other side. I think my presence comforted him now. I suddenly felt like crying, feeling the loss and trauma of this poor little animal as if it were my own.

I wondered what I was doing by bringing this deer out of the forest and commiting him to life imprisonment in a zoo. Perhaps facilitating a quick death was really the most humane thing I could do for him. I had a strong urge to sneak into his room, while Salisa and the others were sleeping, and put him to sleep quietly and painlessly with an injection. No one would know what had happened, and he would soon be forgotten.

But that was the problem, I thought. Death was just too easy and acceptable here. The responsibility of life was the far greater burden. I felt his breath on my lips and saw one eye watching me through an opening in the rattan. I knew I could never purposefully end the life of this little innocent. The burden was mine now. I had to make sure his life had some meaning.

When we reached Putao, Khaing radioed to the director of the Yangon Zoo, explaining what we had with us and asking if they would accept it. I couldn't chance a refusal. I told Khaing that, besides emphasizing that this deer would be the only one of its kind in captivity in the world, he should tell the director that I would pay for building a new enclosure and caring for the animal. The zoo wasted no time in accepting the offer. Now I had to get it to Yangon.

U Than Myint suggested that we leave the deer with the Forest Department officers in Putao and arrange for special transport once we got to Yangon. It was a reasonable suggestion, but Salisa and I both worried that if we let Phet Gyi out of our sight now, we'd never see him alive again. I'd come too far to risk that.

"Khaing, radio the Yangon Zoo again and tell them to meet us at the Yangon Airport with a truck to take the leaf deer from us as soon as we arrive," I said.

"We could do that." Khaing smiled. He didn't even want to know what I had in mind.

The Myanmar Airlines jet stood on the tarmac of the Putao airstrip, already thirty minutes behind schedule. The pilot stood before me, his demeanor having already shifted from amused to annoyed. We had made a new, smaller cage for Phet Gyi that I knew could fit in the aisle of the airplane, and we had brought him to the airport as if he were a member of our team. The baggage handlers tried to take the cage from us and store it in the unpressurized compartment beneath the plane, but I refused. The pilot demanded the same thing, but I would not relent.

"This is a new species," I said for the fifth or sixth time, "the only captive animal of its kind in the world, and it must get to the Yangon Zoo alive and well." There was no need for a translator. The pilot spoke English well.

"It is against all rules to allow an animal of this size in the passenger cabin. He must go with the baggage. He will be okay." The pilot was getting angry.

"He will not be okay. He will die," I said. "You allow live chickens on your plane. He's not much bigger. I won't get on the plane without him."

Most of the other passengers had already boarded, but a small group stood behind us, watching the exchange. I refused to budge. If they departed without us, then the pilot would have to explain to the government why two foreigners had been left behind. I felt bad about putting him in such a quandary, but I would have felt worse if Phet Gyi were to die.

It seemed like a stalemate until a senior military officer who had come to the airport to see someone off approached us, wanting to know what the commotion was. After I pleaded my case, he threw up his hand as if it were a trivial matter and snapped something to the pilot. Suddenly, it was agreed that we could place the cage at the rear of the passenger compartment, out of everyone's way.

As we boarded the flight with Phet Gyi, most of the passengers smiled and even nodded their heads, appreciating our little victory over the powers that be. But our agreement to place the deer as far back in the passenger compartment as it could go meant that the cage blocked the door to the only bathroom on the plane during the four-hour flight to Yangon. As the flight progressed, fewer and fewer passengers smiled or seemed as understanding of our predicament as they had been earlier.

## CHAPTER 18

# The Ghost Valley

After victory, tighten your helmet cord.

—Ancient Japanese proverb

I was on my first cup of coffee when I heard the fax machine in my study at 6 A.M. Seeing the letterhead from the WCS Myanmar Program in Yangon was no surprise. I'd been communicating regularly with Khaing since my return to New York six months earlier, asking for periodic updates on the health of Phet Gyi.

I remembered clearly the day we brought Phet Gyi to Yangon from Putao. Before leaving the plane, we covered Phet Gyi's cage with a blanket to minimize the noise and curious stares from the crowd of people we'd have to pass through at the airport. We also thanked the pilot, who now seemed pleased to have an interesting story to tell his circle of friends. There had been a truck and a veterinarian from the Yangon Zoo waiting for us outside, as promised.

By the time we reached the zoo and unloaded Phet Gyi into a bare, concrete holding cage, he was frightened and shaking. The zoo's director was clearly disappointed that our new, previously unknown species looked just like a smaller version of all the common barking deer he had on exhibit. I looked at Phet Gyi and wondered again if I should have just put him to sleep and left his body in the forest where he was born. Salisa squeezed my arm, knowing my thoughts.

"It's better that he is alive," she said. "No one cares about the dead."

I pulled the paper from the fax machine and started to read, picturing Khaing's frustration with me because he had had to send out yet another message that Phet Gyi was *still* doing well. In the few months since he had been at the zoo, Phet Gyi had grown a little, put on weight, and seemed to be adjusting well, already trying to mate with juveniles of the common muntjac species, with whom he was temporarily housed. The zoo was building a separate enclosure for him with funds I had provided for his upkeep, and there were plans to erect a sign to educate visitors about the importance of this species and the region where it was found.

But the content of this fax actually had nothing to do with the leaf deer. The message was both stunning and brief:

> Alan—We did it! With much patience and frustration, finally Hkakabo Razi has become a national park. The date is November 12, 1998 and the notification number is 79/98 of the Forestry Ministry. The government acted on our proposal and used our suggested boundaries, designating 1,472 square miles as Mount Hkakabo Razi National Park. Now we've got to make it work. Let me know what you think. Khaing.

What did I think? This was what I had hoped for ever since first looking at a map of Myanmar. This is what I had felt must be done ever since taking my first steps into the rugged mountains of the far northern frontier. This is what I had worked toward ever since leaving Tahundan more than two years earlier. I was elated at the news. If we could help the government do it right, animals would be protected and people's lives would be better. And scientists now had a living laboratory to probe beyond the surface we had scratched.

Fifteen years previously, when I was told that my efforts to create the world's first jaguar preserve in Belize had succeeded, I felt incredibly lucky to have been involved in one such major accomplishment in my life. Since then, I had helped to establish the Tawu Mountain Nature Reserve in Taiwan and the Lampi Island Marine National Park in southern Myanmar. Now it had happened again, and to an area unlike any other I'd ever seen. I hadn't even had my second cup of coffee yet.

I started to think about everything that had to be done in the months and years ahead. The most difficult and unpredictable part of our work would now begin. I was elated, but I was also disquieted by the realization that I had helped set in motion a process that would take on a life of its own, affecting people and wildlife half a world away. I wanted to run up to the bedroom and wake Salisa. I needed her to wrap her arms around me, tell me I had done the right thing, and say that everything would be okay. So many times in our marriage she had done just that.

But I didn't go to her. The emotional seesaw of our relationship was on the downswing again, and it had been awhile since we had laughed together and shared secrets. We weren't even talking much to each other now, and our lovemaking, on the rare occasions it occurred, had gone from passionate to mechanical. After we had returned from Myanmar, everything was good for a while. Then Salisa got pregnant a second time. Within the first month, a second miscarriage brought the house of cards crumbling down.

In the emotional outpourings that followed, Salisa said she knew she had failed me. I tried to comfort her, but the walls that had taken so long to dismantle before were quickly resurrected. Secretly, I began to question whether I could still love a woman who couldn't give me the child I now wanted so badly. Perhaps Salisa sensed this.

So now, fax in hand, I sat alone in the darkness of my study, my coffee long cold, thinking about Hkakabo Razi and Htawgyi.

❦

The last day of 1998 marked my forty-fifth birthday. For more than twenty years, I had tried to be in the field on this day each year, someplace far removed from my native soil. That was my annual present to myself. This year I stayed home, hoping that my physical presence would comfort Salisa. It didn't. She knew my heart wasn't in it.

After learning of the declaration of Hkakabo Razi, I immediately sent the government a proposal for another expedition, this one to give me the opportunity to train the new park staff and start implementing some management activities in conjunction with the local people. I needed to meet with the village headmen, explain the new status of the area, and get their approval and cooperation for ideas that would go into a long-term management plan. I also needed to organize a schedule with the park staff for bringing salt, basic medicines, clothing, and tea to distribution points within the park. We could stockpile goods at Putao and Naung Mung. It also had to be clearly conveyed to the villagers that the continuation of the system we were putting in place hinged on the presence and increased abundance of wildlife around their villages, which both hunters and park staff would monitor.

For this expedition, I had little desire to repeat the grueling hike to Tahundan. Instead, I asked Khaing to help explain the purpose of the trip to the director-general of the Forest Department and request two-way helicopter support for us at the outset, at the same rate we had paid the last time. Still riding high from the success of our previous expeditions, which had now been reported in the Myanmar newspapers and on television, we were informed by the new minister of forestry that he would consider our request. But because putting such a request through proper channels was so complex, we were told, it could take up to a *year* to work its way through the system.

I couldn't stay in the United States waiting for another year. There was too much to do in Myanmar, and while I had once felt that another long separation from Salisa would hurt our marriage, now I thought it might help. Furthermore, there was another area I was eager to explore, another biologically unknown part of the Kachin State, with a long history of turmoil and death: the Hukaung Valley, originally called *ju-kawng* in the Jinghpaw dialect, meaning "cremation mounds." The cremations were a result of the battles that took place there over centuries, when the Kachin pushed the Shan, the Chin, and the Palaung out of most of northern Burma.

I had first heard of the Hukaung Valley when looking at the heads of gaur in the Putao marketplace. The specimens had come from there, I'd been told—an area mostly devoid of people yet still filled with animals such as tigers and elephants. Since that time, I'd always made a point of peering west through the window of the airplane whenever I flew between Myitkyina and Putao. That was where the Hukaung Valley lay, and all I ever saw was an unbroken expanse of green.

A trip to the Hukaung Valley, situated about 75 miles southwest of Putao as the crow flies and easily accessible by car and on foot, was not unrelated to our efforts in the Hkakabo Razi region. The Sangpaung Bum, Patkai Bum, and Kuomon mountain ranges surrounding and isolating the Hukaung Valley were part of the southeast Himalayan web, connected to Hkakabo Razi and probably containing some of the same wildlife. Beyond wanting to explore the area more generally, I needed to see if the leaf deer's territory extended this far to the southwest.

The only biological survey that had been done anywhere close to the Hukaung Valley had been in the 1960s, when two American scientists visited Chakuan Pass, on the border with India, and recommended that a national park be designated there. Their recommendations were never acted upon, and now was a good time to look again. Khaing had no problem pushing through approval for this one-month trip with a planned departure date of March 1999. In the meantime, we'd wait to hear about the request for a helicopter for another trip to what was now Hkakabo Razi National Park.

In late February came an unexpected surprise, but what should have been a joyous occasion filled me instead with almost unbearable anxiety. Salisa was pregnant again. It was unexpected because we had stopped trying, and our sexual encounters had been few and far between. We foolishly hadn't even thought of the possibility of another pregnancy.

This time, planning for the worst, we acted properly. Salisa started immediate visits to a prenatal specialist recommended by our friend Jane Alexander. Jane understood how important it was for Salisa to completely trust this doctor; right now, Salisa herself had no confidence that she could carry a baby to term.

After the first visit, our fears were calmed as we realized that this gentle man of Polish descent, Janus Rudnicki, would be more than our doctor, he would be our friend. At the end of the first month, Rudnicki looked us both in the eyes and stated emphatically, "This baby is not going away." I believed him, and I felt that my life would, from that point forward, be irrevocably altered. Salisa, on the other hand, remained unconvinced until well into the second trimester. She would not allow me to discuss the pregnancy with her or with anyone else.

Salisa underwent a strange transformation during this time. The strong, educated, outgoing Thai woman I had married took on a protective, almost tribalistic personality. Thai beliefs and folklore that she would have scoffed at earlier now played a major role in her daily actions. She would do nothing that might cause her to see the death or dying of any living thing. She would avert her eyes if we came upon roadkills. She would not approach a pregnant animal. And most importantly, she would not speak about or plan for the baby as if it were going to be born.

By the second month, she let me begin reading to her belly at night again. Whether or not it did anything for the fetus was of little concern to me. It brought us closer and made me feel more a part of the pregnancy. But I was no longer allowed to read Conrad or anything else that was dark or serious. Salisa restricted me to fairy tales with happy endings.

I had pushed back my departure for the Hukaung Valley trip until May 1999, near the end of the first trimester. I couldn't delay it any longer without canceling the trip. Salisa encouraged me to go, knowing how important the trip was and how badly I needed to get back into the field. I was of two minds. If I canceled the trip now, I feared it would likely never happen. But worse was the lingering fear that something would go wrong with the pregnancy and I wouldn't be there.

During the last week of April, Salisa cuddled against me one night and placed her hand on my cheek. Anything she asked of me right then, I knew I would do.

"I can feel the baby now," she said. "And for the first time, I can feel my body changing to hold and protect it. It would be nice to have you here, but we're okay now. You can go."

The words were spoken with such tenderness and finality that I was filled with a deep sadness. The words "we're okay now" resonated in my head. I was already on the outside and, for a second, I was jealous of my unborn baby. But that feeling passed quickly. This child was everything I wanted. A week later I packed my bags and boarded the plane to Myanmar.

❦

Khaing and I flew to Myitkyina, where we were met by the rest of the team. They had been sent ahead in our Land Cruiser, driving three days from Yangon. In Myitkyina we rented a second vehicle and drove on a muddy road for ten hours to the town of Tanaing, 120 miles away, gateway to the Hukaung Valley. Our rented truck broke down once, when the steering rod came off. We squeezed everyone into one vehicle and continued, leaving the second truck to catch up when it was fixed.

Tanaing was a bustling frontier town with none of the quiet charm of Putao. Everyone seemed self-absorbed, seduced by the prospect of the quick wealth being made from robbing the forests of their bamboo, rattan, and amber, and from mining gold using high-powered water hoses to blast away at the riverbanks. Young girls with stylishly cut short hair walked barefoot in the muddy roads, while men sat around tables at outdoor food stalls sharing bottles of expensive whiskey in the early afternoon.

The quantity of bamboo I saw being rafted downstream was a testament to the still extensive forests of this country. This level of resource extraction couldn't continue much longer. Despite the 107 bamboo species known to exist in the country, bamboo was already scarce on the plains of lower Burma by the late nineteenth century. Interestingly, the Forest Department never accorded a high priority to bamboo management, even during the colonial era, when bamboo was classified as a "minor" forest product. The reality was that the sheer scale of the trade dwarfed the ability of forest officials to regulate it effectively. More importantly, unlike teak, bamboo had little potential for large-scale commercial exploitation, which meant that becoming involved in conflicts surrounding its harvesting was, in the government's eyes, more effort than it was worth.

With drunks staggering in the streets of Tanaing and altercations a nightly occurrence, we were warned not to be out after dark. Khaing and the other members of the team were clearly embarrassed, telling me repeatedly that this was unusual for Myanmar and that most people in the countryside were not like the residents here. Having seen too many towns like Tanaing throughout the world, I thought the behavior here was probably more common than Khaing realized. Still, we kept our stay in town short.

Though home to Naga, Bamar, and Lisu as well as to Kachin peoples, the Hukaung Valley remained a stronghold of the Kachin Independent Army, so after checking in with the regional Myanmar army commander, we also filed our trip plan with local KIA officials. The next morning we hired a boat to cross the Tanai River and took off walking toward the Indian border.

Over the next ten days we covered 122 miles through the Hukaung Valley. The weather alternated between battering rains and scorching sun. I cursed the sun when it burned into my skull and baked my brain; then I cursed the relentless rain when it soaked me to the skin, brought out armies of leeches, and made my steps heavier. Of the two, I preferred the rain. The terrain was easier for walking than it had been on the Naung Mung expedition and soon, as had been the case on all my previous trips, none of the soldiers wanted to be assigned to walk with me. They asked Khaing why I walked so fast, and he told them it was because I took strong vitamins from the United States. Only U Than Myint and U Thein Aung made an effort to keep up, although they would have preferred to walk slower.

Unbelievably, in this remote valley we were walking on one of the best and most expensive roads in the country. Only the lack of bridges over major river crossings prevented us from using our vehicle. But the skeletons of bridges, along with miles of old rusting pipe, battered oil drums, and numerous unrecognizable pieces of military hardware, now taken over by the jungle, begged explanation.

This was the Ledo Road, begun in 1942 by U.S. Army engineers and considered one of the greatest engineering feats of World War II. With the Japanese army controlling much of this region during the war, and Chiang Kai-shek's resistance forces becoming increasingly isolated in China, this 1,000-mile road with some 700 bridges was built to create a supply route from India to China and a fuel pipeline for the Allied forces. The idea was to link the town of Ledo, on the Assam border, with the existing Burma Road, which connected Lashio in Myanmar with Kunming in the Yunnan Province of China. The Americans believed that the road was crucial for communication with the Chinese Nationalists who were trying to contain the large Japanese forces. For more than two years, 28,000 engineers and 35,000 native workers cut through more than 300 miles of jungle, negotiating steep defiles, gorges, and raging rapids to complete the road, at a cost of U.S.$150 million and an estimated human toll of "a man a mile."

Ironically, the highway—renamed the Stillwell Road in honor of General Joseph Stillwell, who first proposed the idea—was so difficult to construct that it became passable only seven months before the end of the war and was used only a few times. It was abandoned in November 1945 when it proved economically unfeasible to maintain. Once the road fell into disrepair, anything and everything salvageable was used or hauled away by the local people. When the KIA controlled the area during the civil conflicts of the 1980s, many of the bridges that hadn't already collapsed were intentionally destroyed to hamper movement of the Myanmar army from Yangon.

It was a strange feeling, walking among the ghosts of warfare past. I called the area "the ghost valley" because so many lives had been cut short here, first by tribal fighting and then by the convoluted politics of international warfare. It reminded me of a time when I'd camped along the former Ho Chi Minh Trail, at the base of the Annamite Mountains between Laos and Vietnam.

We followed the Ledo Road to Shingbwiyang, a former staging area for the American forces coming over the mountains from India. There was a large airstrip cut out of the jungle that still looked usable, and the remains of a American-built motor pool facility in the village. As we got closer to the border of Assam in

India, most of the villagers were of Naga descent. From here, we ascended into the mountains.

With an annual rainfall of 150 inches, the nearly 5,600 square miles of the Hukaung Valley was covered with dense evergreen forests. Although a fertile alluvial plain, it showed little cultivation and less settlement. The only signs of human activity were close to the road. Rice was the major crop, but most villagers also planted tapioca, maize, yams, corn, and pumpkins. Sometimes there were small village gardens with tea, bananas, grapefruits, and limes. The Naga also raised goats.

At every village, people wanted rice instead of money because they were suffering a food shortage. I'd wondered about the extensive areas of bamboo along the Ledo Road that appeared broken and dead, as if a disease or fire had swept through. A rare bamboo flowering had occurred the previous year, we were told, resulting in a massive dropping of seeds and the death of the bamboo. As a result, the rodent population exploded and, after consuming the seeds, devastated the villagers' plantation crops.

We had constant trouble with our Naga porters, who enjoyed the food and money we provided but didn't seem to want to carry any load to speak of. In several villages, Naga men ran off or hid to avoid being chosen as porters by the village headman. On the sixth day out, three of our young Naga porters brought from Tanaing ran off in the middle of the night with some of our extra rations.

Part of the problem was that the Naga were clearly uncomfortable with the soldiers who accompanied us. Violent conflicts between the Naga and Myanmar soldiers stationed along the Indian border were regular occurrences. By the end of the trip, we had given up on hiring Naga and instead arranged for four domesticated elephants with handlers at a daily wage of 800 kyats, double what we had paid the porters.

Hunting was not a major activity for most of the people here, and there was no evidence of an active wildlife trade such as I had seen farther north. Most of the hunting was of such animals as deer, porcupines, and birds around plantations, and was done using black powder rifles and snares. When they needed money or rice, as they did now, many villagers panned the rivers for gold or killed animals from small boats at night, using flashlights.

Some local hunters occasionally went deeper into the valley if they wanted to kill gaur or capture elephants for domestication. One old elephant hunter told us how he had captured nearly a hundred elephants in his time using the lasso method, in which the wild elephants were approached on elephant-back and roped. The animals were sold to the timber industry for 1,200 kyat per foot, measured to the elephant's shoulder. Since the 1990s, however, wild elephants had become scarce, he said, with perhaps only 400 left in the Hukaung Valley.

The indomitable Lisu, coming down from the north, were regular visitors to the interior here to hunt tigers and elephants. Some of the Lisu killed elephants with a special dart made from a long wooden shaft shaped, on one end, to fit the barrel of their rifle and fitted, on the other end, with a metal arrow tip coated in poison. They didn't discriminate according to the sex or age of an animal; any elephant hide was marketable.

Despite the hunting, there were many indicators of a relatively healthy, intact forest, including our almost daily sightings of great hornbills and gibbons, the pugmarks of leopards and dholes, and the sign of tigers, wild elephants, and gaur. Only the rhino was gone, as was true everywhere else I went throughout Myanmar. One old man told of his father's seeing a rhino track in 1935. Since then— nothing.

After a day's rest in Shingbwiyang, we continued into the Tawang Bum mountain range, camping at an army outpost in the village of Namyun and then hiking to Kyang Hlaing, a Naga village high in the mountains. Tawang Bum was the northern boundary of the Hukaung Valley, connecting the Sangpaung Bum and Patkai

Bum mountains on the west to the Kuomon Range on the east. The Naga villages here reminded me of Hmong settlements high in the Annamites—dirty and unsanitary, on cold, bare, mist-enshrouded mountaintops. Both groups preferred to live apart from others. The Naga still occasionally used spears, along with their crossbows and black powder rifles, to hunt wild pigs. Here, every part of the hunted animal was eaten, the Naga said, including the skin.

We remained in these mountains for three days, sending out runners to remote Naga villages to tell them that I was interested in buying any small deer parts they wanted to sell me. The wait paid off. By the time we left, I had two skulls of the leaf deer from Namli, a village high up in the mountains. It confirmed what I'd hoped for. The range of the leaf deer was not just restricted to the mid-elevation mountains between Putao and the Nam Tamai. The deer was more widely distributed, dispersing along the rugged mountain corridors extending down from the north and almost certainly traveling along the Indian side of the border as well.

When we descended the mountains, we returned first to Shingbwiyang. Instead of walking back the way we had come, we arranged for two boats to take us on a two-day, 61-mile river ride along the Tanai River back to Tanaing. This would give me a better look at parts of the Hukaung Valley not easily accessible on foot, and would allow us to record riverine bird species we couldn't see elsewhere.

Our boats averaged only four to five miles an hour moving upstream against currents made stronger, faster, and more dangerous by recent rains. We stayed close to the banks to avoid large trees and other debris barreling past us. Both boats developed engine trouble our first day out and, with darkness already upon us, we spent the night among the Wa, who had traveled far from their territory in the eastern Shan State. The Wa were notorious for their headhunting practices in the past, when they believed that human skulls provided protection against evil spirits, but many were now impoverished, having denuded and ruined their land through timbering and slash-and-burn agriculture. They'd come here, like so many others, in search of gold.

The long hours on the boat allowed Khaing and me to do what now had become a standard part of our trips. We rehashed what we had seen each day and discussed what we'd recommend to the Forest Department. This area clearly was not as spectacular or unique as the Hkakabo Razi region, but it was important for similar reasons.

There was abundant wildlife here, particularly large mammals that had already been eliminated from many of Myanmar's other forested areas. The Hukaung Valley was also an important watershed. The streams originating in the mountains surrounding the Hukaung Valley came together on the flatland to form the Tanai River, which then became part of the Chindwinn River farther south. The largest branch of the Ayeyarwady River, the Chindwinn was the river on which I'd first journeyed in 1994 to get to Htamanthi Wildlife Sanctuary.

Rumors that much of the Hukaung Valley was uninhabited turned out to be true. The view from the Tanai River helped explain why. Seasonal inundations of the lowlands made agriculture almost impossible and turned the jungle into a swamp during the months of heavy rains. We were just now at the beginning of the rainy season, and the streams and rivers were already rising quickly, making even travel by small boat dangerous. Not only would plantations be difficult to maintain under such conditions, but malaria and other diseases also flourished in this environment, as the builders of the Ledo Road had experienced firsthand decades earlier. A 30-year-old woman died of malaria while we stayed overnight in her village. Tuberculosis was also a problem among the Naga, who attributed this affliction to the smoke from their fires and the poor ventilation in their houses.

Back at our the WCS office in Yangon, still flush with the success of getting Hkakabo Razi protected, we pored over maps and considered strategies for protecting the Hukaung Valley. In the end, we proposed nearly 2,500 square miles as Hukaung Valley Wildlife Sanctuary, bounded by the Ledo Road, the Kuomon Range, and the Tawang Bum mountains. This was not a place for tourists or recreational activities but, if protected, it would be one of the country's most important wildlife sites.

Apart from the settlements right along the road, no one lived in the interior of the area we delineated, and there were no large stands of commercially valuable trees. The Tanai River, which was heavily used, was kept outside the proposed boundaries, but the surrounding mountains and all the major feeder streams coming down from them were left inside. These mountains were home to the leaf deer, which still remained unprotected. As I had done with our Hkakabo Razi proposal, I promised to commit WCS funds to develop a management plan and help set up the new wildlife sanctuary once it was declared.

When the trip report and proposal for Hukaung were complete, we sent it off to the director-general of the Forest Department. At the same time, we asked if there was any word about our request to return to Hkakabo Razi by helicopter. It was still sitting with the minister, we were told.

Before leaving Myanmar, I went to visit Phet Gyi. He was in his own enclosure now, seemingly well adjusted and with a healthy appetite. His small spiked antlers were just starting to poke through the hair atop his head, and his body had filled out nicely. When I moved along the perimeter of his enclosure to get closer to him, he ran into a distant corner. But when I pursed my lips and made an almost kissing sound, as I used to just after he was first caught, his big, round ears perked up. He tilted his head to one side, almost as if trying to remember something, and then took a few hesitant steps toward me. I reached out my hand. Suddenly, perhaps realizing his folly, he spun around and ran back into the corner, his head turned away from me.

Salisa was again waiting for me upon my arrival at Kennedy Airport, smiling in a way I hadn't remembered seeing in years. As I approached her, I realized she hadn't seen me yet. I'd been gone only a little more than a month this time, but the change in her was noticeable. She was in her fifth month now and knew with certainty that she would soon be a mom. I looked at the swell of her belly and fervently hoped that the baby, boy or girl, would have her gentle nature. Then she spotted me and realized I'd been looking at her new curves. The smile broadened. This time it was just for me.

# Through the Looking Glass

In the depths of winter, I finally learned there was within
me an invincible summer.

—Albert Camus

THE NEXT FOUR MONTHS passed like a dream.
Thoughts of the first expedition and the time spent in Tahundan,
two years in the past, were never far from my mind. I was occupied
now in writing up the data, publishing our findings, and giving slide
shows to raise funds for the management of Hkakabo Razi National
Park. The discovery of the leaf deer and its close genetic affiliation
to another new species of barking deer, the Truongson muntjac in
the Annamite Mountains, supported my original speculation that
these mountainous regions were connected at one time.

I continued to help Khaing lobby for the protection of the
Hukaung Valley. It was currently the only proposed protected area
that was home to the leaf deer, and I worried about the future of
this heavily hunted species. But conservation was more difficult
now that we had lost our most important ally, General Chit Swe.
The new minister of forestry had allowed us to continue our work,

but he was not nearly as committed to conservation as was his predecessor. Still, in the end, the minister signed off on our request to return to Hkakabo Razi and even helped push through approval for a helicopter.

Salisa's due date was October 28, and during the days preceding I couldn't keep my mind on anything other than thoughts of impending fatherhood. I was going to turn 46 in two months, and I was a basket case. I kept waking Salisa during the night to discuss possible names for the baby; I wanted a name that would lend strength to his life but could not be made into some aberration by teasing youngsters. I kept the car filled with gas. I had Salisa's bags packed, and I knew the fastest route to the hospital. The doctor's number was in my wallet. Salisa would moan in the middle of the night, and I would be out of bed and half dressed before realizing that she was just talking in her sleep.

The due date came and went, and I was surprised at how rattled I was. I had helped deliver a Mayan baby in the back of a pickup truck on a bumpy dirt road in southern Belize. I had sewn up my dog, Cleo, after his neck was ripped open by a jaguar. I had ridden for help on a motorcycle in Thailand with a broken leg and a bamboo stake through my foot. I had had to find my way out of the jungle with a subdural hematoma after a plane crash. But nothing compared to this. This was my child.

In the end, everything went wonderfully. A little after noon on November 3, 1999, Alexander Tyler Rabinowitz was born. At 6 pounds, 4 ounces, and 19 inches long, he didn't look that much bigger than the leaf deer fetus I had pulled from its mother's womb a year earlier. But the wail that arose from this little bloody bundle, already showing my pronounced chin and Salisa's beautiful eyes, indicated that his fate would be far different.

As I had done throughout my life, I sublimated my emotions

until I was alone. Salisa was sleeping, the doctor and nurses had cleaned up, and Jane, who had come to help Salisa, had gone home to shower and change. The baby lay in a heated crib next to Salisa's bed. I stood over him, fingering his little appendages and marveling at the miracle of birth, as every other father in the world must have done before me. He crinkled his little pug nose and gripped my pinkie with his tiny hand. I smiled. Then I cried.

I stayed home with Salisa for the first two months. On Christmas Day I sat in my office at home, all my bags, cameras, and medical supplies sprawled around me in various stages of organization and packing. I was devouring Mary Lovell's new biography of the explorer Richard Burton, *A Rage to Live.* She wrote of Burton's relief when he left behind daily routine and the constraints of civilization: "Of the gladdest moments methinks in human life is the departing upon a distant journey into unknown lands. . . . " It was as if a piece of the man lived within me. Yet my endeavors seemed paltry compared to his.

After returning from the Hukaung Valley, I finally went to see an orthopedic surgeon about my knee problems. The results of the MRI showed no tears in the meniscus; instead, my patella was laterally displaced, causing bone to rub on bone. I decided to forgo surgery and opted for a knee brace and physical therapy sessions, which I stopped attending after realizing that I knew more about anatomy than my therapist who, not long before, had been a stockbroker. I stayed home and did my own exercises.

My forty-sixth birthday was the best of my life. Alexander was the greatest present I could have been given. That and a card from Salisa reminding me how old I was compared to my new son. My response was a marathon exercise session in my log cabin-cum-gym, something I had not had the chance to undertake since the birth. I finished off the three-hour session with ten two-minute rounds of boxing on a black leather punching bag filled with dirt and rags.

The sweat pouring off me and the lactic-acid burn in my shoulders reminded me of similar sessions on the sand-filled canvas bag of my youth. My father taught me to box on that old canvas bag. He taught me how to wrap my hands with cloth and tape and punch with the flat of my fist, between the middle finger joints and the knuckles. But from my earliest days, I remembered my eyes always focusing on the little red bloodstains splattered over the bag, evidence of my father's own bare-knuckled sessions with his demons. Then, one day, I decided to forgo the hand wraps and add my own blood to his.

It was four days before my fifteenth birthday. I let the screen door slam as I entered the house, dropped the bag of groceries on the kitchen counter, and went straight to my room, locking the door. My father came home a few hours later while I was lying on the bed staring up at the ceiling. I heard the doorknob turn. No one respected privacy in this house.

"You want to come down to the basement and box a little?" My father's voice filled the room despite the locked door. He knew. My mother had said something to him. She had no idea what had happened, but she had seen the pattern often enough. Now my father would try to make the hurt go away, the only way he knew how.

I followed him into the basement and we put on the gloves in silence. The routine was always the same. I punched and he blocked, just barely. He wanted me to hit him. I think he wanted me to hurt him. It was the only way he knew to try to share my pain. Finally, between punches, he'd talk to me, telling me one of the stories about his own youth that I'd heard at least a dozen times before. I think he knew I'd start talking to him just to avoid hearing the stories again.

I told him about the supermarket, where I'd stopped to pick up the groceries my mother had bought and left there earlier in the day. There was a girl I'd never seen before at the counter, maybe 18 years old. I waited on line, practicing in my mind the easiest words I'd use to ask for the groceries. But when my turn came, I felt the familiar churning in my stomach and sweat on my forehead. I pointed to the bags behind her, hoping somehow she'd know which one was mine.

"Your name, please," she said. Those hated words. I started feeling the beginning of a grimace and the facial contortions.

"Ra . . . ra . . . ra . . . bi . . . bi . . . " It was a bad one this time.

"Poor thing, must be retarded," a woman's voice said behind me.

"Bi . . . bi . . . bi . . . " Red in the face now. I had to stop for breath.

"Binowitz!" finally exploded from my mouth, after I had stomped my foot and swung my head to help the sound come out.

"How could his parents let him out alone like this?" the counter girl asked the woman behind me, as if I couldn't understand her words. She turned and looked through the bags behind her, finally realizing that the one marked "Rabinowitz" was the closest thing to the sounds I'd been making.

"This one?" she asked, mouthing the words carefully, as if I were deaf as well as dumb. Her look of pity burned through me. I nodded my head, then looked at the floor and clenched my fists.

"Now, go straight home with this, and tell your mother to come with you next time." I grabbed the bag, keeping my eyes on the floor.

"Poor dumb thing," I heard as I walked out the door.

⚶

I stopped punching the bag long before I would have when I was younger. I removed the gloves, then slowly and methodically unwrapped my hands, wanting to remember, needing to remember everything. The concentration, the focus, the use of my mental and physical strength—it was a gift from my father. Only now I no longer needed to rage against the world. My last thought while locking the cabin was that I would give my son a happier childhood than my own.

My return in January 2000 was my fifth trip to northern Myanmar since 1996, when I first came there searching for a reason to journey farther into the hinterland. In some ways, I felt this was the most important trip I'd be making toward helping shape the future of the region. I wasn't sure what we would do after this trip since the government had informed Khaing that helicopter support would be impossible to get again at the rate we were paying. My knees didn't feel the same after the walk to Tahundan, and there were many other places I wanted to explore while I was still physically capable of doing so.

Khaing had sent WCS funds on ahead so that U Thein Aung, the new chief of Hkakabo Razi National Park, could buy supplies and hike with his seven new park staff from Putao to Tahundan, where they would meet our helicopter. This would familiarize them with the route and the people. My main objective for this trip was to bring together the village headmen from different areas of the park at Tazundam, a central location. I was hoping for agreement on a vision for the future, before we formalized a management plan and initiated a distribution and monitoring system to curtail hunting and trade in animal parts while providing for the needs of the villagers. We were bringing in salt and clothing by helicopter as an initial gift to the village representatives.

The ostensible purpose of going first to Tahundan, which was at least a three-day walk from Tazundam, was to make plans for a guard post and research station we were thinking of building there. Personally, I had other motives as well. I wanted to see my friends again, particularly Htawygi. I wanted to return to the village of Karaung and visit with the Taron. And Khaing wanted to see his adopted daughter's natural mother and give her pictures of the little girl's new life in Yangon.

The helicopter to take us to Hkakabo Razi was already waiting when we arrived at the Putao airport. The pilot, a 40-year-old major with twenty years of flying experience, had been trained in Russia but had never flown in terrain of high mountains and deep canyons before. Still, he appeared confident. His copilot, a 25-year-old captain, was still cutting his teeth.

We took off only a day late, during a break in the weather. When we reached the pass that would take us over to the Nam Tamai, however, it was completely obscured. As the pilot looked for breaks in the cloud bank, we came uncomfortably close to the mountains, the ride got rough, and our visibility dropped to near zero. The pilot, clearly nervous, aborted the attempt, and we returned to Putao.

We were disappointed but glad to be back safely. Steve Winter, a talented photographer whom I had asked to join us on this trip, occupied himself by shooting pictures of the Putao market. Khaing and I went to meet a man whom we were told was very influential in the Church of Christ. From our earlier trips, I'd learned that there were three main religious groups in the wider Putao District, the most influential being the Church of Christ, followed by the Assembly of God and then the Baptists. If we were going to try to change the basic attitudes of the Rawang toward wildlife, we needed to do more than just provide material goods. I was hoping we could appeal to their Christian beliefs.

Sitting in his yard drinking tea, we described to this man what was being taught to the people by most of the Rawang preachers— that animals had been put on earth to be used and exploited by humans in any way that we see fit. Such proselytizing contributed to a wildlife trade that would eventually wipe out most, if not all, of the larger species, I said, describing in detail the indiscriminate, and sometimes irresponsible, use of jaw traps and snares. Finally, I tactfully mentioned that much of the wildlife trade in the region involved the local preachers.

He listening politely, shaking his head sadly. "It is true that the Bible speaks of animals and other things being put on earth by God for man's use," he said after I was finished. "But the use has to do with survival, with providing food for oneself and one's family. If life is taken for any other reason, then it is wrong. And if the life is made to suffer when it does not have to suffer, that too is wrong."

I was pleased to hear these words. If we could set up a proper distribution system to provide people with what they needed, he agreed that they should stop or at least curtail the killing of animals for their parts.

"When the time comes, would you or one of your preachers come with us into the Hkakabo Razi and tell the Rawang what you are saying now? Will you help us save wildlife?" I asked.

He smiled and nodded. "It is God's work," he said. Then he added, almost to himself, "No Christian should be surviving on the death and suffering of other living things."

❧

When the helicopter remained idle for the next two days despite a clear sky and favorable weather reports, Khaing and I were puzzled. We invited the pilot and copilot to meet us at the coffee shop in Putao so that we could talk in private. The pilot was clearly worried. He was concerned about clouds, downdrafts, and icing on the blades when he went above 8,000 feet. As far as I knew, these were all valid concerns, but they were normal considerations for flying in this region.

"Don't worry," he said to us finally. "Whatever happens, I have been instructed to get you safely to Tahundan. If the weather is good, we will try again tomorrow."

I watched his face as he spoke. His words belied the fact that his confidence had been badly shaken after the last attempt. The question was, how badly shaken?

❧

That night I suggested to Khaing that, if we had to abort again, we should ask to be dropped off at Naung Mung. U Than Myint could return to Putao with the helicopter and make sure the pilots came back to pick us up and take us to Tahundan when the weather cleared. We could start our work in Naung Mung, where we hoped to build a guard station for park staff to monitor trade and to set up a distribution point for goods going into the park.

We took off the next morning at 11:45, after getting favorable weather reports from Tahundan and Naung Mung and after a test flight by the pilot. It was a clear day and everything went smoothly. We got through the pass easily, followed the Nam Tamai, and then headed north at Tazundam into the Adung Wang Valley. We anticipated an imminent arrival at Tahundan, so no one was paying much attention to what the pilot did next. But when we saw canyon walls closing in around us and realized that we should have arrived at our destination already, we knew something was wrong.

At Talahtu, just miles from our destination, the pilot had turned east up the Htala Wang River instead of continuing straight up the Adung Wang to Tahundan. The canyon that we'd been following had started to narrow and required a sharp, tight turn up ahead. We'd warned him of this in Putao and told him that just afterward the canyon opened up again. But instead, the pilot had decided to turn east into the wider-looking Htala Wang canyon, hoping to find a quicker way to cut over to Tahundan. If it didn't work, he planned to turn around and come back to the junction of the rivers.

What seemed like a wide canyon at first closed in on us quickly. By the time the pilot realized his mistake, the canyon walls were too close for us to safely turn around. There was complete silence in the helicopter now as everyone stared out the windows at the steep canyon slopes. We had no choice but to keep going deeper, hoping the canyon walls would open up.

Steve was by the door, the best position from which to see what was ahead of us and take photographs. Suddenly, all the color drained from his face. He had just realized that, instead of opening up, the canyon ended. A huge rock wall loomed directly in our path.

Before I had time to ask what was wrong, the helicopter seemed to come to an abrupt midair stop and then tilted into a tight 180-degree turn that I wouldn't have thought possible this close to the canyon walls. The whole helicopter was vibrating. Steve, who had flown in small aircraft most of his life, looked as if he were ready to leap out the door. We were more than 1,000 feet above the river and would not have survived a crash. As we turned, I glimpsed the huge looming rock wall that might have been our headstone.

We were more than 10 miles up the canyon, and as we tried to make it back out to the junction, we were assaulted by severe downdrafts. The helicopter kept dropping in altitude despite the pilot's efforts to keep it up. I opened the field notebook that I had been clutching tightly in my lap. On the back inside cover was a photo of Alexander that I had glued in before leaving New York. I looked at the picture and realized how scared I was at the thought of never seeing him again, never being able to tell him how much he had changed my life just by being born.

It took nearly ten long minutes before the pilot stabilized our speed and altitude. The helicopter had stopped shaking and we could see more open sky than rock around us. Once we neared the river junction, we saw the cultivated fields of a village ahead, and the pilot aimed for a fallow open plot near the river.

After landing, the pilot turned to us and said that this was Tahundan and we needed to disembark so that he could get back to Putao. Still shaken, I looked at him as if he were crazy. The copilot said nothing. I knew exactly where we were, and it wasn't Tahundan. But we disembarked from the helicopter with our belongings anyway, all of us happy just to have solid ground under our feet again.

The pilot, strangely uncommunicative now, took off immediately and flew high above the mountains, seeming to circle almost aimlessly for nearly thirty minutes. We were in Talahtu, a village where we'd spent a night during our first trip. The headman was not there. He had gone with a small contingent to greet us at Tahundan. We went into the village and watched from the doorway of the headman's hut as the helicopter came back and landed where it had dropped us off. The pilot shut down the engines and approached our hut. They were too low on fuel to get out now, he said. They needed to spend the night here and radio for another helicopter to bring in more fuel. The pilot looked shaken and unsteady, while his copilot remained silent.

We were at least two hours overdue at Tahundan before the pilot finally sent a radio message to Putao explaining our situation. Then a barrage of panicked messages flew between Talahtu, Tahundan, Putao, and Myitkyina. Having had no word from our party for so long, the soldiers who had accompanied the park staff to Tahundan had already been ordered by the northern commander in Myitkyina to find us, dead or alive. Rumors had begun circulating throughout the government offices in Yangon about what had happened to us: either we had crashed into a mountain or we had been kidnapped by a local tribal group.

That evening the pilot, seeming almost shell-shocked, told us that when the extra fuel came, we could return to Putao with him, but he would not take us on to Tahundan. We passed on his offer. Since no one was injured and we were only 11 miles from our destination, we decided to continue on foot.

The next day we hired porters and went on to Tahundan, staying a night in Karaung. I assumed, as did Khaing, that this whole situation would straighten itself out once the pilot returned and explained what had happened. Despite our anger at the pilot, we were willing to excuse his arrogance, poor judgment, and lack of cooperation once he got us down safely. What we didn't anticipate was how he would distort the truth of the incident. When we reached Karaung and met up with the soldiers coming down from Tahundan, we were shocked at the radio message they had for us. We were told to cancel our trip and start walking back out.

Only later did I learn what had happened. When the second helicopter arrived at Talahtu with more fuel, it brought in another pilot. Our pilot was grounded immediately and, upon his return to Myitkyina, was called before the northern commander. Trying to save himself, he reported that he had not been able to make it to Tahundan because of the tight canyons combined with gusty winds and icing on the blades at high altitudes. He had told us to stay with him but we left against his orders, he went on, never mentioning his having turned into the wrong canyon, mistaking Talahtu for Tahundan, or ordering us out of the helicopter. When the minister of defense heard the pilot's version of the events, he was furious. We were ordered out of the area immediately because we had disobeyed orders and "walked off into the forest on our own."

To make matters worse, in the midst of it all, the director-general of the Forest Department and the director-general of Planning and Statistics were told that they would lose their jobs if anything happened to "the Americans." The minister of forestry developed chest pains after being berated by the minister of defense, and the northern commander, I was told, went on a drinking binge after realizing he had nearly lost a helicopter and two Americans.

Knowing nothing of these developments, when we learned of the radio order, we decided to go on to Tahundan anyway and try to straighten out the matter from there. We felt we had done nothing wrong and couldn't imagine what we were being blamed for. I had forgotten we were dealing with a government where logic did not always prevail.

# CHAPTER 20

# The Return

We shall not cease from exploration
And the end of all our exploring
Will be to arrive where we started
And know the place for the first time.

—T. S. Eliot

IN TAHUNDAN, several hundred people from outlying villages, some as far away as Madaing, had gathered to see the helicopter and welcome us with orchids and milk. When they learned that we had landed in Talahtu and were coming in on foot instead, they all dispersed. Apparently, we were not the main attraction. Only the headman, U Ga Nar, was there to greet us upon arrival.

Within hours of reaching Tahundan, we received another radio message. Since I had disobeyed orders (the emphasis was now placed on *me* having disobeyed orders), we would not be picked up by helicopter. We were told to file a new schedule for an immediate walk out. We replied that we were not equipped to walk out and that we didn't understand why we were being accused of disobeying orders. After having spent so much time and money getting here, we needed to get our work done for the Forest Department, we added.

Among ourselves that night, we discussed what we should do if the government insisted that we change our plans. I suggested that we could shorten the trip by two weeks by hiking south to Tazundam, as originally planned, but then remaining there for the scheduled helicopter pickup instead of returning to Tahundan. We all agreed that this seemed reasonable. It let the government "punish" us for whatever misdeeds they thought we had committed, while allowing us enough time to get the most important work done.

The next day we sent a radio message suggesting our changed itinerary. We received a response within hours: our plan was unacceptable. And no helicopter would be sent to pick us up, the government said again. It dawned on us that the truth about what had happened on our helicopter ride was not getting through to the highest levels. And we didn't have our staunch ally General Chit Swe to turn to.

Khaing was clearly worried. He and I decided to circumvent the chain of command that we were currently dealing with and send a radio message directly to the director-general of the Forest Department. In the message, Khaing explained in detail what had happened, mentioning that we had photographs and video to corroborate our version of the events. We stated again that we were not equipped to walk out and that we would wait in Tahundan until we heard back from the Forest Department.

Htawgyi was by my side almost from the moment I arrived in Tahundan. He had a basket of dry leaves on his back that he and other villagers were spreading over the fallow land before they plowed it for the next crop. Around his neck was the black plastic whistle I had given him two years earlier. But the shy little boy I had known was gone. He was now 15 years old and, in this culture, he was a young man with adult responsibilities. Soon he would be given his own crossbow and taken out on his first hunt. When I asked after his family, I was saddened to learn that Ma Phae Darae, the little four-year-old with pinkeye, had died less than a month after we left. Several other villagers I had known had died as well.

I gave Htawgyi a new pocketknife that I had brought for him, and then I opened my field book and showed him the picture of my new son, Alexander. Htwagyi took the book from my hands and stared at the picture hard for a while. Then he looked up at me. I didn't know what to expect from him—sadness, jealously, or perhaps complete apathy. Instead he smiled, held the picture up to my face, and pointed to the chin, the ears, and the hairline, all matching my own. Then he took a leaf from his basket and, placing it next to the picture, closed the book gently and pressed it hard into my hands.

I wasn't sure what was in Htawgyi's mind, but I felt that in his own way he was connecting his own life to my son's and telling me that I should never let go of either of them. I wondered if he was thinking of his father's death, or how his mother had left him and never come back. During the week we were in Tahundan, I went back to our special place by the river several times and waited by the rocks. Htawgyi never came.

Since U Tilawka was not often at Tahundan, I was not surprised to learn that the Tibetans were looking elsewhere for spiritual guidance. When the passes were open, they invited Tibetan monks from across the border to their villages to give prayers in return for food, lodging, and trade goods. I was leaving the headman's house one afternoon when I heard melodic chanting coming from somewhere in the village, accompanied by what sounded like periodic beatings on a drum. I followed the sounds to a villager's house.

As I entered the doorway I saw a dark-skinned man bent over

by the fire, rocking slightly to the rhythm of his own voice. He wore a fur-lined aviator hat with earflaps hanging down, dark brown monklike robes, and a leather jacket with a Harley-David-son symbol on the upper left breast. Every few moments he gently put to one side a page from an ancient-looking unbound book.

In his right hand was a small double-sided drum, with a ball hanging from a string attached to a piece of wood that extended above the drum. At certain junctures in his reading, he swung his hand from side to side, causing the ball to beat each of the drums alternately and creating a deep, resonating sound that filled the hut. I had seen an instrument like this in India, in one of the arms of a depiction of the goddess Shiva. The sound of the drum was meant to mimic the rhythm of creation.

I went over to join the family sitting around him by the fire. As I sat down, the monk looked up at me and smiled. It was a boyish smile, although he looked to be in his late 30s. For a moment I thought of U Tilawka, with his funky WCS hat and shaved head.

The man was not a "real" monk, Khaing told me later, more like an itinerant lay preacher following the basic Buddhist precepts. He was married with four children, but he didn't smoke or drink alcohol. His profession, passed on to him by his father, was to travel to remote Tibetan villages reciting prayers and offering spiritual guidance.

I was fascinated by the man's book of prayers and asked if I could examine it more closely. The corners of each page were dirtied with wear; the edges of some had broken off after so many years of use. The paper was like old parchment, with writing on both sides, the likes of which I'd seen only in museums. Only the most gentle touch prevented the paper from cracking or breaking when handled.

The book had been written by five different monks, the man told Khaing as I held it in my hands. After completing it, the monks died and their bodies were said to have suddenly disappeared. His father, still a youth at the time, had been a disciple of one of those monks and was given the book. When his father was dying, he gave the book to his son.

I showed the man my picture of Alexander and asked him to say a special prayer so that my son would grow to be strong and intelligent yet remain a gentle and kind person. He started going through his prayer book until close to the end and then began to read. I handed him my notebook and asked if he would write down the prayer so that my son could have it throughout his life. He looked sad and said he could not; he hadn't learned how to write.

That evening the lay preacher showed up at the door to the monastery and, to my amazement, handed me the three pages from his book containing the prayer he'd read for Alexander.

"This is for you," he said. Then he paused for a few moments. "But you need to remember that the power of this prayer is not only in the words themselves. Once they are taken into the mind, their power will work for you. Give these to your son when he is old enough to understand what I tell you."

In the days that followed, we anxiously awaited a response from the Ministry of Forestry. Steve continued to photograph the villagers and their day-to-day activities, while I trained the park guards on data collection, species identification, and interview techniques.

When one of the villagers killed a red goral and brought it to us, I showed the guards how to examine the animal, what to look for, and what to save intact before skinning and cleaning it. It was a female, with a tiny fetus that would have been easily overlooked had we not cut open the womb. I explained the importance of such information and how, by the size of the fetus, we could estimate when this animal had gotten pregnant and when it would have given birth. This animal, for example, would probably not give birth until after the winter season, when food was more readily available for the mother and when chances of survival for the newborn were better.

We discussed how rare and unusual the red goral was, despite its seeming abundance in this region. I encouraged all the villagers, including women and children, to join these training sessions, and I made sure my words were translated for all of them. U Thein Aung set up nets to catch birds and bats and demonstrated how even delicate animals such as these could be handled, examined, and measured without injuring them. We spoke of treating animals with respect, even in death, because of their value to the natural system upon which everyone in this region depended.

As soon as he had time, Khaing set about trying to find the mother of his adopted daughter. He was pleased to learn that she had remarried, to a younger man from Karaung. When word reached her that Khaing was looking for her, she and her family came immediately.

The family looked much better now than when we had left them standing in the clearing two years ago. She smiled when Khaing gave her the bundle of clothes he'd brought for them. But when she saw Khaing pull out a folder filled with photos, she suddenly looked apprehensive, almost scared. As soon as she saw the first picture of her now two-year-old daughter playing in Yangon, she burst into tears and hid her face behind her mother's back.

Khaing told me later that she had apologized to him, explaining that the tears were due to happiness, and that she truly appreciated what Khaing had done to give her daughter a better life. But I'd watched her carefully, just as I had that day two years before when the helicopter flew in. I remembered the look of sheer terror on her face when confronted with the reality of giving up her baby. Today I had seen a similar look of deep anguish, along with the obliteration of whatever hope had remained in her mind until now. She knew that she had lost her daughter forever.

⤞✕⤝

We finally received a radio message in response to Khaing's report. It was good news and bad news. Although the higher officials now understood the truth about what had happened to us on this trip, decisions had been made and orders had been given that were not easily rescinded. It was a matter of "face." The northern commander would send in a helicopter to get us, but the pickup point would be in Talahtu, where we had first landed, not in Tahundan or Tazundam. And they wanted us out now. They would not risk anything else happening to us. This was the final order, and it was clear that if I didn't abide by it, my ability to help protect Hkakabo Razi and other areas in Myanmar in the future would be severely compromised.

We prepared to leave Tahundan the next day. Since there was no longer time to hold the big meeting of villagers that I had hoped for, the process of getting a consensus from village headmen would now have to be conducted by U Thein Aung's staff in a piecemeal fashion during their hike out. I would spend at least a few days in villages along the way to Talahtu talking to the staff about what they should say to village headmen, what questions should be asked, and what kind of additional village data should be collected.

That evening I sat in front of the monastery sipping Johnnie Walker and soaking in the magnificent landscape around me for what could be the last time. Htawgyi had come by earlier to shake my hand and say good-bye. He had never gotten the father he so desired, but he was almost a man himself. Perhaps his pain would make him a better father to his children, I thought.

I thrilled to the biting chill of the evening temperature, which, before tonight, would have made me rush to the warmth of the nearest fire. Everything seemed indescribably real: the heartfelt smiles, the inner peace, the acceptance of that which cannot be changed. It was there despite the pain, suffering, and hardship. As the sun sank from the sky, the valley darkened, contrasting sharply with the snowcapped peaks reflecting the last of the evening light. God, what beauty!

I left Tahundan the next morning feeling strangely content, despite the knowledge that I might never return. As much as I had come to love it here, this was not "my" place. My place was with my wife and son.

A few hours later, my thoughts took a new turn as I crossed a mountain and spotted the village of Karaung below me. I had never forgotten the Taron. Dawi's face as he looked into the fire still haunted me. If my understanding of his words was correct, the Taron had become active participants in their own extinction. Many times, rereading my notes, I wondered if I had misunderstood what Dawi had said to me or if the translation had just failed completely. I had to see him and the other Taron again.

We were expected in Karaung. The house we had stayed in two years earlier was prepared for us. Sadly, three of the Taron I'd met the last time were already dead: one had fallen off a cliff while collecting pine resin, and two—one of whom was Dawi's mother—had died of illness.

The weather had turned bad again, and there was little chance that a helicopter would come in over the next couple of days. We sent a radio message that we would be staying in Karaung to get some work done and would leave for Talahtu at the first sign of good weather. A message came back later that same day: we should stay put in Karaung; they would pick us up here when the weather improved. We gladly acquiesced. Whatever complex machinations went on in the minds of the government were way beyond my ken.

Over dinner that night we told the headman the full story of what had happened to us in the helicopter. He had heard all about the aborted landing at Talahtu, but he knew nothing about our near crash into the rock wall. He seemed so taken aback by the story that I wondered how much Khaing was embellishing it in the telling. But his next words explained his response.

"Before we all became Christians," he said, "the Taron worshiped many spirits. But the most powerful among them was the Spirit of the Mountain, called La."

Someone suddenly opened the door of the hut, and the headman jumped at the sound. Then he turned back toward the fire.

"The Spirit of the Mountain lives in that big rock you saw. Everyone knew about this big rock in the old days, but very few people had ever visited it. It's a ten-day walk from here, and a very hard journey."

I nodded my head in agreement, recalling the sight of the steep canyon walls and the raging river below.

"The Taron and some Htalu made sacrifices to La," the headman continued. "If you wanted a good hunt, you pounded millet into the shape of the animal you were hunting, then faced the direction of the rock and offered the animal to La. If someone was sick, you killed a pig or a chicken as an offering. Some people long ago could communicate directly with La and the other spirits. But no more," he said. "No more."

I remembered the Taron telling me during the last trip about an old ritual of burning corn flour after a child was born in order to appease the Spirit of the Mountain. It must have been the same spirit.

The headman was quiet, looking into the fire.

"We don't believe in these things anymore," he blurted out, as if feeling guilty for what he'd just said to us. The look on his face told another story.

At my invitation, Dawi came by for dinner. He seemed so much more at ease with us now than during the first trip, and he enjoyed having Steve follow him around to take photographs. After dinner, Dawi went over and opened one of the books lying near my sleeping bag, *The Mammals of Thailand*. I sat next to him and we went through the pictures together. I showed him a tapir and he laughed. The sound warmed my heart. I had heard that laugh only once before, when I'd nearly set myself on fire in his house two years ago. It reminded me how little I knew of his thoughts, and how much I wanted to spend more time with him. The helicopter could arrive to take us back out at any hour now. For the first time during the trip, I wished for bad weather.

Perhaps the pages that the Tibetan monk had given me for Alexander were more powerful than I'd realized, or maybe La was giving me a break after nearly killing us. In any case, that night a completely unexpected snowstorm swept in and closed the canyon passes for a week. Dawi became a frequent visitor to our house. Despite the language barrier, we began to establish what might have blossomed into a real friendship had there been more time. The initial sadness I detected in Dawi on my first trip ran deep indeed, but so did the spontaneous laughter that occasionally burst forth.

Once we felt comfortable together, Dawi talked easily about the end of the Taron line, reaffirming what I thought he had said to me two years earlier. He didn't like to dwell on the subject. What he enjoyed more than anything was talking about animals and looking over and over again at the pictures in my books. He asked how people hunted the bigger animals in other places, and acted out how he would use his own crossbow to bring them down. His crossbow seemed huge for a man of his stature, but it was actually of average size and had been made right here in the village. Only four hunters in Karaung still made crossbows, he told me.

The next day Dawi brought us to the best crossbow maker in the village. I gave him 1,000 kyats for a crossbow he'd recently finished, and he agreed to take it apart and explain each piece to us as he reassembled it. The main straight stock of the crossbow was oak, a hard, brittle wood, while the crosspiece was magnolia, a more pliable wood that was first shaped and smoothed with a knife and then boiled in water in a bamboo container to soften it further. After the boiling, the crosspiece was elevated on a block with its ends tied down to form just the right arc. It was kept that way until it retained its new shape.

The trigger of the crossbow was made from the thickest part of the front leg bones of a Himalayan black bear. About ten crossbow triggers could be made from a bear's two front legs. I had seen other crossbows that used cattle bone for the trigger, but this hunter insisted that bear bone didn't eat away at the string as fast as other bone. He restrung the crossbow, explaining that the twisted fibers of the string were from a stinging-nettle-like shrub that grew above Tahundan.

"Finding the wood for the crosspiece of these bows is becoming harder and harder," he said, answering a question Khaing had posed. "And I have to collect the wood myself. When I find the right tree, I say a prayer. I thank the tree for its wood, and I ask it for good hunts for the crossbow."

"So you actually pray to the tree, asking for the crossbow to be a good one?" I asked. Finally, it seemed, someone was admitting that the culture's underlying animistic beliefs remained despite the official conversion to Christianity. I was mistaken, however.

"Yes, I pray to the tree," he responded. "But since the tree was created by God, I am speaking to God."

⚶

The heaviest snowfall was on a Sunday, and everyone stayed in the village to attend church services. We were given permission by the preacher to observe. Steve wanted to take pictures and I wanted to see what, if anything, I was not understanding about this religion that exerted such a powerful influence in this region.

We stood outside the church, a one-room cabin with a cross carved into its side, watching the scantily clad villagers scurry through the snow. Dawi walked at his usual slow pace, his blackened bare feet in stark contrast to the white snow.

The service was like so many others I'd been through in different parts of the world. There were announcements, proselytizing, and singing. It was a social event, a break from the drudgery of daily lives, an excuse to do nothing other than sing and rest. Beyond that, I couldn't see how it made the villagers' lives any better than before, when they had prayed to the mountains and the trees. Dawi was the only one of the remaining pure Taron who attended. And the look on his face, while the others sang, clearly indicated that he was there in body alone.

The next day the weather broke. As soon as the sun came out, the snow began to melt and was gone from the valley within hours. A radio message from Putao told us that, given a clear sky, the helicopter would pick us up by noon the next day. This would be my last day in Karaung.

That night, before Dawi arrived, I thought about how, in almost every way, my work here had been one of the greatest successes of my career. I had discovered a new species that might help us understand the origin and evolution of deer and other large vertebrates. I had extended the known range of several other large mammal species—blue sheep, stone marten, black muntjac—never even believed to exist in the country. We had successfully pushed for the creation of a new national park, home to perhaps the world's largest populations of the rare red goral and the black barking deer as well as numerous other important Himalayan species that were being wiped out elsewhere. We were working with the government and the residents of the park to establish a participatory management scheme that would protect the cultures of this region and help meet their nutritional and medical needs. As a result of these activities, I expected a decrease in hunting and a drop-off in the trade of wildlife parts.

But whatever our achievements now and in the future, there was nothing that could be done for the Taron, the last remnants of a tribe whose lives had been so pitiful that they had decided to help close the chapter on their own existence. I tried to tell myself that, in the scheme of things, the Taron had taken the best course of action for the well-being of future generations. I remained unconvinced.

That night I tried explaining to Dawi again exactly what my job was and why we were in Hkakabo Razi. I felt the need for his approval or, at the very least, his understanding. I tried to paint a picture of what the future would be like for others in this area that was now a national park. When I told him that I did what I did because of my love for animals, more than because of my love for people, he smiled, seeming to understand that more than anything else I'd said.

Then I tried telling Dawi that he and the other Taron had played an important part in everything that had happened since my first trip here. They had helped me better understand the value of the people as well as the wildlife in this region. They had helped me better understand myself. And my knowing him had made me a better person.

As always, I had no idea whether Dawi really understood, or for that matter cared, what I said to him. When I spoke, he looked at me almost curiously. I think he understood my sincerity, and that was enough. But the best moment came when I showed him the photograph of Alexander, and he let out raucous laughter that rocked him backward. Before I had a chance to be surprised, he pounded me on the back in a gesture unlike any I had seen from him or any other villager in this region. It was clear that he was truly happy for me and proud of my having fathered a son, despite the fact that he would never have a child of his own. I felt great, as if he were in some small way sharing my good fortune.

☙

As the helicopter lifted off, I searched for only one face among the more than a hundred people who had gathered from this and nearby villages to get a look at the big machine from the sky. I found him, just before the helicopter turned toward the river and disappeared into the canyon. While everyone ran for shelter to escape the downdraft from the helicopter blades, Dawi stood there like a stone, looking up at me, watching the helicopter grow smaller.

I could do nothing to strengthen the tenuous thread that held Dawi and the other Taron to what remained of their existence. But I could do something to ensure that children like Htawgyi had a chance. And I could do something to keep every red panda, red goral, and black barking deer from ending up as clothing or medicine or food. The future would be better for the people and animals here; I felt confident of that now. And I felt confident that the pieces of myself that had come together here in this remote northern region, and that had been completed with the birth of Alexander, would never break apart. The little stuttering boy had found his way. He would never have to hide in the darkness again.

# Epilogue

The events of that fateful trip in January 2000 were to have lasting repercussions. After the helicopter mishap, the minister of forestry stopped issuing permits for foreigners to travel into the backcountry. He refused to jeopardize his position again by risking another incident. I was told that I could get permission by working through another ministry instead, but I worried that such a move might hurt WCS's relationship with the Forest Department.

I had seen enormous achievements for conservation during the time I'd been in Myanmar. Before 1990, there had been eighteen parks and wildlife sanctuaries, comprising only 1.1 percent of the land area in the country. Seventy-five percent of these areas were smaller than 100 square miles. Since 1994, twelve new parks and sanctuaries had been designated, more than doubling the protected land area of Myanmar to 2.3 percent. The largest protected site, Hkakabo Razi National Park (1,472 square miles), was nearly twice the size of the previously largest site, Htamanthi Wildlife Sanctuary (830 square miles). Only in the large areas did the most endangered large mammals, such as tigers, elephants, and bears, or the smaller, fragmented populations of animals, such as serows, gorals, takins, and red pandas, have a chance to survive in viable numbers.

Yet I still felt the same sense of urgency as when I first arrived in Myanmar in 1993. We'd accomplished a lot since then, but Myanmar was still well below the 5 to 10 percent of land that many other countries in the world had set aside for their protected area systems. Furthermore, simply designating protected areas was only the beginning if conservation was to be effective in the long term. Good management had to be put in place that served the needs of the people and the wildlife both within and outside these protected areas. As we entered the year 2000, there was still no effective management throughout most of Myanmar's forests. In Hkakabo Razi National Park, we had an opportunity not just to preserve an important area but to create a model showing how wildlife protection and management could work and, at least in these circumstances, benefit the local people as well.

We had no time to waste. Unexpected shifts on Myanmar's political stage could shut down our efforts at any time. The biologically important transition zone, home to the leaf deer, remained unprotected, although the Forest Department supported our idea for delineating protected forest areas as a buffer to the park. Meanwhile, the increasingly lucrative trade in animal parts threatened to deplete the region's wildlife resources. Administrative control of the Kachin State, which contained much of northern Myanmar's forests, was still contentious, forcing the park staff based in Putao to tread carefully when enforcing Forest Department rules and regulations handed down from Yangon.

By February 2000, despite the difficulties of previous expeditions, I had decided it was important for me to return to Hkakabo Razi and finish what we had hoped to accomplish during the aborted January trip. Expecting that I would have to walk from Putao to Tahundan again, I had a special brace made for my knee that would make the trip bearable. For many months I implored the minister to change his mind about permitting me to go back north, but he remained unresponsive to my request and to that of the director-general of the Forest Department. I started to wonder if all our hard work and planning for Hkakabo Razi would be in vain.

Then, in November, I received an unexpected fax from Khaing who, half a world away, had developed similar concerns:

> We can't wait any longer. I will go back to Hkakabo Razi myself. You have already trained the park staff on our last trip. As for me, I think I have been with you long enough to know what to do. I will start the distribution of salt and other goods, and I will hold a meeting with all the headmen. We will discuss hunting and wildlife monitoring. I will walk very slowly so that I can make the whole trip. I will be gone for at least three months.

In December 2000, I flew to Yangon for two weeks to help Khaing plan the trip. When I asked him why he insisted on making the arduous journey again at the age of nearly 57, he smiled and told me that it was not his choice; he was being "called" by the icy mountains. His departure was scheduled for January 19, 2001, with a return date of early May if all went well.

On January 14, I received another fax:

> Alan—Just got a call from the senior vet at the Yangon Zoo. Our leaf deer is dead. She died this morning. The autopsy showed internal hemorrhage due to rupture of the spleen. I know that you and Salisa will be upset. I am sorry. Now you know why I really must go to Hkakabo Razi. The animals of my country cannot be saved by putting them in zoos and museums. It is something you have helped teach me. Khaing.

I sat alone for a long time in my study in New York, remembering Phet Gyi and all the events that had brought his life into contact with mine. He had been doomed from the moment his mother stepped into the hunter's snare. What affected me even more than Phet Gyi's death, however, were Khaing's last words.

I had been convinced that Khaing was going on this trip

because he viewed it as his job and he enjoyed being in the wilderness. I hadn't realized how deeply his emotions ran concerning the wildlife of his country. It was partly because I was too caught up in my own emotions and desires, thinking of Hkakabo Razi as *my* area, with *my* discoveries, and believing that I was the only one who could do what needed to be done now.

But the task of lasting conservation in Hkakabo Razi, as in the rest of the country, had to be pursued by Khaing and the many competent, caring people like him in Myanmar. It was only appropriate that he and the Forest Department staff take the burden of this trip onto their shoulders. They were fully capable of doing that now, and it was their commitment and passion that had to shine forth. By leading this expedition, Khaing would set an example for the park staff, for the people in Hkakabo Razi, and for other Myanmar people in a way that I could never do. After this, the Forest Department staff would truly be invested in the process. They would be the ones to ensure that their people shared the land with wildlife, and that local people benefited more from wildlife being alive than from being dead.

This is what has to be done throughout much of the world if conservation is to succeed and become a lasting part of people's mind-set everywhere. Biologists like me have to know not only when to step in to try and make conservation happen, but also when to step out to allow conservation to work. But stepping out doesn't necessarily mean walking away. Organizations like WCS, as well as international funding agencies, have a role to play in providing financial or intellectual assistance until it is no longer needed or, perhaps, wanted. In many cases, assistance will be needed indefinitely. Outside the most affluent countries, asking local people or even local governments to pay the full costs of saving their lands' biodiversity "for the greater good" is untenable. The entire world must pay for conservation, and unending vigilance will be needed to ensure success.

My trips to Hkakabo Razi were finished; I was fairly certain of that now. I would continue to watch, advise, and cheer from the sidelines. The lives of the Tibetans, the Rawang, and the ancient lineages of the Himalayan species in that far northern outpost of Myanmar were in capable hands. I knew there were other places I had yet to explore and other discoveries to make before my days in the field were over. But the icy mountains would always call to me. And I would always dream of the last village.

### Postscript

On April 3, 2001, the Ministry of Forestry acted on our proposal submitted two years earlier and declared an uninhabited 2,494-square-mile area as Hukaung Wildlife Sanctuary. This meant that 3.2 percent of the land area in Myanmar was now protected as either a national park or a wildlife sanctuary.

Four days later, U Saw Tun Khaing and his team returned safely to Yangon. He had successfully organized meetings with all of the village headmen and many of the hunters within Hkakabo Razi National Park and had received approval for our plan to protect the forests and wildlife while improving the lives of the people living within the park.

# *Acknowledgments*

Almost all of the travel, exploration, and research described in this book was made possible through funding provided by the Wildlife Conservation Society, founded in 1895 as the New York Zoological Society. WCS is the only organization I have chosen to work for during the two decades spanning my professional career. It has remained true to the ideal that wildlife has an innate right to share this planet with us and to the philosophy that only through good science can one accomplish lasting conservation.

One of the hallmarks of WCS has been its practice of finding passionate, self-motivated people and then setting them loose in the field to study and do whatever they can to save wildlife. Over the course of more than a century, these people have made the world a better place. I have been fortunate to have been given the rare opportunity to follow in the footsteps of William Beebe, Fairfield Osborn, George Schaller, and William Conway. In whatever I have accomplished, I have been guided by their examples, while being assisted by the emotional and financial support of my colleagues at WCS.

I would like to thank especially John Robinson, executive vice president of the international division, who has always encouraged my efforts and who continues to patiently negotiate with me when we disagree. I would also like to thank George Schaller, my mentor and my friend. Through our years together, he has believed in me, he has helped point the way, and I always knew he would come to my aid if things went wrong. His wife, Kay, is a dear friend who helped me adjust to the trauma of fatherhood and helped my wife adjust to the trauma of having me as a husband.

For my work in Myanmar, I wish to thank U Tint Lwin Thaung, who first helped me set up the WCS program in the country, and my good friends U Uga and U Aung Than, who were my first government contacts. I also wish to thank U Than Myint, U Saw Lwin, and the members of our various expedition teams over the years who helped calm my spirit and taught me patience and tolerance despite the continual roadblocks placed in our way. Sincere gratitude goes to General Chit Swe, former minister of forestry, who believed in what I and WCS stand for, and who pushed for a strong conservation agenda in Myanmar despite opposition. Finally, I thank U Saw Tun Khaing, friend and teacher throughout my years in Myanmar. His passion, tenacity, and moral character continue to set an example for me in my own life.

Back at home, there are several people who have added immeasurably to my life and work. Their support while I was writing this book was of great comfort, although I never told them so at the time. I would like to acknowledge the friendship and support especially of Sal and Sue Polifemo, who made sure I never went too long without a home-cooked meal; Jane Alexander and Ed Sherin, kindred spirits and godparents to my son; and Gregg and Kim Manocherian, who watched over me whenever I seemed to be slipping too far from my fellows. For helping to make sure this book was published, I thank my agent, Owen Laster, who continues to believe I have some writing talent, and my editor at Island Press, Jonathan Cobb. Jonathan critiqued the manuscript several times and showed me that there are still editors who take their job seriously and really care about their writers. *Natural History* and *Wildlife Conservation* magazines kindly gave permission for me to use portions of previously published articles in this book. Steve Winter kindly gave permission for use of his photographs. Finally, I give heartfelt thanks to Michael Cline and Joyce Moss, who helped to fund the research and travel that are detailed in this book and who have always been there when I needed them.

As I write these words, my father sits at home writing a book about his own incredible life, while taking care of my mother, whose inner light is beginning to flicker. Whenever I visit their home, he reads to me his latest chapter, filled with stories I have heard innumerable times since childhood. But now, as the stories are woven together to create the summation of my father's life, I can finally see the larger picture. It is clear to me now that I am my father's son. I thank him for helping make me the man I am. I also thank my mom and my two sisters, Suzan and Sharon, for always supporting my dreams, even when they were frightened about where such dreams were taking me.

Finally, there is my wife, Salisa. How do I thank someone who chose to love me more than I ever loved myself? How do I acknowledge one who held me to her breast when I was delirious with fever, put up with my tirades against the world, and helped lift me out of an inner darkness from which I saw no absolution? What can I say to someone who has given me the greatest present and the greatest challenge of my life—my son, Alexander? My heart is yours.

# Selected Bibliography

The references listed here are mostly those that describe the people and the region of northern Myanmar, including some recent publications by the author. This is by no means an exhaustive list. For the reader who wishes to learn more about the history or the current politics of Myanmar, many excellent books and publications are available that are not listed here. For those interested in learning more about the life of Frank Kingdon Ward, who made at least eight trips to northern Myanmar between 1914 and 1953, see the books by Charles Lyte and Jean Kingdon Ward that are listed below.

## *Books*

Aung, Maung Htin. *Folk Elements in Burmese Buddhism.* Buddha Sasana Council Press, Yangon, 1981.

Barua, S. N. *Tribes of Indo-Burma Border.* Mittal Publications, New Delhi, 1991.

Beebe, W. *Pheasant Jungles.* Blue Ribbon Books Inc., New York, 1927.

Bigandet, P. A. *The Catholic Burmese Mission.* White Orchid Press, Bangkok, 1996. (First published in 1887 by Hanthawaddy Press, Rangoon.)

Brunner, J., K. Talbott, and C. Elkin. *Logging Burma's Frontier Forests: Resources and the Regime.* World Resources Institute, Washington, D.C., 1998.

283

Bryant, R. L. *The Political Ecology of Forestry in Burma: 1824–1994.* Hurst and Co., London, 1997.

Carrapiett, W. J. S. *The Salons.* Ethnographical Survey of India, No. 2. Government Printing Office, Rangoon, 1909.

———. *The Kachin Tribes of Burma.* Government Printing Office, Rangoon, 1929.

Cox, E. M. *Farrer's Last Journey: Upper Burma, 1919–1920.* Dulau & Co., Ltd., London, 1926.

Cutting, S. *The Fire Ox and Other Years.* Charles Scribner's Sons, New York, 1940.

Diran, R. K. *The Vanishing Tribes of Burma.* Amphoto Art, New York, 1997.

Enriquez, C. M. *Races of Burma,* 2nd ed. Handbooks for the Indian Army. Manager of Publications, Delhi, 1933.

Evans, G. P. *Big-Game Shooting in Upper Burma.* Longmans, Green and Co., London, 1911.

Fielding Hall, H. *The Soul of a People.* White Orchid Press, Bangkok, 1995. (First published in London, 1898.)

Fischer, E. *Mission in Burma: The Columban Fathers' Forty-three Years in Kachin Country.* Seabury Press, New York, 1980.

Gilhodes, A. *The Kachins: Religion and Customs.* White Lotus Press, Bangkok, 1996. (First published in 1922.)

Hla, Tha. *Report on the Triangle Expedition, Kachin State, North Burma.* Government Printing Office, Rangoon, 1955.

Hundley, H. G., and Chit Ko Ko. *List of Trees, Shrubs, Herbs and Principal Climbers, etc. Recorded from Burma,* 4th ed. Government Printing Office, Rangoon, 1987.

Ivanoff, J. *Moken: Sea-Gypsies of the Andaman Sea.* White Lotus Press, Bangkok, 1997.

Kaulback, R. *Salween.* Hodder & Stoughton, London, 1939.

———. *Tibetan Trek.* Hodder & Stoughton, London, 1943.

Keeton, C. L. *King Thebaw and the Ecological Rape of Burma. Period of 1878–1885.* Manohar Book Service, Delhi, 1974.

Kingdon Ward, F. *In Farthest Burma.* Seeley, Service & Co. Ltd., London, 1921.

————. *The Romance of Plant Hunting.* Edward Arnold & Co., London, 1924.

————. *Burma's Icy Mountains.* Jonathan Cape, London, 1949.

————. *Return to the Irrawaddy.* Andrew Melrose, London, 1956.

————. *Plant Hunter's Paradise.* Waterstone, London, 1985.

————. *Plant Hunting on the Edge of the World.* Cardogan Books, London, 1985. (First published in 1930.)

————. *Himalayan Enchantment: An Anthology.* Serindia Publications, London, 1990.

Kingdon Ward, J. *My Hill So Strong.* Jonathan Cape, London, 1952.

Lintner, B. *The Kachin: Lords of Burma's Northern Frontier. People and Cultures of Southeast Asia.* Teak House, Bangkok, 1994.

Lowis, C. C. *The Tribes of Burma.* Ethnographical Survey of India, No. 4. Government Printing Office, Rangoon, 1919.

Lyte, C. *The Last of the Great Plant Hunters.* John Murray, London, 1989.

Milton, O., and R. D. Estes. *Burma Wildlife Survey, 1959–1960.* American Committee for International Wildlife Protection Special Publication No. 15, New York, 1963.

Morse, E. *Exodus to a Hidden Valley.* Readers Digest Press, New York, 1974.

Mya-Tu, M., U Ko Ko, Aung Than Batu, Kywe Thein, and Than Tun Aung Hlaing. *The Tarons in Burma.* Special Report Series No. 1. Burma Medical Research Institute. Central Press, Rangoon, 1967.

Peacock, E. H. *A Game-Book for Burma and Adjoining Territories.* H. F. & G. Witherby, England, 1933.

Sangermano, V. *The Burmese Empire a Hundred Years Ago.* White Orchid Press, Bangkok, 1995. (First published in 1833.)

Stanford, J. K. *Far Ridges: A Record of Travel in North-Eastern Burma.* C. & J. Temple Ltd., London, 1944.

Tu, Sein. *Large Mammals of Myanmar.* Innwa Publishing House, Yangon, 1998.

Yin, Tun. *Wild Mammals of Myanmar.* Department of Forestry, Yangon, 1993. (First published by Rangoon Gazette Ltd., Rangoon, 1967.)

## *Articles*

Amato, G., M. G. Egan, and A. Rabinowitz. "A New Species of Muntjac, *Muntiacus putaoensis* (Artiodactyla: Cervidae) from Northern Myanmar." *Animal Conservation,* vol. 2, 1999, pp. 1–7.

Anthony, H. E. "A Winter in Remote Burma." *Natural History,* vol. 44, 1939, pp. 263–276, 297.

————. "Mammals Collected by the Vernay-Cutting Burma Expedition." *Publication of the Field Museum of Zoology,* Chicago, vol. 27, 1941, pp. 37–123.

Dollman, G. "Mammals Collected by Lord Cranbrook and Captain F. Kingdon Ward in Upper Burma." *Proceedings of the Linnean Society,* London, vol. 145, 1932/1933, pp. 9–11.

Forrest, G. "The Land of the Crossbow." *National Geographic,* vol. XXI, 1910, pp. 132–156.

Gely-Ozaki, F. "Hkakabo Razi—Joint Friendship Expedition to Myanmar." *Himalayan Journal,* vol. 52, 1996, pp. 16–28.

Hayman, R. W. "The Red Goral of the North-East Frontier Region." *Regional Proceedings of the Zoological Society,* London, vol. 136, no. 3, 1961, pp. 317–324.

————. "Note on a Reputed Skull of *Nemorhaedus cranbrooki.*" *Journal of the Bombay Natural History Society,* vol. 58, no. 3, 1961, pp. 792–796.

Kingdon Ward, F. "Glacial Phenomena on the Yunnan-Tibet Frontier." *Geographical Journal,* London, vol. 48, 1916, pp. 55–68.

————. "From the Yangtze to the Irrawaddy." *Geographical Journal,* London, vol. 60, 1923, pp. 6–20.

————. "The Sino-Himalayan Flora." *Proceedings of the Linnean Society,* London, vol. 139, 1927, pp. 67–74.

————. "Botanical Exploration on the Burma-Tibet Frontier." *Proceedings of the Linnean Society,* London, vol. 144, 1930, pp. 140–143.

————. "Explorations on the Burma-Tibet Frontier." *Geographical Journal,* vol. 80, no. 6, 1932, pp. 465–483.

————. "The Irrawaddy Plateau." *Geographical Journal,* London, vol. 94, 1936, pp. 293–308.

————. "Ka Karpo Razi: Burma's Highest Peak." *Himalayan Journal,* vol. 9, 1939, pp. 74–88.

————. "Botany and Geography of North Burma." *Journal of the Bombay Natural History Society,* vol. 44, 1944, pp. 550–574.

————. "A Sketch of the Botany and Geography of North Burma— Part II." *Journal of the Bombay Natural History Society,* vol. 45, 1944, pp. 16–30.

————. "A Sketch of the Botany and Geography of North Burma— Part III." *Journal of the Bombay Natural History Society,* vol. 45, 1944, pp. 133–148.

————. "Botany and Geography of North Burma." *Journal of the Bombay Natural History Society,* vol. 45, 1945, pp. 16–30.

————. "Caught in the Assam-Tibet Earthquake." *National Geographic,* vol. CI, 1952, pp. 402–416.

————. "Report on the Forests of the North Triangle, Kachin State, North Burma." *Journal of the Bombay Natural History Society,* vol. 52, 1954, pp. 304–320.

Kinnear, N. B. "On the Birds of the Adung Wang Valley, North-East Burma." *Journal of the Bombay Natural History Society,* vol. 37, 1934, pp. 347–368.

Lu, H-G., and H-L. Sheng. "Status of the Black Muntjac, *Muntiacus crinifrons,* in Eastern China." *Mammal Review,* vol. 14, no. 1, 1984, pp. 29–36.

Martin, E. B. "Wildlife Products for Sale in Myanmar." *Traffic Bulletin,* vol. 17, no. 1, 1997, pp. 33–44.

Mya-Tu, M., U Ko Ko, Aung Than Batu, Kywe Thein, C. J. R. Francis, and Than Tun Aung Hlaing. "Tarong Pygmies in North Burma." *Nature,* vol. 195, 1962, pp. 131–132.

Pocock, R. I. "The Serows, Gorals, and Takins of British India and the Straits Settlements. Part I—Introductory Remarks Upon the Structural Characters of Serows, Gorals and Takins and Descriptions of the Known Species of Takins." *Journal of the Bombay Natural History Society,* vol. 19, 1910, pp. 807–819.

————. "The Serows, Gorals, and Takins of British India and the Straits Settlements. Part II—On the Serows (*Capricornis*) and Gorals (*Naemorhedus*)." *Journal of the Bombay Natural History Society*, vol. 23, 1913, pp. 296–318.

Rabinowitz, A. "Notes on the Rare Red Goral (*Naemorhedus baileyi*) of North Myanmar." *Mammalia*, vol. 63, no. 1, 1999, pp. 119–123.

————. "The Price of Salt." *Natural History*, vol. 109, no. 7, 2000, pp. 52–57.

Rabinowitz, A., G. Amato, and Saw Tun Khaing. "Discovery of the Black Muntjac, *Muntiacus crinifrons,* in North Myanmar." *Mammalia*, vol. 62, no. 1, 1998, pp. 105–108.

Rabinowitz, A., and Saw Tun Khaing. "Status of Selected Mammal Species in North Myanmar." *Oryx*, vol. 32, no. 3, 1998, pp. 201–208.

Rabinowitz, A., G. Schaller, and U Uga. "A Survey to Assess the Status of Sumatran Rhinoceros and Other Large Mammal Species in Tamanthi Wildlife Sanctuary, Myanmar." *Oryx*, vol. 29, no. 2, 1995, pp. 123–128.

Rabinowitz, A., Than Myint, Saw Tun Khaing, and S. Rabinowitz. "Description of the Leaf Deer (*Muntiacus putaoensis*), a New Species of Muntjac from Northern Myanmar." *Journal of Zoology*, London, vol. 249, 1999, pp. 427–435.

Rao, M., A. Rabinowitz, and Saw Tun Khaing. "A Status Review of the Protected Area System in Myanmar with Recommendations for Conservation Planning." *Conservation Biology*, in press.

Stanford, J. K., and E. Mayr. "The Vernay-Cutting Expedition to Northern Burma with Notes on the Bird Collection by Dr. E. Mayr." *Ibis*, October 1940, pp. 679–711.

Stanford, J. K., and C. B. Ticehurst. "On the Birds of Northern Burma." *Ibis*, vol. 2, 1938, pp. 65–102(I), 197–229 (II).

Weatherbe, D. Burma's Decreasing Wildlife. *Journal of the Bombay Natural History Society*, vol. 42, 1939, pp. 149–160.

Yin, Tun. "Wildlife Preservation and Sanctuaries in the Union of

Burma." *Journal of the Bombay Natural History Society,* vol. 52, 1954, pp. 264–284.

———. Rhinoceros in the Kachin State. *Journal of the Bombay Natural History Society,* vol. 53, 1956, pp. 692–694.

# Index

291

ALAN RABINOWITZ is Director of Science and Exploration for the Wildlife Conservation Society (WCS). Educated at the University of Tennessee, with degrees in ecology and wildlife biology, and the author of more than fifty popular articles and scientific papers, Rabinowitz has conducted surveys and led expeditions in diverse parts of the globe, making important scientific discoveries and often serving as the catalyst for creation of new wildlife preserves.

In 1982, Rabinowitz traveled to the Central American country of Belize to conduct the first ecological research on jaguars in rain forest habitat. His work led to the creation of the world's only jaguar preserve and inspired the author's first popular book, *Jaguar: One Man's Struggle to Establish the First Jaguar Preserve*. Rabinowitz went on to survey clouded leopards throughout Asia, and then lived and worked for five years in Thailand studying tigers, leopards, leopard cats, and civets, as described in *Chasing the Dragon's Tail: The Struggle to Save Thailand's Wild Cats*. He also has led wildlife research training courses in Malaysia, Myanmar, Taiwan, and China, conducted the first systematic survey of Sumatran rhinos in Sabah, and initiated some of the first biological surveys in remote areas of Laos.

The author began the scientific and conservation work in Myanmar described in *Beyond the Last Village* in 1993.